Odoo 11 Development Essentials
Third Edition

Develop and customize business applications with Odoo 11

Daniel Reis

BIRMINGHAM - MUMBAI

Odoo 11 Development Essentials
Third Edition

Commissioning Editor: Aaron Lazar
Acquisition Editor: Larissa Pinto
Content Development Editor: Flavian Vaz
Technical Editor: Sachin Sunilkumar
Copy Editor: Safis Editing
Project Coordinator: Devanshi Doshi
Proofreader: Safis Editing
Indexer: Aishwarya Gangawane
Graphics: Jason Monteiro
Production Coordinator: Aparna Bhagat

First published: April 2015
Second edition: November 2016
Third edition: March 2018

Production reference: 1230318

Published by Packt Publishing Ltd.
Livery Place
35 Livery Street
Birmingham
B3 2PB, UK.

ISBN 978-1-78847-779-6

www.packtpub.com

`mapt.io`

Mapt is an online digital library that gives you full access to over 5,000 books and videos, as well as industry leading tools to help you plan your personal development and advance your career. For more information, please visit our website.

Why subscribe?

- Spend less time learning and more time coding with practical eBooks and Videos from over 4,000 industry professionals

- Improve your learning with Skill Plans built especially for you

- Get a free eBook or video every month

- Mapt is fully searchable

- Copy and paste, print, and bookmark content

PacktPub.com

Did you know that Packt offers eBook versions of every book published, with PDF and ePub files available? You can upgrade to the eBook version at `www.PacktPub.com` and as a print book customer, you are entitled to a discount on the eBook copy. Get in touch with us at `service@packtpub.com` for more details.

At `www.PacktPub.com`, you can also read a collection of free technical articles, sign up for a range of free newsletters, and receive exclusive discounts and offers on Packt books and eBooks.

Contributors

About the author

Daniel Reis has had a long career in the IT industry, most as a consultant implementing business applications in variety of sectors, and today works for Securitas, a multinational security services provider.

He has been working with Odoo (formerly OpenERP) since 2010, is an active contributor to the Odoo Community Association projects, is currently a member of the board of the Odoo Community Association, and collaborates with ThinkOpen Solutions, a leading Portuguese Odoo integrator.

I would like to thank my wife, Maria, for all the patience and support.

My thanks also to Olivier Dony, for agreeing to be part of this project and for all the valuable feedback given.

About the reviewer

Olivier Dony is a Belgian engineer specialized in network engineering, databases, and information security. He enjoys analyzing and solving complex problems and getting to the bottom of seemingly inexplicable bugs.

He joined Odoo Belgium in 2009, where he had the chance to take on many roles, such as working with the community, running the cloud platform with his team, setting up the security response team, or just as importantly, solving interesting problems everyday within the Odoo R&D.

Packt is searching for authors like you

If you're interested in becoming an author for Packt, please visit authors.packtpub.com and apply today. We have worked with thousands of developers and tech professionals, just like you, to help them share their insight with the global tech community. You can make a general application, apply for a specific hot topic that we are recruiting an author for, or submit your own idea.

Table of Contents

Preface

Odoo is a full featured open source platform to build applications. Based on this core framework, a suite of integrated applications was built, covering all business areas from CRM and Sales to Stocks and Accounting.

Beyond these out-of-the-box features, Odoo's framework was built with extensibility in mind. Extensions and modifications can be implemented as modules, to be applied over the module with the feature being changed, without actually changing it. This provides a clean and easy -to-control and customized applications.

This capability to combine several modules into feature-rich applications, along with the open source nature of Odoo, are probably important factors explaining the community that grew around Odoo. In fact, there are thousands of community modules available for Odoo, covering virtually every topic, and the number of people getting involved has been steadily growing every year.

Odoo 11 Development Essentials provides a step-by-step guide to Odoo development, allowing readers to quickly climb the learning curve and become productive in the Odoo application platform. At the same time, it tries to provide good reference materials, to be kept nearby every time you are working with Odoo.

Who this book is for

This book was written keeping in mind developers with minimal programming knowledge but a strong will to learn. We will use a lot the Python language and explain how to run Odoo in a Ubuntu/Debian system, but little previous knowledge on them is assumed. The code examples are kept simple and clear, and they are accompanied with appropriate explanations to help build up the knowledge on them.

Experienced developers, already familiar with Odoo, should also be able to benefit from this book. Not only does it allow them to consolidate their knowledge, it also provides an easy way to get up to date with all the details that changed with Odoo 11.0. In fact, special care was taken to highlight all the relevant changes between Odoo versions since 8.0.

Finally, this book should provide a solid reference to be used daily, both by newcomers and experienced developers. The documentation of the relevant differences between the several Odoo versions should also be a good resource for any developer working with different Odoo versions at the same time or porting modules to other versions.

What this book covers

This books contains 14 chapters, which can be seen to be organized in five parts, roughly, introduction, models, business logic, views, and deployment.

The first part introduces the Odoo framework, explains how to set up your development environment and provides a tutorial with thorough, step-by-step creation of a new Odoo module:

Chapter 1, *Quick Start – The Odoo Developer Mode and Concepts*, visually introduces the Odoo development concepts, creating a simple Odoo application directly from the user interface. An existing Odoo installation, or an Odoo.com instance, can be used, so no local setup is needed.

Chapter 2, *Installing and Organizing the Development Environment*, explains how to install Odoo from source and how to set up the development environment to be used throughout the book. We choose to install Odoo in an Ubuntu host, but guidance is given to have a perfectly functioning development environment in a Windows machine with an Ubuntu virtual machine.

Chapter 3, *Your First Odoo Application – A Practical Overview*, provides a step-by-step guide through the creation of our first Odoo module. While the example is kept simple, it covers all the different layers and components that can be involved in an Odoo application: models, business logic, backend views, and web frontend views.

The second part of the book introduces Models, responsible for the data model structures around which the application is built:

Chapter 4, *Models – Structuring the Application Data*, discusses the Model layer in detail, introducing the framework's **Object-Relational Mapping (ORM)**, the different types of models available, and the field types, including relational and computed fields.

Chapter 5, *Import, Export, and Module Data*, covers the most used Odoo data file formats—XML and CSV—the external identifier concept, how use to data file in modules, and data import/export operations.

In the third part, we explain how to write the business logic layer on top of the Models—the "Controller "component of the architecture:

Chapter 6, *The ORM API – Handling Application Data*, goes further into the ORM, explaining how it can be used to manipulate the data in the Models. The API for social features, such as followers and notifications, is also explained.

Chapter 7, *Business Logic – Supporting Business Processes*, explains how to program business logic on the server side, leveraging the ORM concepts and features. It also explains how to use wizards for a more sophisticated user interaction.

Chapter 8, *External API – Integrating with Other Systems*, shows how to implement Odoo external applications by implementing a command-line client that interacts with our Odoo server. There are several alternative client programming libraries available, which are introduced and used to implement our showcase client utility.

The fourth part explores the "View" layer and the several technologies that can be used for that layer:

Chapter 9, *Backend Views – Design the User Interface*, covers the web client's View layer, explaining the several types of views in detail and all the elements that can be used to create dynamic and intuitive user interfaces.

Chapter 10, *Kanban Views and Client-Side QWeb*, keeps working with the web client, but introduces Kanban views and explains the QWeb templates used to design the Kanban board elements.

Chapter 11, *Reports and Server-Side QWeb*, discusses using the QWeb-based report engine and everything needed to generate printer-friendly PDF reports.

Chapter 12, *Creating Website Frontend Features*, introduces Odoo website development, including web controller implementations and using QWeb templates to build frontend web pages.

Finally, the fifth part covers deployment and maintenance practices. Some special considerations, not relevant for development environments, need to be taken into account when deploying for production use.

Chapter 13, *Debugging and Automated Tests*, shares some debugging techniques to be used when developing Odoo modules. How to implement automated tests is also explained, since this is an essential practice to produce reliable code.

Chapter 14, *Deploying and Maintaining Production Instances*, shows us how to prepare a server for production prime time, explaining what configuration should be taken care of and how to configure an Nginx reverse proxy for improved security and scalability.

At the end of the book, the reader should have a solid understanding of all the steps and components involved in the Odoo application development cycle, from the drawing board to production deployment and maintenance of these applications.

To get the most out of this book

Other than being familiar with programming, no particular knowledge is expected to be able to take advantage of this book.

Odoo is built using the Python programming language, so it is a good idea to get solid knowledge of it. We also choose to run Odoo in an Ubuntu host, and will do some work on the command line, so it will help to be familiar with it.

To get the most out of this book, we recommend that you find complementary readings on the Python programming language, Ubuntu/Debian Linux operating system, and the PostgreSQL database.

While we will run Odoo in an Ubuntu host (a popular cloud hosting option), we will provide guidance on how to set up our development environment in a Windows system with the help of VirtualBox. Of course, working from an Ubuntu/Debian system is also a possible choice.

All the required software is freely available, and the instructions on where to find it will be given.

Download the example code files

You can download the example code files for this book from your account at `www.packtpub.com`. If you purchased this book elsewhere, you can visit `www.packtpub.com/support` and register to have the files emailed directly to you.

You can download the code files by following these steps:

1. Log in or register at `www.packtpub.com`.
2. Select the **SUPPORT** tab.
3. Click on **Code Downloads & Errata**.
4. Enter the name of the book in the **Search** box and follow the onscreen instructions.

Once the file is downloaded, please make sure that you unzip or extract the folder using the latest version of:

- WinRAR/7-Zip for Windows
- Zipeg/iZip/UnRarX for Mac
- 7-Zip/PeaZip for Linux

The code bundle for the book is also hosted on GitHub at `https://github.com/PacktPublishing/Odoo-11-Development-Essentials-Third-Edition`. We also have other code bundles from our rich catalog of books and videos available at `https://github.com/PacktPublishing/`. Check them out!

Conventions used

There are a number of text conventions used throughout this book.

`CodeInText`: Indicates code words in text, database table names, folder names, filenames, file extensions, pathnames, dummy URLs, user input, and Twitter handles. Here is an example: "We will have a new `/todo_app` directory alongside the `/odoo` directory containing the modules."

A block of code is set as follows:

```xml
<?xml version="1.0"?>
<odoo>
  <!-- Content will go here... -->
</odoo>
```

When we wish to draw your attention to a particular part of a code block, the relevant lines or items are set in bold:

```
'data': [
  'security/ir.model.access.csv',
  'views/todo_menu.xml',
  'views/todo_view.xml',
  ]
```

Any command-line input or output is written as follows:

```
$ createdb MyDB
$ createdb --template=MyDB MyDB2
```

Bold: Indicates a new term, an important word, or words that you see onscreen. For example, words in menus or dialog boxes appear in the text like this. Here is an example: "In the web client, access the **Apps** top menu and select the **Update Apps List** menu option."

Warnings or important notes appear like this.

 Tips and tricks appear like this.

Get in touch

Feedback from our readers is always welcome.

General feedback: Email feedback@packtpub.com and mention the book title in the subject of your message. If you have questions about any aspect of this book, please email us at questions@packtpub.com.

Errata: Although we have taken every care to ensure the accuracy of our content, mistakes do happen. If you have found a mistake in this book, we would be grateful if you would report this to us. Please visit www.packtpub.com/submit-errata, selecting your book, clicking on the Errata Submission Form link, and entering the details.

Piracy: If you come across any illegal copies of our works in any form on the Internet, we would be grateful if you would provide us with the location address or website name. Please contact us at copyright@packtpub.com with a link to the material.

If you are interested in becoming an author: If there is a topic that you have expertise in and you are interested in either writing or contributing to a book, please visit authors.packtpub.com.

Reviews

Please leave a review. Once you have read and used this book, why not leave a review on the site that you purchased it from? Potential readers can then see and use your unbiased opinion to make purchase decisions, we at Packt can understand what you think about our products, and our authors can see your feedback on their book. Thank you!

For more information about Packt, please visit packtpub.com.

1
Quick Start – The Odoo Developer Mode and Concepts

Odoo provides a rapid application development framework that's particularly suited to building business applications. This type of application is usually concerned with keeping business records, centered around **create, read, update, and delete** (**CRUD**) operations. Not only does Odoo makes it easy to build this type of application, it also provides rich components to create compelling user interfaces, such as Kanban and Calendar views.

This book is organized into five parts. We start by providing an overview of the Odoo framework, setting up a development environment, and building our first Odoo app. Being generally familiar with the main Odoo components, we will dive, in more detail, into each of the three main application layers: models, business logic, and views. Once we have built our app, it needs to be tested, deployed to a production environment, and maintained. The final part of the book will cover these topics.

In this chapter, we will quickly get into the action, exploring the Odoo internals directly from the web user interface, even before having set up our local development environment.

We will learn about the Odoo architecture, to understand where each of the components fit. Then we will use the **Developer mode** to create a simple `Library` app, learning how to add fields to existing **Models**, add new **Models**, create our custom **Views** for them, and make them available to users through **Menu Items**.

We will next provide a high-level overview of the Odoo architecture, before we perform a hands-on customization using the **Developer mode**.

The Odoo architecture

Odoo follows a multi-tier architecture, and we can identify three main tiers: Data, Logic, and Presentation:

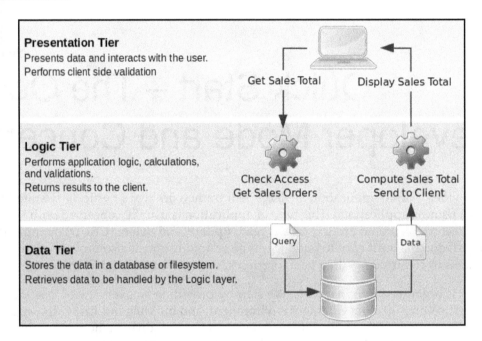

The **Data tier** is the lowest-level layer, and is responsible for data storage and persistence. Odoo relies on a PostgreSQL server for this. PostgreSQL is the only supported RDBMS, and this is a design choice. So, other databases such as MySQL are not supported. Binary files, such as attachments of documents or images, are usually stored in a filesystem.

The **Logic tier** is responsible for all the interactions with the data layer, and is handled by the Odoo server. As a general rule, the low-level database should only be accessed by this layer, since it is the only way to ensure security access control and data consistency. At the core of the Odoo server, we have the **Object-Relational Mapping (ORM)** engine for this interface. The ORM provides the **application programming interface (API)** used by the addon modules to interact with the data.

For example, the **Partner** data entity, such as a Customer or a Supplier, is represented in the ORM by a model. This model is a Python object class supporting several interaction methods, such as `create()` to create new **Partner** records, or `read()` to query existing records and their data. These generic methods can implement specific business logic in particular **Models**. For example, the `create()` method might implement default values or enforce validation rules; the `read()` method might support some automatically computed fields, or enforce access controls depending on the user performing that action.

The **Presentation tier** is responsible for presenting data and interacting with the user. It is implemented by a client responsible for all the user experience. The client interacts with the ORM API to read, write, verify, or perform any other action, calling ORM API methods through **remote procedure calls (RPCs)**. These are sent to the Odoo server for processing, and then the results are sent back to the client for further handling.

For the Presentation tier, Odoo provides a full-featured web client out of the box. The web client supports all the features needed by a business application: login sessions, navigation menus, data lists, forms, and so on. The global look and feel are not as customizable as a frontend developer might expect, but it makes it easy to create a functional and consistent user experience.

A complementary presentation layer is the included website framework. It gives full flexibility to create web pages as the exact user interface intended, like in other CMS frameworks, at the expense of some additional effort and web expertise. The website framework supports web controllers to implement code for presenting specific logic, keeping it separate from the model intrinsic logic. Frontend developers will probably feel very much at home in this space.

Due to the openness of the Odoo server API, other client implementations are possible, and could be built in almost any platform or programming language. Desktop and smartphone apps can be built to provide specific user interfaces, leveraging the Odoo Data and Logic tiers for business logic and data persistence.

A particular example of a third-party Odoo client is **ERPpeek**. It is a command- line client, allowing you to connect and interact with remote Odoo servers. It can be useful for developers or system administrators with Odoo technical knowledge, to inspect data on the server, script advanced operations, or perform maintenance operations. We will present an overview of ERPpeek in `Chapter 8`, *External API – Integrating with Other Systems*.

The Developer mode

Many Odoo customizations can be made directly from the user interface.

This has the advantage of being a rather quick way to make changes to applications. It can be used from small modifications, such as adding a field, to larger customizations, such as creating an app with several models, views, and menu items.

These customizations done directly from the user interface have some limitations, when compared to customizations done with programming tools, covered throughout the rest of this book. For example, you can't add or extend ORM methods (although **Automated Actions** can be used as a close alternative to that). They also can't be easily integrated into a structured development workflow, such as running automated tests and deploying into several environments (for example, quality assurance, pre-production, and production).

Odoo 10.0 introduced Odoo Studio, an app designer to create customizations from the user interface. We won't discuss Odoo Studio here, but it ends up being a user-friendly frontend for the developer tools we introduce throughout this chapter, so the limitations on customizations possible are about the same. Odoo Studio does include an important additional feature, that is, the ability to export the customizations done in a convenient module package. It can be very helpful to allow power users to create customizations in a SaaS instance or simpler self-hosted technical environments.

The remainder of this book explains how to develop for Odoo in a structured way, creating addon modules with your code editor.

But in this chapter, we will be using the **Developer mode** features to perform customizations directly from the web client user interface, since it is important for an Odoo developer to have a good understanding of these tools and what can be achieved with them.

But more importantly, the goal for this exercise is to gain a good understanding of the several layers involved in an Odoo application, and how their components are organized.

Enough talk; let's get busy trying out these tools.

Introducing the Library project

To explain the developer tools, we will use a simple project: we will create a very simple `Library` app. Our `Library` aims to keep a record of our Books and their Authors. It should keep a list of the Authors and the Books authored by each Author.

Our Library app needs two Models: Authors and Books. These two Models have a many-to-many relationship between them: each Author can have many Books, and each Book can have many Authors.

Odoo already provides the built-in **Partner** Model, with the `res.partner` technical name, to represent people, organizations, and addresses. For example, customers, suppliers, contact people, and application users are all Partners.

We will make our life simpler if we reuse it for the Authors of our `Library` app. We will be adding an **Is Book Author?** flag to this Model, and a menu item showing only the Author Partners.

The book we will create has a completely new Model, the corresponding form, and list views, and a menu item to access them.

Creating a work database

We will be needing an Odoo test database to work with.

In `Chapter 2`, *Installing and Organizing the Development Environment*, we will explain how to install Odoo from source and set up our development environment. But we want to skip that for now, and start working directly from the user interface of some existing Odoo server.

If by chance you have a self-hosted Odoo installation working, that's perfect; we can use it to go through the rest of this chapter. At the login screen, access the **Manage Databases** menu option and create a new database to play with.

If you don't have an Odoo installation available, you can instead create a test database at `Odoo.com` to follow this chapter. The user interface there will be from the Odoo Enterprise Edition, so it will be a little different from the screenshots you will find here, but that should not be a problem. To create a new database, you will probably be asked to select a starting app. No specific app is required to follow this chapter, but if you're unsure on what to pick, CRM would be fine.

Odoo follows an "open core" business model, where the product is published in two editions, Community and Enterprise. The Enterprise edition is built on top of the Community edition, adding some premium features to it, including an improved user interface. At Odoo.com, you will be using the Enterprise edition, and in the public GitHub repository, you will find the Community edition. While the user interface looks different in both editions, they are just cosmetic changes; the user interface features are the same in both editions.

Now, access the Odoo database with your browser and log in. For Odoo online, the address should be something like `https://<mydbname>.odoo.com`. For a self-hosted instance, it should be something like `http://<server-address>:8069`. The 8069 port is the Odoo default. If your installation uses a different port, you should change it accordingly.

We will be using the **Contacts Directory** app, so the first thing to do is to install it. Open the **Apps** top menu, look up this app, and install it, if you have not already done so:

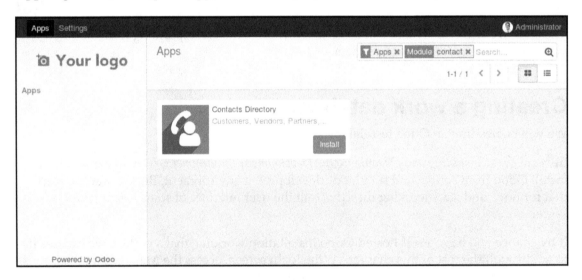

Now that we have an Odoo instance to work with, the next step is to enable the developer tools, that give us the access to the Odoo internals.

Enabling the developer tools

In **Settings** | **Dashboard**, at the bottom right, you can find the **Activate the developer mode** link. Clicking on it enables the **Developer mode** features for this browser window.

For Odoo 9.0 and before, the **Developer mode** is activated in the **About** dialog window, available from the **User** menu, at the top-right corner of the web client.

We also have available an **Activate the developer mode (with assets)** option. What it does is to prevent web client asset minification. It is useful to debug the web client itself, at the expense of making the navigation a little slower.

For faster load times, the web client minifies the Javascript and CSS assets into compact files. Unfortunately, that makes web client debugging nearly impossible. The **Activate the developer mode (with assets)** option prevents this minification and loads the web assets in individual, non-minified files.

You can enable the **Developer mode** without having to leave your current screen to open settings. Just edit the current URL to insert ?debug, or ?debug=assets, just after the /web part.
For example, http://myserver/web#home would be changed to http://myserver/web?debug#home.
Although there is no link to enable it, the frontend framework also supports the debug flag. To disable asset minification in a frontend web page, add ?debug=assets to the corresponding URL. Take note that the option will probably not persist when navigating through links to other frontend pages.

Once the **Developer mode** is enabled, we will see two additional menus available:

- The Debug menu, the bug icon at the right-hand side of the top menu bar, just before the username and avatar
- The **Technical** menu item, in the **Settings** app:

 The **Developer mode** also enables additional information on form fields: when pausing the mouse pointer over a field, a tooltip will display technical information on it.

We will be explaining and making use of these **Developer mode** features in the next sections of this chapter.

Adding a field to an existing Model

Adding a custom field to an existing form is a common customization, and it can be done from the user interface, without the need to create a custom module.

For our `Library` app, we want to add the **Is Book Author?** flag to the **Partner** model, to make it easier to list everyone who is a book author.

To do this, in the **Settings** app, go to the **Technical** | **Database Structure** | **Models** menu item, and look up the `res.partner` model, with **Contacts** for **Model Description**. Click on it to open the corresponding form view, and you will see all the specific details about the **Partner** model, including the field list:

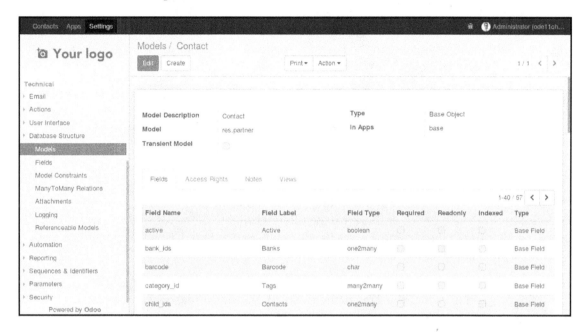

Now, **Edit** the form and click on **Add an item** at the bottom of the **Fields** list. A pop-up window will be presented for the new field creation.

Let's fill in the configuration:

- Field Name: `x_is_book_author`
- Field Label: **Is Book Author?**
- Field Type: **boolean**

The **Field Name** must start with x_. This is mandatory for **Models** and **Fields** created directly through the user interface. Customizations made through addon modules don't have this limitation.

That's it. Click **Save & Close** and our new field should have been added to the **Fields** list. Chances are that this model has more than 80 fields, and so you might need to navigate to the next page of the **Fields** list to see it. To do so, use the right arrow at the top left of the **Fields** list.

Now, click on the top-left **Save** button to make this change permanent.

Our new field is now available in the Partners model, but it is not yet visible to users. For that, we need to add it to the **Views**.

Still, on the Partner/Contact Model form, click on the **Views** tab, and we will be able to see all the View definitions for the res.partner model. As you can see, each View is a record in the database. Changing or adding View records is immediately effective, and will be visible the next time that View is reloaded.

There are a couple of important things to notice in the Views list.

We can see that there are several **View Type**, such as **Form**, **Tree**, **Search**, or **Kanban**. The **Search** views are actually definitions on the filters available in the top-right search box. The other view types are the different ways the data can be displayed. The basic ones are **Tree**, for list views, and **Form**, for the detailed form view.

 Both **Tree** and **List** can be used to refer to the same view type. They are in fact lists, and the Tree name exists for historical reasons: in the past list views used to have a "tree" hierarchical mode.

If you sort the list by **View Type**, you will notice that the same view type can have multiple definitions. In fact, we can have several **Base view** definitions, the ones with an empty **Inherited View** field. And we can have several **Extension view** definitions, also called **Inherited Views**, adding incremental changes to a base view, for example, to add a field to an existing form.

 Extension views can themselves be extended by other extension views. In this case, the later extension is applied to the base view after all preceding extensions have been already applied to it.

For the res.partner model, we can see that there are two base forms: res.partner.form and res.partner.simplified.form. Client Actions, such as the ones in menu items, can specify the particular base view to use. If none are defined, the one with the lowest **Sequence** is used. You can think of it as being the default view. Clicking on a **Views** line, we will see a form with the View's details, including the Sequence value.

To learn what the specific view used somewhere in the user interface is, we can inspect it using the **Debug** menu. Let's try it now. Click on the **Contacts** app and we will be presented with a list of contact cards. Clicking on any of the cards will show us the corresponding **FormView**. Now, on the **Debug** menu (the bug icon at the top right), select the **Edit FormView** option:

This will show the same view details form we saw before in **Models**, but positioned on the actual view definition used here. As you can see, it is the `res.partner.form` view.

In the **Architecture** field, we can see the XML with the view definition. We could just edit it to add our new field. While that works, in the long run it is not a good idea. This view is owned by an addon module, and if some time in the future that module is upgraded, these customizations would be overwritten and lost. We can learn about the owner module through the **External ID** field. In this case, it is `base.view_partner_form`, so we know that this view belongs to the `base` module.

The proper way to modify a view is to create an **Inherited View** extension.

First, we need to pick an element from the original view to use as the extension point. We can do that by inspecting the base view and choosing an XML element with a `name` attribute. Most of the time, this will be a `<field>` element. Here, we will pick the `<field name="category_id" ...>` element.

Now, open the **Debug** menu, click on the **Edit Form View** option, select the **Inherited Views** tab, and click on **Add an item** at the bottom of the list.

A pop-up window, **Create: Views which inherit from this one,** will be shown, and we should fill it with the following values:

- **View Name**: **Contacts - Custom Is Book Author Flag**
- **Architecture**: Use the following XML:

```
<field name="category_id" position="after">
  <field name="x_is_book_author" />
</field>
```

The other important fields, such as the **Model, View Type,** and **Inherited View**, already have correct default values.

We can now **Save & Close**. **Save** in the **Edit Form View** window and then close it. We will be able to see the change done once we reload the **Contacts** form view. This means reloading the page in your web browser. In most browsers, you would do that by pressing **F5**.

Adding Menus, Models, and Views

Now we will be creating new application features, rather than extending already existing ones. We will continue working on our `Library` project.

First, we want to add a **Library** top menu, and we can already add the **Books Authors** menu item to it. Next, we will create a new Model for **Books**, and make it available to users by adding a menu item for it. Finally, we will create the list and form views for the **Books** model.

Creating menus

We now have a way to list Authors. It is the list of all Partners with the **Is Book Author?** flag checked.

Now, we want to add an **Authors** menu item that opens that list, filtering away the other Partners that are not Authors. The good news is that we can do this pretty easily by reusing the already existing Partner views.

Before that, we want to create the top menu item for our shiny new **Library** app, under which we will be including the menu item for the Authors, and later a menu item for Books.

The menu definitions can be seen in the **Settings** app, at **Technical | User Interface | Menu Items**. Create a new menu item using the following values:

- Menu: **Library**
- Parent Menu: (empty)
- Action: (empty)

In the **Submenus** tab, click on **Add an item** to add a sub-menu using these values:

- Menu: **Book Authors**
- Parent Menu: **Library** (the default value)
- Action: Select ir.actions.act_window, and in the selection list on the right click on **Create and Edit**, opening a form to create the related Window Action. Set the following values on the Window Action:
    - Action name: **Book Authors**
    - Object: res.partner (the technical name of the target Model):

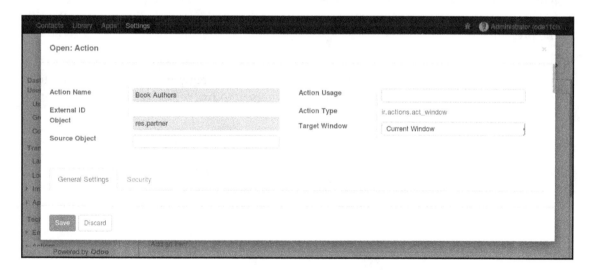

Save all the forms we opened, and the menu tree for our **Library** app should be ready to use:

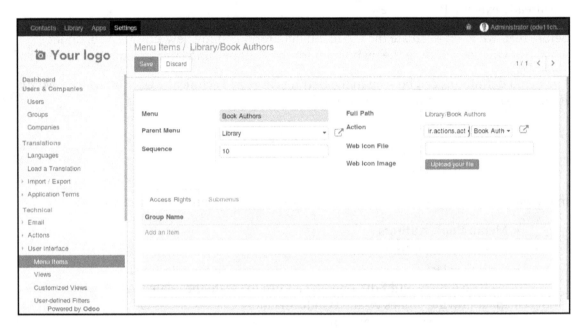

To see changes in the menu, we need to reload the web client. We can see that the menu is a tree of menu items, with parent/child relations. The leaf menu items have a related **Action**, defining what happens when it is selected. This Action name is what will be used as the title of the presented views.

There are several Actions types available, and the most important ones are Window, Reports, and Server Actions. Window Actions are the most frequent ones, and are used to present Views in the web client. Report Actions are used to run reports and Server Actions are used to define automated tasks.

At this point, we are concerned with Window Actions that are used to display views.

The Menu Item we just created for Book Authors uses a Window Action, which was created directly from the Menu Item form. We can also view and edit it from the **Settings |
Technical | Actions** menu options. In this particular case, we are interested in the **Window
Actions** menu option.

It happens that the **Book Authors** Action we created is too simple, and does not perform what we want: it opens a list with all Partners, regardless of whether they have the **Is Book
Author?** set. We need to fix that.

Open the **Window Actions** menu item, look up our recently created **Book Authors** action, and edit it. We are interested in the **Filters** section, found inside the **General Settings** tab.

In many cases, it is more convenient to use the **Edit Action** option in the **Debug** menu, providing a convenient shortcut to edit the Window Action that was used to access the current view.

The **Domain Value** field can have an expression defining a filter for the records to be presented. This "domain expression" follows an Odoo-specific syntax that will be explained in later chapters. For now, it's enough to know that it is a list of triplets, where each triplet is a filter condition.

In our case, the expression to use for the **Domain Value** is:

```
[('x_is_book_author', '=', True)]
```

For usability, we would also want new records created to have the **Is Book Author?** flag checked by default. An Action is able to do this, allowing us to set default values on the views it presents. This is done using the **Context Value**. The *Context* is the way Odoo passes around session information, including default values to be used. It will be discussed in detail in later chapters, and for now we just need to know that it is a dictionary of key-value pairs. Values prefixed with default_ provide the default value for the corresponding field.

In our case, the expression needed for the **Context Value** is:

```
{'default_x_is_book_author': True}
```

That's it. If we now try the **Library | Book Authors** menu option, it should list only Partners with the **Is Book Author?** flag checked, if any. And if we try to create a new **Book Author**, we will see that the **Is Book Author?** checkbox will be conveniently checked by default.

 The Domain filter we used can't be removed by the user. It is possible to set default filters that can be removed, using the Context to enable a default Search filter instead. This is done with a `search_default_<field>` key, as explained in `Chapter 9`, *Backend Views – Design the User Interface*.

Creating a Custom Model

We now have a Library top menu with a menu item for Book Authors. It's time to add a Books menu item to hold the records for books.

Let's visit again, in **Settings**, the **Technical | Database Structure | Models** menu, and click on **Create**. Fill in the Model form with these values:

- Model Description: **Book**
- Model: x_library_book

We should save it before we can properly add new fields to it. So click on **Save** and then **Edit** it again. You can see that a few fields were automatically added. The ORM includes them in all Models, and they can be useful for audit purposes.

The x_name (or name) field is a title representing the record in lists or when it is referenced in other records. For us, it makes sense to use it for the book title. You may edit it and change the **Field Label** to a more meaningful *Title*.

We also add a field for the book authors. A book can have many authors, and any author can have many books. So this is a many-to-many relationship.

On the **Fields** list, click on **Add an item** to create a new field with these values:

- Field Name: x_author_ids
- Field Label: **Authors**
- Field Type: many2many
- Object Relation: res.partner
- Domain: [('x_is_book_author', '=', True)]

The many-to-many field has a few specific definitions: the **Relation Table**, **Column1**, and **Columns2** fields. These are automatically filled out for you and the defaults are good for most cases, so we don't need to worry about them now. These will be discussed in more detail in Chapter 4, *Models – Structuring the Application Data*.

The Domain attribute is optional, but we used it so that only book authors are selectable from the list. Otherwise, all Partners would be available for selection.

We now need to make this Model available in the user interface. If we create a menu item for a new model, it can be used right away, since Odoo will automatically generate default views for it.

In **Settings**, navigate to **Technical** | **User Interface** | **Menu Items** and create a new record with the following values:

- Menu: **Books**
- Parent Menu: **Library**
- Action: Select `ir.actions.act_window`, and in the selection list on the right, click on **Create and Edit** to open a form for the creation of the related Window Action:
    - Action name: **Books** (will be the title used for the presented views)
    - Object: `x_library_book` (the technical name of the target Model)

Save the Action and Menu Item, and once we reload the web client the **Library** top menu app will show the **Books** option alongside the **Book Authors** option.

Try it and you will see the basic, but functional, automatically generated views. We will want to create our own views, so that's what we will be working on in the next section.

Creating Views

We have created the Books model and made it available in the user interface with a Menu Item. Next, we will be creating the two essential views for it: a list (also called a tree) and a form.

In **Settings**, navigate to **Technical** | **User Interface** | **Views** and create a new record with the following values:

- View Name: **Books List View**
- View Type: **Tree**
- Model: `x_library_book`

In the **Architecture** tab, we should write XML with the view structure. Use the following XML code:

```
<tree>
  <field name="x_name" />
  <field name="x_author_ids" widget="many2many_tags" />
</tree>
```

The basic structure of a list view is quite simple: a `<tree>` element containing one or more `<field>` elements for each of the columns to display in the list view. We added the `widget` attribute to the Authors field, to have it presented as button-like tags.

We can do a few more interesting things with list views, and will explore them in more detail in `Chapter 9`, *Backend Views – Design the User Interface*.

Next, we will create the form view. Create another new record, and use the following values:

- View Name: **Books Form View**
- View Type: **Form**
- Model: `x_library_book`

In the **Architecture** tab, type the following XML code:

```
<form>
  <group>
    <field name="x_name" />
    <field name="x_author_ids"
            widget="many2many_tags"
            context="{'default_x_is_book_author': True}" />
  </group>
</form>
```

The form view structure has a root `<form>` element, containing elements such as `<field>`, among others that we will learn about in `Chapter 9`, *Backend Views – Design the User Interface*. Here, we also chose a specific widget for the Authors field, to be displayed as tag buttons instead of a list grid. We also added a `context` attribute, so that when new Authors are created directly from here, they will already have the **Is Book Author** checkbox enabled.

Configuring access control security

Odoo includes built-in access control mechanisms. A user will only be able to use the features he was granted access to. This means that the Library features we created are not accessible by users. The `admin` user can because it is a special case; the access control mechanisms don't apply to it.

The access control is based on Groups. A security **Group** is given access to Models, and this will determine the menu items available to the users belonging to that Group. For more fine-grained control, we can also give access to specific Menu Items, Views, Fields, and even data records (with Record Rules).

The security Groups are also organized around apps, and usually each app provides at least two Groups: User, capable of performing the daily tasks, and Manager, able to perform all configurations for that app.

We cover this topic in more detail in Chapter 5, *Import, Export, and Module Data*, but will give a short introduction to it here, so that our users can use the Library app.

Let's create a new security Group. In the **Settings** top menu, navigate to **Users & Companies** | **Groups**. Create a new record using the following values:

- Application: Type **Library**, and select the **Create "Library"** option in the popup
- Name: **User**
- Inherited tab: Add the item **Employees / Employee:**

The Library app is not available yet in the Application selection list, so we added it directly from the Group form.

We also made it "inherit" the **Employee** Group. This means that members of this Group will also be made members of the inherited Groups (recursively), effectively having the permissions granted to all of them. **Employee** is the basic access Group, and app security Groups usually inherit it.

Now we can grant access to specific Models to the **Library / User** Group. We can use the **Access Rights** tab of the **Groups** form for this. Add an item there, using these values:

- Object: select **Library Book** from the list
- Read, Write, Create and Delete Access: Checked
- Name: **Library Book User Access**

The Name attribute is just informative but is mandatory. The Model access can also be managed from the **Technical** | **Security** | **Access Control List** menu item.

We don't need to add access to the **Partner** model because we inherit the **Employees** Group that already has access to it.

We can now try this new security group on a user. If you are using an Odoo instance with demo data installed, you should have the **Demo User** that we can use for this. If not, no problem, you can create or use an existing user. The point here is to not use the admin user, since it has special security privileges and bypasses access control.

Select the **Users & Companies** | **Users** menu item and edit the **Demo User** form:

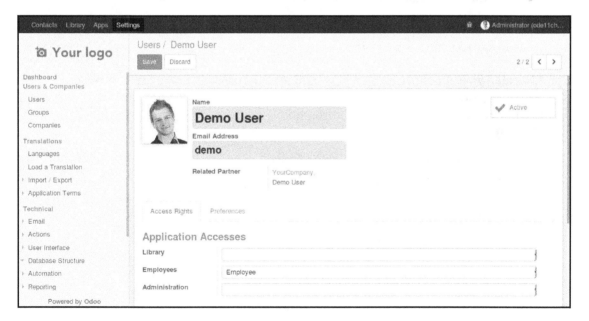

In the **Access Rights** tab, in **Application Accesses** section, we should see a **Library** option, where we can select the **User** security group. Select it, save, log out from the Administrator account, and log in with the `demo` user (the default password is `demo`).

If everything was done correctly, you should be able to see the Library top menu, and use it to add books and authors.

About Odoo base Models

Throughout this chapter, we have had the chance to create a new **Books** Model, but also to make use of the already existing **Partners** Model. It is worth learning more about these out-of-the-box models.

At the core of Odoo, we have the `base` addon module. This provides the essential features needed for Odoo apps. Then, we have a set of built-in addon modules, providing the official apps and features made available with the standard product.

The base module provides two kinds of Models:

- Information Repository, `ir.*` models
- Resources, `res.*` models

The **Information Repository** is used to store data needed by Odoo to know how to work as an application, such as Menus, Views, Models, Actions, and so on. The data we find in the **Technical** menu is usually stored in Information Repository models. Some relevant examples are:

- `ir.action.act_window` for Windows Actions
- `ir.ui.menu` for Menu Items
- `ir.ui.view` for Views
- `ir.model` for Models
- `ir.model.fields` for Model Fields

The resources contain basic data about the world, which can be useful for many of the applications. These are a few relevant resource models:

- res.partner for business partners, such as customers, suppliers, and so on
- res.company for company data
- res.currency for currencies
- res.country for countries
- res.users for application users
- res.groups for application security groups

This should provide you with a useful context to better understand where the Models come from whenever you come across them in the future.

Summary

In this chapter, not only did we present an overview of how Odoo components are organized, but we also made use of the Developer mode to dive into the Odoo internals and understand how these components work together to create applications.

We used these tools to build a simple application, with Models, Views, and the corresponding Menu. We also learned the usefulness of the developer tools to inspect existing applications or make quick customizations directly from the user interface.

In the next chapter, we will start getting more serious about Odoo development, and will learn to set up and organize our development environment.

2
Installing and Organizing the Development Environment

Before we dive into Odoo development, we need to set up our development environment and learn the basic administration tasks for it.

In this chapter, we will learn how to set up the working environment where we will build our Odoo applications. We will set up an Ubuntu system to host the development server instance. This can be a cloud server, a local network server, or a virtual machine in your workstation.

This simplifies the explanation, since we don't have to worry about the specifics of each platform. People not familiar with Ubuntu/Debian should find it easy to follow the steps. People confident with other operating systems, such as CentOS or macOS, should be able to adapt the instructions to their preferred system.

Another benefit from using a remote system for development is that when the time comes to deploy our Odoo solution for production use, we will already be familiar with the techniques to remotely work with that server.

For those more at home with Windows operating systems, we will cover how to set up a virtual machine to host the Odoo server. This is useful for learning since it simulates on your machine a setup where the Odoo server is in a cloud Linux server, which is a common deployment scenario. Of course, you can try other options, such as the all-in-one Windows install. In previous Odoo versions, it shipped with only compiled Python code, but since 11.0 it has the proper source code files and is developer friendly.

We will also learn how to set up file sharing with Samba, which may be a practical solution to work on the Odoo server files from our workstation running Windows or other operating systems.

In case you are using Ubuntu or Debian for your workstation, then things will be simpler for you: your workstation can also act as your server, so you can start setting up Odoo right away.

Setting up a host for the Odoo server

A Debian/Ubuntu system is recommended to run Odoo servers. While Odoo is multi-platform and can run on a variety of operating systems, it's also true that the Odoo R&D team considers Debian the reference deployment platform. In fact, Odoo's own SaaS operations are known to be Debian-based. It is also the most popular choice in the community. This means that it will be easier to find help or advice if you use Debian or Ubuntu. Even if you're from a Windows background, it will be important that you have some knowledge about it.

You will still be able to work from your favorite desktop system, be it Windows, Mac, or other Linux flavors, such as CentOS.

 Keep in mind that these instructions are intended to set up a new system for development. If you want to try some of them in an existing system, always take a backup ahead of time in order to be able to restore it in case something goes wrong.

Using a virtual machine

You're welcome to choose your preferred virtualization software to get a working Ubuntu system in a virtual machine, and there are a few options to choose from.

Microsoft Windows 10 includes Hyper-V as a feature. It just needs to be enabled in the **Programs and Features** menu.

The VMWare Workstation Player can also be a good option. Free to use downloads can be found at `https://my.vmware.com/web/vmware/downloads`. For macOS, VMWare Fusion should be used instead.

Virtualbox is free software and is available for a wide range of platforms, and so can be a good choice. It can be downloaded from `https://www.virtualbox.org`.

When writing this chapter, we used Windows 10 and Virtualbox 5.1. Since VirtualBox is free software and supports a wide range of platforms, it seems to be the most versatile choice. Windows 10 was chosen as the example host platform because of its popularity.

A particular configuration important to get right is networking. We want our guest machine to be reachable from the host, so that a web browser in the host can access an Odoo server running in the guest system. And we want our guest system to share the host's internet connection. With VirtualBox, we can achieve these two goals by configuring two network adapters for the guest system.

We first need to ensure connectivity between the host and the guest. This can be done using host-only networking. First, we need to add a network configuration to the VirtualBox host:

1. From the **File** menu, select **Global Settings**. In the Linux edition, the option is **File | Preferences**

2. From the list on the left-hand side, select **Network**, select the **Host-only Networks** tab, and click on the icon to add a network configuration

3. In the configuration's **Adapter** tab, set an IP address for the host, such as 192.168.122.1

4. In the configuration's **DHCP Server** tab, enable it and set these suggested values:
   - **Server address** (for the DHCP): 192.168.122.100
   - **Server mask**: 255.255.255.0
   - **Initial Address**: 192.168.122.101
   - **Final Address**: 192.168.122.254

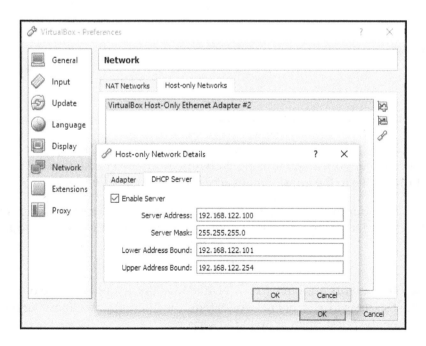

This configures the network between the host and the guest machines, including a DHCP server that will assign IP addresses to the guest machines.

Now we can go to our Odoo guest settings and add a Network Adapter using the host-only network we just created. Using the suggested configuration, the first IP address assigned will be `192.168.122.101`:

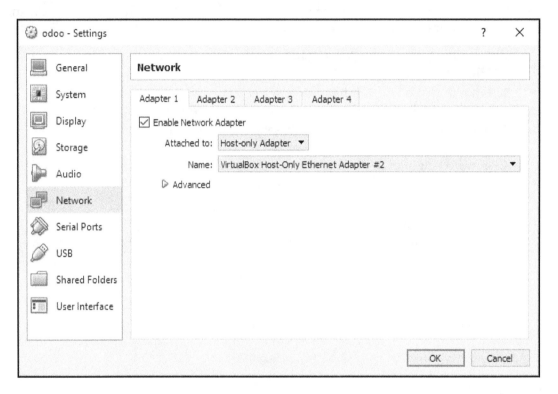

However, it does not provide external access to the guest system. For that, we should configure a second network adapter using **Network Address Translation** (**NAT**). This is the simplest option to give to the guest system access to external networks.

 The Ubuntu guest system might need additional network configuration to be able to use the second adapter. Detailed instructions can be found at `https://askubuntu.com/a/876579/88156`

Adding these two network adapters to our virtual machine should achieve our two goals: sharing the host's access to external networks (and the internet), and allowing the host to access services on the guest, such as an Odoo server.

Installing a Linux server

We will need a Debian-based server for our development Odoo server. If these are your first steps with Linux, you may take note that Ubuntu is a Debian-based Linux distribution, so they are very similar.

Odoo is guaranteed to work with the current stable version of Debian or Ubuntu. At the time of writing, these are Debian 9 Stretch and Ubuntu 16.04 LTS Xenial Xerus.

We do recommend you choose Ubuntu, since it is easier to install than Debian. Ubuntu ISO images can be downloaded from `https://www.ubuntu.com`. It is recommended to use the latest LTS (long-term support) version available.

If you're just getting started with Linux, a ready-to-use image can be easier to start with. TurnKey Linux provides easy-to-use preinstalled images in several formats, including ISO. The ISO format will work with any virtualization software you choose, even on a bare-metal machine you might have. A good option might be the LAPP image, which includes Python and PostgreSQL, and can be found at `http://www.turnkeylinux.org/lapp`.

We should make sure we have an OpenSSH server installed, to be able to remotely work on the server. Ubuntu has that option available in the setup assistant, but it can also be installed from the following command line:

```
$ sudo apt-get install openssh-server
```

After this, we can use any SSH client to connect to our Odoo host. In a Windows machine, a popular option is to use PuTTY. It can be downloaded from `http://www.putty.org`.

We can check our server's IP address, using:

```
$ ip addr show
```

Using an SSH client not only allows you to work on a remote server, it is also more comfortable to work with than the virtual machine console screens, providing better copy/paste support, and allowing you to choose window size, font type, and so on.

Installing Odoo from source

Ready-to-install Odoo packages can be found at `https://nightly.odoo.com`, available as Windows (`.exe`), Debian (`.deb`), CentOS (`.rpm`), and source code tarballs (`.tar.gz`).

As developers, we will prefer installing them directly from the GitHub repository. This will end up giving us more control over versions and updates.

Odoo is built using the Python programming language, and it uses the PostgreSQL database for data storage; these are the two main requirements of an Odoo host. To run Odoo from the source, we will first need to install the Python libraries it depends on. The Odoo source code can then be downloaded from GitHub. While we can download a ZIP file or tarball, we will see that it's better if we get the sources using the Git version control application; it'll help us to have it installed on our Odoo host as well.

To keep things tidy, let's work in a `/odoo-dev` directory inside our `home` directory.

 Throughout the book, we will assume that `/odoo-dev` is the directory where your Odoo server is installed.

First, make sure you are logged in as the user we created here or during the installation process, not as the `root`. Assuming your user is `odoo`, confirm it with the following command:

```
$ whoami
odoo
$ echo $HOME
/home/odoo
```

Now we are ready, we start by installing some basic dependencies needed by Odoo:

```
$ sudo apt-get update
$ sudo apt-get upgrade
$ sudo apt-get install python3-dev python3-pip # Python 3 for dev
$ sudo apt-get install wkhtmltopdf  # For report printing
$ sudo apt-get install git  # Install Git
$ sudo apt-get install npm  # Install NodeJs and its package manager
$ sudo ln -s /usr/bin/nodejs /usr/bin/node  # node runs nodejs
$ sudo npm install -g less less-plugin-clean-css  # Install less
```

Starting from version 9.0, the Odoo web client requires the `less` CSS preprocessor to be installed in the system in order for web pages to be rendered correctly. To install this, we need Node.js and npm.

Previous Odoo versions only supported Python 2.7, but starting from version 11.0 Odoo runs on Python 3.5 or later. This is the primary Python version supported. It should still work with Python 2.7, but this is not guaranteed to hold true in the future.

Be aware that your operating system can have both Python versions installed, but the `python` and `pip` commands by default point to Python 2.7. Both installations will have their own installed package index, so if you are missing some Python library, make sure that you are using `python3` and `pip3` commands.

To install Odoo from the source, we should follow these steps:

1. Clone the Git repository.
2. Install Odoo dependencies.
3. Install the PostgreSQL database.

We start by cloning the Odoo source code directly from GitHub:

```
$ mkdir ~/odoo-dev   # Create a directory to work in
$ cd ~/odoo-dev   # Go into our work directory
$ git clone https://github.com/odoo/odoo.git -b 11.0 --depth=1   # Get Odoo
sources
```

At the end, Odoo should be ready to use. The ~ symbol is a shortcut for our `home` directory (for example, `/home/odoo`). The `-b 11.0` option tells Git to explicitly download the 11.0 branch of Odoo. At the time of writing, this is redundant since 11.0 is the default branch; however, this may change, so it may make the script future-proof. The `--depth=1` option tells Git to download only the last revision, instead of the full change history, making the download smaller and faster.

In previous editions, the Odoo source code included a utility script, inside the `odoo/setup/` directory, to help us install the required dependencies in a Debian/Ubuntu system. As of Odoo 11, this script is not available.

Odoo is a Python application, depending on other Python packages installable using `pip`. Some of these packages require some system packages to be installed. To install all that is needed, we can use:

```
$ sudo apt-get install libxml2-dev libxslt1-dev libevent-dev \
libpq-dev libjpeg-dev poppler-utils # Odoo system dependencies
$ sudo apt-get install libldap2-dev libsasl2-dev  # for LDAP
$ pip3 install -r ~/odoo-dev/odoo/requirements.txt
```

Alternatively, we could have installed the system packaged versions of these libraries, such as `python3-lxml`, using the apt-get package manager. The list of dependencies used can be found in the `./odoo/debian/control` file.

 The correct dependency installation may vary depending on your operating system and on the Odoo version you are installing. If you have trouble with any of the previous steps, make sure you check the official documentation at `https://www.odoo.com/documentation/11.0/setup/install.html`. Instructions for previous editions are also available there.

We still need to install the PostgreSQL database, required to run Odoo:

```
$ sudo apt-get install postgresql  # Install PostgreSQL
$ sudo su -c "createuser -s $(whoami)" postgres # Create db superuser
```

The last command creates a PostgreSQL user for the current system user. We need that so that we can create and drop the databases to be used by our Odoo instances.

Now, we can start the Odoo server instance by running:

```
$ ~/odoo-dev/odoo/odoo-bin
```

 Since Odoo 10.0, the server is started using the `./odoo-bin` executable. In former Odoo versions, the `./odoo.py` script was used instead.

By default, Odoo instances listen on port `8069`, so if we point a browser to `http://<server-address>:8069`, we will reach these instances. When we access it for the first time, it shows us an assistant to create a new database, as shown in the following screenshot:

As a developer, we will need to work with several databases, so it's more convenient to create them from the command line, and we will learn how to do this. Now, press *Ctrl + C* in the terminal to stop the Odoo server and get back to the command prompt.

Initializing a new Odoo database

To create and initialize an Odoo database with the Odoo data schema, we should run the Odoo server using the -d option:

```
$ ~/odoo-dev/odoo/odoo-bin -d testdb
```

This will take a couple of minutes to initialize the testdb database, and it will end with an INFO log message, **Modules loaded**. Note that it might not be the last log message, and it can be in the last three or four lines. With this, the server will be ready to listen to client requests.

Since Odoo 9.0, the database is automatically created if it doesn't exist yet. In version 8.0, this was not so, and you needed to create the database manually, using the `createdb` command.

By default, this will initialize the database with demonstration data, which is often useful for development databases. This is the equivalent to having the **Load demonstration data** checkbox ticked when creating a new database from the user interface.

To initialize a database without demonstration data, add the `--without-demo=all` option to the command.

To be able to create a new database, your user must be a PostgreSQL superuser. The PostgreSQL setup script used in the previous section takes care of that. Just in case you also need it for some other user, this is the command to make the current Unix user a PostgreSQL superuser:

```
$ sudo createuser --superuser $(whoami)
```

 For a development environment, it is fine for the user running the Odoo instance to be a database superuser. However, for a production environment, Odoo security best practices recommend to never run a production instance with a database user that is a superuser.

Now that we have a running Odoo instance, we can access it by opening the `http://<server-name>:8069` URL with a web browser. This should present us with the Odoo login screen. If you don't know your server name, type the `hostname` command in the terminal in order to find it or the `ifconfig` command to find the IP address.

The default administrator account is `admin`, with its password `admin`. Upon login, you are presented with the **Apps** menu, displaying the available applications.

To stop the Odoo server instance and return to the command line, press *Ctrl + C* at the terminal window running the server. Pressing the up arrow key will bring us the previous shell command, so it's a quick way to start Odoo again with the same options. The *Ctrl + C* keys followed by the up arrow key and *Enter* is a frequently used combination to restart the Odoo server during development.

Managing Odoo databases

We've seen how to create and initialize new Odoo databases from the command line. There are more commands worth knowing about for managing databases.

Although the Odoo server automatically takes care of that, we can manually create PostgreSQL databases from the command line, using:

```
$ createdb MyDB
```

More interesting, it can also create a new database by copying an existing one, using the `--template` option. For this to work, the copied database can't have open connections to it, so make sure your Odoo instance is stopped and there is no other connection open for it. The command to use looks like this:

```
$ createdb --template=MyDB MyDB2
```

In fact, every time we create a database, a template is used. If none is specified, a predefined one called `template1` is used.

To list the existing databases in your system, use the PostgreSQL `psql` utility with the `-l` option:

```
$ psql -l
```

Running it will list the two databases we have created so far: `MyDB` and `MyDB2`. The list will also display the encoding used in each database. The default is UTF-8, which is the encoding needed for Odoo databases.

To remove a database you no longer need (or want to recreate), use the `dropdb` command:

```
$ dropdb MyDB2
```

Now you know the basics to work with databases. To learn more about PostgreSQL, refer to the official documentation at `http://www.postgresql.org/docs/`.

WARNING: The `drop database` command will irrevocably destroy your data. Be careful when using it and always keep backups of important databases before using this command.

A word about Odoo product versions

At the time of writing, Odoo's latest stable version is version 11, marked on GitHub as branch 11.0. This is the version we will work with throughout the book.

 It's important to note that Odoo databases are incompatible between Odoo major versions. This means that if you run an Odoo 11 server against a database created for a previous major version of Odoo, it won't work. Non-trivial migration work is needed before a database can be used with a later version of the product.

The same is true for addon modules: as a general rule, an addon module developed for an Odoo major version will not work with other versions. When downloading a community module from the web, make sure it targets the Odoo version you are using.

On the other hand, major releases (10.0, 11.0) are expected to receive frequent updates, but these should be mostly bug fixes. They are assured to be "API stable," meaning model data structures and view element identifiers will remain stable. This is important because it means there will be no risk of custom modules breaking due to incompatible changes in the upstream core modules.

Be warned that the version in the `master` branch will result in the next major stable version, but until then, it's not "API stable" and you should not use it to build custom modules. Doing so is like moving on quicksand: you can't be sure when some changes will be introduced that will break your custom module.

More server configuration options

The Odoo server supports quite a few other options. We can check all the available options with `--help`:

```
$ ./odoo-bin --help
```

We will review some of the most important options in the following sections. Let's start by looking at how the currently active options can be saved in a configuration file.

Odoo server configuration files

Most of the options can be saved in a configuration file. By default, Odoo will use the `.odoorc` file. In Linux systems, its default location is in the `home` directory (`$HOME`), and in the Windows distribution, it is in the same directory as the executable used to launch Odoo.

 In older Odoo/OpenERP versions, the name for the default configuration file was `.openerp-serverrc`. For backward compatibility, Odoo 10 will still use this if it's present and no `.odoorc` file is found.

On a clean install, the `.odoorc` configuration file is not automatically created. We should use the `--save` option to create the default configuration file, if it doesn't exist yet, and store the current instance configuration into it:

```
$ ~/odoo-dev/odoo/odoo-bin --save --stop-after-init
```

Here, we also used the `--stop-after-init` option to stop the server after it finishes its actions. This option is often used when running tests or asking to run a module upgrade to check whether it is installed correctly.

Now we can inspect what was saved in this default configuration file:

```
$ more ~/.odoorc   # show the configuration file
```

This will show all the configuration options available with their default values. Editing them will be effective the next time you start an Odoo instance. Type `q` to quit and go back to the prompt.

We can also choose to use a specific configuration file, using the `--conf=<filepath>` option. Configuration files don't need to have all the options you've just seen. Only the ones that actually change a default value need to be there.

Changing the listening port

The `--http-port=<port>` command option (or just `-p <port>`) allows us to change the listening port of a server instance from the default `8069`. This can be used to run more than one instance at the same time, on the same machine.

The `--http-port` server option was introduced in Odoo 11.0 and replaces the old `--xmlrpc-port` option, used in previous versions.

Let's try this out. Open two terminal windows. On the first, run this:

```
$ ~/odoo-dev/odoo/odoo-bin --http-port=8070
```

Run the following command on the second terminal:

```
$ ~/odoo-dev/odoo/odoo-bin --http-port=8071
```

There you go, two Odoo instances on the same server listening on different ports! The two instances can use the same or different databases, depending on the configuration parameters used. And the two could be running the same or different versions of Odoo.

The database filter option

When developing with Odoo, it is common to work with several databases, and sometimes even with different Odoo versions. Stopping and starting different server instances on the same port, and switching between different databases, can cause web client sessions to behave improperly. This is because the browser stores session cookies.

Accessing our instance using a browser window running in private mode can help avoid some of these problems.

Another good practice is to enable a database filter on the server instance to ensure that it only allows requests for the database we want to work with, ignoring all others.

Since Odoo 11.0, the `--database` (or `-d`) server option accepts a comma-separated list of database names, and only these can be used.

However, in Odoo versions before 11.0, the `--database` option only indicates a database to be initialized, but the other existing databases are accessible. We need to also add a filter limiting the databases that can be accessed.

This is done with the `--db-filter` option. It accepts a regular expression to be used as a filter for valid database names. To match an exact name, the expression should begin with ^ and end with $.

For example, to allow only the `testdb` database, we would use this command:

```
$ ~/odoo-dev/odoo/odoo-bin --db-filter=^testdb$
```

Managing server log messages

The `--log-level` option allows us to set the log verbosity. This can be very useful to understand what is going on in the server. For example, to enable the debug log level, use the `--log-level=debug` option.

The following log levels can be particularly interesting:

- `debug_sql` to inspect SQL queries generated by the server
- `debug_rpc` to detail requests received by the server
- `debug_rpc_answer` to detail responses sent by the server

In fact, `--log-level` is a simplified way to set the Odoo logging verbosity. You might like to know that the more complete `--log-handler` option allows you to selectively turn on/off specific loggers.

By default, the log output is directed to standard output (your console screen), but it can be directed to a log file with the `--logfile=<filepath>` option.

Finally, the `--dev=all` option will bring up the Python debugger (pdb) when an exception is raised. It's useful for doing a postmortem analysis of a server error. Note that it doesn't have any effect on logger verbosity. More details on the Python debugger commands can be found at `https://docs.python.org/3/library/pdb.html#debugger-commands`.

Developing from a remote workstation

You may be running Odoo with a Debian/Ubuntu system either in a local virtual machine or in a server over the network, but you may prefer to do the development work at your personal workstation, using your favorite text editor or IDE. This may frequently be the case for developers working from Windows workstations, but it also may be the case for Linux users who need to work on an Odoo server over the local network.

A solution for this is to enable file sharing in the Odoo host so that files are made easy to edit from our workstation. For Odoo server operations, such as a server restart, we can use an SSH shell (such as PuTTY on Windows) alongside our favorite editor.

Using a Linux text editor

Sooner or later, we will need to edit files from the shell command line. In many Debian systems, the default text editor is vi. If you're not comfortable with it, you probably could use a friendlier alternative. In Ubuntu systems, the default text editor is nano. You might prefer it since it's easier to use. In case it's not available in your server, it can be installed with:

```
$ sudo apt-get install nano
```

In the following sections, we will assume nano as the preferred editor. If you prefer any other editor, feel free to adapt the commands accordingly.

Installing and configuring Samba

The Samba service helps make Linux file-sharing services compatible with Microsoft Windows systems. We can install it on our Debian/Ubuntu server with this command:

```
$ sudo apt-get install samba samba-common-bin
```

The `samba` package installs the file-sharing services. The `samba-common-bin` package might be needed in order to have the `smbpasswd` tool available. Users that are allowed to access the shared files need to be registered with it. We will register our `odoo` user, and set a password for it:

```
$ sudo smbpasswd -a odoo
```

After this, we will be asked for a password to use to access the shared directory, and the odoo user will be able to access shared files for its home directory, although it will be read-only. We want to have write access, so we need to edit the Samba configuration file to change it, as follows:

```
$ sudo nano /etc/samba/smb.conf
```

In the configuration file, look for the [homes] section. Edit its configuration lines so that they match these settings:

```
[homes]
    comment = Home Directories
    browseable = yes
    read only = no
    create mask = 0640
    directory mask = 0750
```

For the configuration changes to take effect, restart the service:

```
$ sudo /etc/init.d/smbd restart
```

On Windows, we can now access the network shared files with File Explorer, using a \\<my-server-name-or-IP> address. In our example, we used \\odoo or \\192.168.56.101.

When accessing for the first time, we will be asked for the Samba login created just now. Following our example, use the odoo user with the chosen password. You might encounter trouble with Windows adding the computer's domain to the username (for example, MYPC\odoo). To avoid this, use an empty domain by prepending a \ character to the login (for example, \odoo).

After this, we will be able to access and edit the contents of the odoo user's home directory:

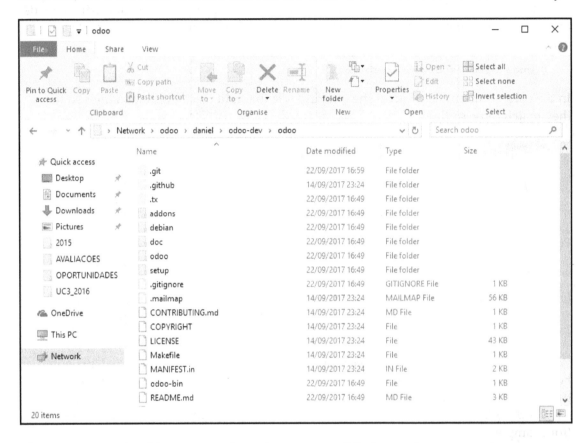

This is more comfortable to use, and persistent across Windows reboots, mapping a network drive for the path \\<my-server-name>\odoo.

Installing additional modules

Making new modules available in an Odoo instance so they can be installed is something that newcomers to Odoo frequently find confusing. But it doesn't have to be, so let's get familiar with that.

Finding community modules

There are many Odoo modules available on the internet. The Odoo apps store at apps.odoo.com is a catalog of modules that can be downloaded and installed on your system. Another important resource are the **Odoo Community Association (OCA)** maintained modules, also available on GitHub at https://github.com/OCA/. The OCA is a non-profit organization created to coordinate community contributions, promoting quality, software best practices, and open source values.

To add a module to an Odoo installation, we could just copy it into the addons directory alongside the official modules. In our case, the addons directory is at ~/odoo-dev/odoo/addons/. However, this is not a good idea. Our Odoo installation is a Git version-controlled code repository, and we want to keep it synchronized with the upstream GitHub repository. Polluting it with foreign modules will make it hard to manage.

Instead, we can select one or more additional locations for modules, which will also be used when the Odoo server looks for modules. Not only can we keep our custom modules in a different directory, without having them mixed with the official ones, we can also have them organized in several directories.

We can try this now by downloading the code from this book, available in GitHub, and making those addon modules available in our Odoo installation. To get the source code from GitHub, run the following commands:

```
$ cd ~/odoo-dev
$ git clone https://github.com/dreispt/todo_app.git -b 11.0
```

We used the -b option to make sure we are downloading the modules for the 11.0 version.

After this, we will have a new /todo_app directory alongside the /odoo directory containing the modules. Now we need to let Odoo know about this new module directory.

Configuring the addons path

The Odoo server has a configuration option called addons_path to set where the server should look for modules. By default, this points to the /addons directory, where the Odoo server is running. We can provide not only one, but a list of directories where modules can be found. This allows us to keep our custom modules in a different directory, without having them mixed with the official addons.

Let's start the server with an addons path that includes our new module directory:

```
$ cd ~/odoo-dev/odoo
$ ./odoo-bin -d testdb --addons-path="../todo_app, ./addons"
```

If you look closer at the server log, you will notice a line reporting the addons path in use: `INFO ? odoo: addons paths: [...]`. Confirm that it contains our `todo_app` directory.

Updating the apps list

We still need to ask Odoo to update its module list before these new modules are available to be installed.

This has to be done from the Odoo web user interface, and we need the developer mode to be enabled. In the web client, access the **Apps** top menu and select the **Update Apps List** menu option.

After updating the modules list, we can confirm the new modules are available for installation with the **Apps** menu option, looking them up in the available apps list:

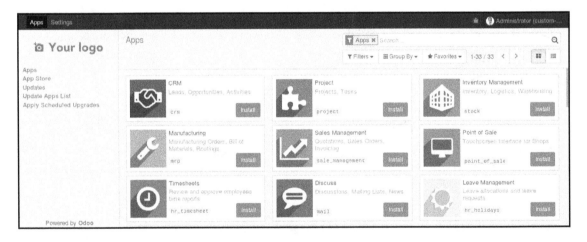

Summary

In this chapter, we learned how to set up an Ubuntu system to host Odoo and install it from the GitHub source code. We also learned how to create Odoo databases and run Odoo instances. To allow developers to use their favorite tools in their personal workstation, we explained how to configure file sharing in the Odoo host.

We should now have a functioning Odoo environment to work with and be comfortable with managing databases and instances.

With this in place, we're ready to go straight into action. In the next chapter, we will create our first Odoo module from scratch and understand the main elements it involves.

So, let's get started!

3
Your First Odoo Application – A Practical Overview

Developing in Odoo most of the time means creating our own modules. In this chapter, we will create our first Odoo application and learn the steps needed to make it available to Odoo and install it.

Inspired by the notable `http://todomvc.com/` project, we will build a simple To-Do application. It should allow us to add new tasks, mark them as completed, and finally clear the task list of all the already-completed tasks.

We will get started by learning the basics of the development workflow: we'll set up a new instance for your work, create and install a new module, and update it to apply the changes we make along with the development iterations.

Odoo follows an MVC-like architecture, and we will go through the layers during our implementation of the To-Do application:

- The **model** layer, defining the structure of the app's data
- The **view** layer, describing the user interface
- The **controller** layer, supporting the business logic of the application

Next, we will learn how to set up access control security and, finally, we will add some descriptions and branding information to the module.

Note that the concept of the term controller mentioned here is different from the Odoo web development controllers. These are program endpoints that web pages can call to perform actions.

With this approach, you will be able to gradually learn about the basic building blocks that make up an application and experience the iterative process of building an Odoo module from scratch.

Creating a new addon module

An addon module is a directory containing the files that implement some Odoo features. It can add new features or modify existing ones.

The addon module directory must contain a manifest, or descriptor file, named __manifest__.py, plus the other module files.

Some module addons are featured as Apps. These represent applications available for Odoo, and usually add their own top-level menu item. They provide the core elements for a functional area, such as CRM or HR. Because of this, they are highlighted in the Odoo Apps menu. On the other hand, non-App module addons are expected to add features to these Apps.

If your module adds new or major functionality to Odoo, it probably should be an App. If the module just makes changes to the functionality of an existing App, it probably should be a regular addon module. We will show you this in the next section.

Creating the module's basic skeleton

Following the instructions in Chapter 2, *Installing and Organizing the Development Environment*, we should have the Odoo server code at ~/odoo-dev/odoo/. The best practices say that our code should be kept in its own directory, and never mixed up with Odoo's original code. So, to host our custom modules we will use a new directory alongside Odoo: ~/odoo-dev/custom-addons.

Odoo includes a scaffold command to automatically create a new module directory, with a basic structure already in place. You can learn more about it with the following command:

```
$ ~/odoo-dev/odoo/odoo-bin scaffold --help
```

You might want to keep this in mind when you start working on your next module, but we won't be using it right now since we prefer to manually alter the structure for our module.

An Odoo addon module is a directory containing a __manifest__.py descriptor file. It also needs to be Python importable, so it must also have a __init__.py file.

 In previous versions, this descriptor file was named __openerp__.py. This name is still supported but is deprecated.

The module's directory name is its technical name. We will use todo_app for it. The technical name must be a valid Python identifier: it should begin with a letter and can only contain letters, numbers, and the underscore character.

If using the command line, we can initialize our module directory, with an empty __init__.py file in it, with these commands:

```
$ mkdir -p ~/odoo-dev/custom-addons/todo_app
$ touch ~/odoo-dev/custom-addons/todo_app/__init__.py
```

Next, we need to add the manifest file. It should contain only a Python dictionary, with about a dozen possible attributes. Of them, only the name attribute is required, but the description and author attributes are also highly advised.

Now, create the __manifest__.py file, alongside the __init__.py file, with the following content:

```
{
    'name': 'To-Do Application',
    'description': 'Manage personal to-do tasks.',
    'author': 'Daniel Reis',
    'depends': ['base'],
    'application': True,
}
```

The depends attribute can have a list of other modules that are required. Odoo will have them automatically installed when this module is installed. It's not a mandatory attribute, but it's advised to always have it. If no particular dependencies are needed, we should depend on the core base module.

You should be careful to ensure all dependencies are explicitly set here; otherwise, the module may fail to install in a clean database (due to missing dependencies) or have loading errors if by chance the other required modules are loaded afterward.

For our application, we don't need any specific dependencies, so we depend on the `base` module only.

To be concise, we chose to use only some essential descriptor keys:

- `name` is a string with the addon module title.
- `description` is a long text with the description of the features, usually in RST format.
- `author` is the author name. It is a string, but can contain a comma-separated list of names.
- `depends` is a list of the addon modules it depends on. They will be automatically installed before this module is.
- `application` is a Boolean flag, declaring whether the addon module should be featured as an app in the Apps list.

Since Odoo 8.0, instead of the `description` key, we can use a `README.rst` or `README.md` file in the module's top directory. If both exist, then the manifest description is used.

In a real-world scenario, we recommend that you also use the additional keys, since they are relevant for the Odoo apps store:

- `summary` is a string displayed as a subtitle for the module.
- `version`, by default, is 1.0. It should follow versioning rules (see `http://semver.org/` for details). It is a good practice to use the Odoo version before our module version, for example: 11.0.1.0.
- `license` identifier, by default considered to be LGPL-3.
- `website` is a URL to find more information about the module. This can help people find more documentation or the issue tracker to file bugs and suggestions.
- `category` is a string with the functional category of the module, which defaults to **Uncategorized**. The list of existing categories can be found in the security **Groups** form (at **Settings | User | Groups**), in the **Application** field drop-down list.

These other descriptor keys are also available:

- `installable` is by default `True` but can be set to `False` to disable a module.
- `auto_install`, if set to `True`, will be automatically installed as soon as all its dependencies are already installed. It is used for "glue" modules, connecting two features together as soon as both are installed in the same instance.

Adding an icon

Our module is looking good. Why not add an icon to it to make it look even better? For this, we just need to add a `static/description/icon.png` file to the module, with the icon to be used.

We will be reusing the icon of the existing Notes application, so we should copy the `odoo/addons/note/static/description/icon.png` file into the `custom-addons/todo_app/static/description` directory.

The following commands should do that trick for us:

```
$ cd ~/odoo-dev
$ mkdir -p ./custom-addons/todo_app/static/description
$ cp ./odoo/addons/note/static/description/icon.png ./custom-addons/todo_app/static/description
```

Now, if we update the module list, our module should be displayed with the new icon.

A word about licenses

Choosing a license for your work is very important, and you should consider carefully what the best choice for you is, and its implications. The most used licenses for Odoo modules are the **GNU Lesser General Public License v3 (LGPLv3)** and the **Affero General Public License v3 (AGPLv3)**. The LGPL is more permissive and allows commercial modifications, without the need to share the corresponding source code. The AGPL is a stronger open source license, and requires derivative work and service hosting to share the source code. Learn more about the GNU licenses at `https://www.gnu.org/licenses/`.

Discovering and installing new modules

We now have an addon module with minimal structure, but it can be installed in our Odoo instance. Before we can do that, our Odoo server needs to know about this new directory we are using for our custom modules, and needs to make them available for installation.

That's what we will be doing next.

Adding to the addons path

To have new modules available for Odoo, we need to make sure the directory containing the module is in the addons path, then update the Odoo module list. Both actions have been explained in detail in the previous chapter, but here we will continue with a brief overview of what is needed.

We will position ourselves in our work directory and start the server with the appropriate addons path configuration:

```
$ cd ~/odoo-dev
$ ./odoo/odoo-bin -d todo --addons-path="custom-addons,odoo/addons" --save
```

The `--save` option saves the options you used in a configuration file. This spares us from repeating them every time we restart the server; just run `./odoo-bin` and the last saved option will be used. You can specify the configuration file and location to use (and save to) using the `-c` option.

Look closely at the server log. It should have an `INFO ? odoo: addons paths:[...]` line. It should include our `custom-addons` directory.

Remember to also include any other addon directories you might be using. For instance, if you also have a `~/odoo-dev/extra` directory containing additional modules to be used, you might want to include them also, using the `--addons-path` option:

```
--addons-path="custom-addons,extra,odoo/addons"
```

Now we need the Odoo instance to acknowledge the new module we just added.

Installing the new module

Before a new addon module can be installed, the module list needs to be updated.

This can be done from the **Apps** top menu and the **Update Apps List** option. It updates the module list, adding any modules that may have been added since the last update to the list. Remember that we need the developer mode enabled for this option to be visible.

Make sure your web client session is working with the right database. You can check that at the top-right: the database name is shown in parentheses, right after the username, a way to have the server limited to using only the intended database. Until Odoo 11.0, this was done with the additional option `--db-filter=^MYDB$`. Since Odoo 11.0, this is not required, as by default `-d` (or `--database`) automatically performs that filter.

The **Apps** option shows us the list of available modules. By default, it shows only the application modules. Since we have created an application module, we don't need to remove that filter to see it. Type `todo` in the search and you should see our new module, ready to be installed:

Now click on the module's **Install** button, and we're ready!

Upgrading a module

Developing a module is an iterative process, and you will want changes made on source files to be applied to and made visible in Odoo.

In many cases, this is done by upgrading the module: look up the module in the **Apps** list and once it is already installed, you will have an **Upgrade** button available.

However, when the changes are only in Python code, the upgrade may not have an effect. Instead of a module upgrade, an application server restart is needed. Since Odoo loads Python code only once, any later changes to code require a server restart to be applied.

In some cases, if the module changes were in both data files and Python code, you might need both the operations. This is a common source of confusion for new Odoo developers.

But fortunately, there is a better way. The safest way to make all our changes to a module effective is to stop and restart the server instance, requesting our modules to be upgraded to our work database.

In the terminal where the server instance is running, use *Ctrl + C* to stop it. Then, start the server and upgrade the `todo_app` module using the following command:

```
$ ./odoo-bin -d todo -u todo_app
```

The `-u` option (or `--update` in the long form) requires the `-d` option and accepts a comma-separated list of modules to update. For example, we could use `-u todo_app,mail`. When a module is updated, all other installed modules depending on it are also updated. This is essential to maintain the integrity of the inheritance mechanisms, used to extend features.

Throughout the book, when you need to apply the work done in modules, the safest way is to restart the Odoo instance with the preceding command. Pressing the up arrow key brings to you the previous command that was used. So, most of the time, you will find yourself using the *Ctrl + C*, up, and *Enter* key combination.

 Until Odoo 10.0, before a new addon module could be installed, the module list had to be manually updated from the web client menu option for it to be known to Odoo. Since 11.0, the list of modules available has been automatically updated when a module is installed or updated.

Similarly, a `-i` option, or `--install,` is also available to perform the installation (or reinstallation) of modules. For new modules, you had to update the module list in the web client before they could be installed, but since Odoo 11 this has not been necessary and new modules can immediately be installed.

The server development mode

In Odoo 10, a new option was introduced, providing developer-friendly features. To use them, start the server instance with the additional option `--dev=all`.

This enables a few handy features to speed up our development cycle. The most important are:

- Reload Python code automatically once a Python file is saved, avoiding a manual server restart
- Read view definitions directly from the XML files, avoiding manual module upgrades

The `--dev` option accepts a comma-separated list of options, although the `all` option will be suitable most of the time. We can also specify the debugger we prefer to use. By default, the Python debugger, `pdb`, is used. Some people might prefer to install and use alternative debuggers. The other debuggers supported are `ipdb` and `pudb`.

The server developer mode requires an additional dependency to be installed, `python3-watchdog`. Before you can use it in an Ubuntu/Debian system, install:

```
$ sudo apt-get install python3-watchdog
```

 For versions before Odoo 11 running on Python 2, install `python-watchdog` instead.

The model layer

Now that Odoo knows about our new module, let's start by adding a simple model to it.

Models describe business objects, such as an Opportunity, Sales Order, or Partner (customer, supplier, and so on). A model has a list of attributes and can also define its specific business.

Models are implemented using a Python class derived from an Odoo template class. They translate directly to database objects, and Odoo automatically takes care of that when installing or upgrading the module. The component responsible for this is the **Object Relational Mapping (ORM)**.

Our module will be a very simple application to maintain To-Do tasks. These tasks will have a single text field for the description and a checkbox to mark them as complete. We should later add a button to remove the old, completed tasks from the To-Do list.

Creating the data model

The Odoo development guidelines state that the Python files for models should be placed inside a `models` subdirectory. So, we will create a `models/todo_task_model.py` file in the main directory of the `todo_app` module.

The Odoo official coding guidelines can be found at `http://www.odoo.com/documentation/11.0/reference/guidelines.html`. Another relevant coding standards document is the Odoo Community Association coding guidelines at `https://github.com/OCA/maintainer-tools/blob/master/CONTRIBUTING.md`.

Before that, we need to let Python know that the `models` directory should be used (imported). To do that, edit the module's main `__init__.py` file like this:

```
from . import models
```

We also need to add a `models/__init__.py` file, importing the Python code file to be used:

```
from . import todo_task_model
```

Now we can create the `models/todo_task_model.py` file with the following content:

```
from odoo import fields, models

class TodoTask(models.Model):
    _name = 'todo.task'
    _description = 'To-do Task'
    name = fields.Char('Description', required=True)
    is_done = fields.Boolean('Done?')
    active = fields.Boolean('Active?', default=True)
    user_id = fields.Many2one(
        'res.users',
        string='Responsible',
        default=lambda self: self.env.user)
    team_ids = fields.Many2many('res.partner', string='Team')
```

The first line is a special marker telling the Python interpreter that this file has UTF-8 so that it can expect and handle non-ASCII characters. We won't be using any, but it's good practice to have it anyway.

The second line is a Python code import statement, making the `models` and `fields` objects from the Odoo core available.

The third line declares our new model. It's a class derived from `models.Model`.

The next line sets the _name attribute, defining the identifier that will be used throughout Odoo to refer to this model. Note that the actual Python class name, `TodoTask` in this case, is meaningless to other Odoo modules. The _name value is what will be used as an identifier.

> Only Model names use dots (.) to separate keywords. Everything else uses underscores (_): addon modules, XML identifiers, table names, and so on.

Notice that this and the following lines are indented. If you're not familiar with Python, you should know that this is important: indentation defines a nested code block, so these four lines should all be equally indented.

Then we have the `_description` model attribute. It is not mandatory, but it provides a user-friendly name for the model records, which can be used for better user messages.

The remaining lines define the model's fields. It's worth noting that name and `active` are special field names. By default, Odoo will use the name field as the record's title when referencing it from other models. The `active` field is used to activate records, and by default, only active records will be shown. We will use it to clear away completed tasks without actually deleting them from the database.

We can see also examples of how to add fields with relationships to other models. The user_id field allows for picking the User owner of the Task. We added a default to it, so that the current user is automatically set as responsible for the Task.

Finally, team_ids allows us to select a list of Partners involved in the Task. It is a many-to-many relation, where each Task can have many Team members, and each Partner can be involved in many Tasks.

That's it! For our Python code changes to take effect, the module needs to be upgraded, triggering the creation of the corresponding objects in the database.

We won't see any menu options to access this new model since we didn't add them yet. Still, we can inspect the newly created model using the **Technical** menu. In the **Settings** top menu, go to **Technical** | **Database Structure** | **Models**, search for the `todo.task` model in the list, and click on it to see its definition:

If everything goes right, it is confirmed that the model and fields were created. If you can't see them here, try a server restart with a module upgrade, as described before.

We can also see some additional fields we didn't declare. These are reserved fields Odoo automatically adds to every new model. They are as follows:

- `id` is a unique numeric identifier for each record in the model.
- `create_date` and `create_uid` specify when the record was created and who created it, respectively.
- `write_date` and `write_uid` confirm when the record was last modified and who modified it, respectively.
- `__last_update` is a helper that is not actually stored in the database. It is used for concurrency checks.

Extending existing models

New models are defined through Python classes. Extending models is also done through Python classes, with help from an Odoo-specific inheritance mechanism, the _inherit class attribute. This _inherit class attribute identifies the model to be extended. The new class inherits all the features of the parent Odoo model, and we only need to declare the modifications to introduce.

In our todo.task model, we have a many-to-many field for the team of people (Partners) that will collaborate with us on that Task. We will now add to the Partners model the inverse of that relation, so that we can see, for each Partner, all the Tasks they are involved in.

The coding style guidelines recommend having a Python file for each model. So we will add a models/res_partner_model.py file to implement our extensions on Partners.

Edit the models/__init__.py file to also import this new code file. The content should look like this:

```
from . import todo_task_model
from . import res_partner_model
```

Now create the models/res_partner_model.py with the following code:

```
from odoo import fields, models

class ResPartner(models.Model):
    _inherit = 'res.partner'
    todo_ids= fields.Many2many(
        'todo.task',
        string="To-do Teams")
```

We used the _inherit class attribute to declare the Model to extend. Notice that we didn't use any other class attributes, not even the _name. This is not needed, unless we want to make changes to any of them.

> The _name is the model identifier; what happens if we try to change it? In fact, you can, and if you do it creates a new Model that is a copy of the inherited one. This is called **prototype inheritance** and will be discussed in Chapter 4, *Models - Structure the Application Data*.

You can think of this as getting a reference to a Model definition living in a central registry, and making in-place changes to it. These can be adding fields, modifying existing fields, modifying model class attributes, or even methods with business logic.

In our case, we add a new field, `todo_ids`, with the inverse of the relation between Tasks and Partners, defined in the To-Do Task model. There are some details here that are being automatically handled by the ORM, but they are not relevant for us right now. They are addressed in more detail in `Chapter 4`, *Models - Structure the Application Data*.

Extending existing fields follows a similar logic: we only need to use the attributes to be modified. All omitted attributes will keep the original value.

To have the new Model fields added to the database tables, we should now perform a module upgrade. If everything goes as expected, the newly added field should be seen when inspecting the `res.partner` model, in the **Technical** | **Database Structure** | **Models** menu option.

The view layer

The view layer describes the user interface. Views are defined using XML, which is used by the web client framework to generate data-aware HTML views.

We have **menu items** that can activate actions which can render views. For example, the **Users** menu item processes an action also called **Users**, which in turn renders a series of views. There are several view types available, such as the **list** (sometimes called **tree** for historical reasons) and **form** views, and the filter options made available in the top-right search box are also defined by a particular type of view, the **search** view.

The Odoo development guidelines state that the XML files defining the user interface should be placed inside a `views/` subdirectory.

Let's start creating the user interface for our To-Do application.

In the next sections, we will make gradual improvements and frequent module upgrades to make those changes available. You might also want to try the `--dev=all` server option, which spares us from module upgrades while developing. Using it, the view definitions are read directly from the XML files so that your changes can be immediately available to Odoo without the need for a module upgrade.

If an upgrade fails because of an XML error, don't panic! Read the error message in the server log carefully; it should point you to where the problem is. If you feel in trouble, just comment out the last edited XML portions or remove the XML file from the __manifest__.py and repeat the upgrade. The server should start correctly.

Adding menu items

Now that we have the places to store our data, we want to have them available on the user interface. The first thing to do should be to add the corresponding menu options.

Create the views/todo_menu.xml file to define a menu item and the action performed by it:

```xml
<?xml version="1.0"?>
<odoo>
  <!-- Action to open To-do Task list -->
  <act_window id="action_todo_task"
    name="To-do Task"
    res_model="todo.task"
    view_mode="tree,form"
  />
  <!-- Menu item to open To-do Task list -->
  <menuitem id="menu_todo_task"
    name="Todos"
    action="action_todo_task"
  />
</odoo>
```

The user interface, including menu options and actions, is stored in database tables. The XML file is a data file used to load those definitions into the database when the addon module is installed or upgraded. The preceding code is an Odoo data file, describing two records to add to Odoo:

- The <act_window> element defines a client-side window action that will open the todo.task model with the tree and form views enabled, in that order
- The <menuitem> defines a top menu item calling the action_todo_task action, which was defined before

Both elements include an id attribute. This id attribute, called an **XML ID**, is very important; it is used to uniquely identify each data element inside the module, and is the method other elements can use to reference it. In this case, the <menuitem> element needs to reference the action to process, and so needs to use the <act_window> XML ID for that. XML IDs are discussed in greater detail in Chapter 5, *Access Control and Data Files*.

Our module does not yet know about this new XML data file. For this to happen, it needs to be declared in the __manifest__.py file, using the data attribute. It is a list of the data files to be loaded by the module upon installation or upgrade.

Now add this attribute to the manifest's dictionary:

```
'data': ['views/todo_menu.xml'],
```

We need to upgrade the module again for these changes to take effect. Go to the **Todos** top menu and you should see our new menu option available. Clicking on it displays a basic list view, and we will have available an automatically generated form view:

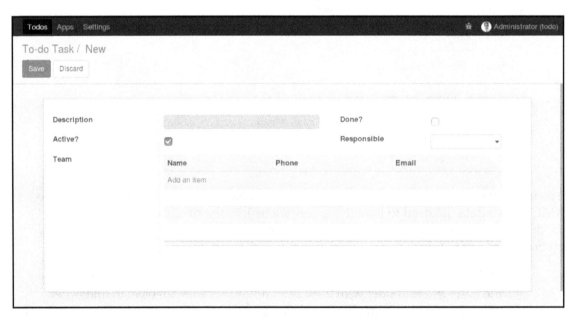

Even though we haven't defined our user interface view, the automatically generated list and form views are functional, and allow us to start editing data right away.

Creating the form view

All views are stored in the database, in the `ir.ui.view` model. To add a view to a module, we declare a `<record>` element describing the view in an XML file, which is to be loaded into the database when the module is installed.

Add this new `views/todo_view.xml` file to define our form view:

```xml
<?xml version="1.0"?>
<odoo>
  <record id="view_form_todo_task" model="ir.ui.view">
    <field name="name">To-do Task Form</field>
    <field name="model">todo.task</field>
    <field name="arch" type="xml">
      <form string="To-do Task">
        <group>
          <field name="name"/>
          <field name="is_done"/>
          <field name="active" readonly="1"/>
        </group>
      </form>
    </field>
  </record>
</odoo>
```

The `ir.ui.view` record has values for three fields: `name`, `model`, and `arch`. Another important element is the record `id`. It defines an XML ID identifier that can be used for other records to reference it.

The view is for the `todo.task` model and is named `To-do Task Form`. The name is just for information; it does not have to be unique, but it should allow one to easily identify which record it refers to. In fact, the name can be entirely omitted; in that case, it will be automatically generated from the model name and the view type.

The most important field is `arch`, as it contains the view definition, highlighted in the XML code listed previously. The `<form>` tag defines the view type, and in this case contains three fields. We added the `readonly` attribute to the `active` field, to make it read-only in the user interface.

Remember to add this new file to the `data` key in the manifest file; otherwise, our module won't know about it and it won't be loaded:

```
'data': [
    'views/todo_menu.xml',
    'views/todo_view.xml',
],
```

 Remember that for the changes to be loaded to our Odoo database, a module upgrade is needed. To see the changes in the web client, the form needs to be reloaded. Either click again on the menu option that opens it or reload the browser page (*F5* in most browsers).

Business document form views

The preceding section provided a basic form view, but we can make some improvements to it. For document models, Odoo has a presentation style that mimics a paper page. This form contains two elements: `<header>` to contain action buttons and `<sheet>` to contain the data fields.

We can now replace the basic `<form>` defined in the previous section with this one:

```
<form>
  <header>
  <!-- Buttons go here-->
  </header>
  <sheet>
    <!-- Content goes here: -->
    <group>
      <field name="name"/>
      <field name="is_done"/>
      <field name="active" readonly="1"/>
    </group>
  </sheet>
</form>
```

Adding action buttons

Forms can have buttons to perform actions. These buttons are able to run window actions such as opening another form or running Python functions defined in the model.

They can be placed anywhere inside a form, but for document-style forms, the recommended place for them is the `<header>` section.

For our application, we will add a button to clear a done task. This button will run the `do_clear_done` object method:

```
<header>
  <button name="do_clear_done" type="object"
          string="Clear Done" />
</header>
```

The basic attributes of a button consist of the following:

- `string` with the text to display on the button
- `type` of action it performs
- `name` is the identifier for that action
- `class` is an optional attribute to apply CSS styles, like in regular HTML

Using groups to organize forms

The `<group>` tag allows you to organize the form content. Placing `<group>` elements inside a `<group>` element creates a two-column layout inside the outer group. Group elements are advised to have a `name` attribute so that its easier for other modules to extend them.

We will use this to better organize our content. Let's change the `<sheet>` content of our form to match this:

```
<sheet>
  <group name="group_top">
    <group name="group_left">
      <field name="name" />
      <field name="user_id" />
      <field name="is_done" />
    </group>
    <group name="group_right">
      <field name="date_deadline" />
      <field name="team_ids" widget="many2many_tags" />
      <field name="active" readonly="1" />
    </group>
  </group>
</sheet>
```

The complete form view

At this point, our `todo.task` form view should look like this:

```
<form>
  <header>
    <button name="do_clear_done" type="object"
      string="Clear Done" />
  </header>
  <sheet>
    <group name="group_top">
      <group name="group_left">
        <field name="name" />
        <field name="user_id" />
        <field name="is_done" />
      </group>
      <group name="group_right">
        <field name="date_deadline" />
        <field name="team_ids" widget="many2many_tags" />
        <field name="active" readonly="1" />
      </group>
    </group>
  </sheet>
</form>
```

The action buttons won't work yet since we still need to add their business logic.

Adding list and search views

When viewing a model in list mode, a `<tree>` view is used. Tree views are capable of displaying lines organized in hierarchies, but most of the time they are used to display plain lists.

We can add the following `<tree>` view definition to `todo_view.xml`:

```
<record id="view_tree_todo_task" model="ir.ui.view">
  <field name="name">To-do Task Tree</field>
  <field name="model">todo.task</field>
  <field name="arch" type="xml">
    <tree colors="decoration-muted:is_done==True">
      <field name="name"/>
      <field name="is_done"/>
    </tree>
  </field>
</record>
```

This defines a list with only two columns: name and is_done. We also added a nice touch: the lines for done tasks (is_done==True) are shown as grayed out. This is done by applying the muted Bootstrap class. Check http://getbootstrap.com/docs/3.3/css/ #helper-classes-colors for more information on Bootstrap and its contextual colors.

> Because is_done is a Boolean field, the "decoration-muted:is_done==True" can elegantly be simplified to "decoration-muted:is_done". Try it!

At the top-right corner of the list, Odoo displays a search box. The fields it searches in and the available filters are defined by a <search> view.

As before, we will add this to todo_view.xml:

```
<record id="view_filter_todo_task" model="ir.ui.view">
  <field name="name">To-do Task Filter</field>
  <field name="model">todo.task</field>
  <field name="arch" type="xml">
    <search>
      <field name="user_id"/>
      <filter string="Not Done"
        domain="[('is_done','=',False)]"/>
      <filter string="Done"
        domain="[('is_done','!=',False)]"/>
    </search>
  </field>
</record>
```

The <field> elements define fields that are also searched when typing in the search box. We added user_id to automatically suggest searching in the Responsible field. The <filter> elements add predefined filter conditions, which can be toggled with a user click, defined using a specific syntax. This will be addressed in more detail in Chapter 9, *Backend Views - Design the User Interface*.

Extending views

Forms, lists, and search views are defined using the arch XML structures. To extend views, we need a way to modify this XML. This means locating XML elements and then introducing modifications at those points.

The XML record for view inheritance is just like the one for regular views, but also using the `inherit_id` attribute, with a reference to the view to be extended.

As an example of this, we will extend the Partner view to make the `todo_ids` field visible, showing all the Tasks that person is involved in.

The first thing to do is to find the XML ID for the view to be extended. We can find that by looking up the view in the Settings app and the **Technical | User Interface | Views** menu. The XML ID for the Partner form is `base.view_partner_form`. While there, we should also find the XML element where we want to insert our changes. We will be adding the list of collaborators at the end of the right columns, after the `Language` field. We usually identify the element to use by its `name` attribute. In this case, we have `<field name="lang" />`.

We will add an XML file for the extensions made to the Partner views, `views/res_partner_view.xml`, with this content:

```xml
<?xml version="1.0"?>
<odoo>
  <record id="my_inherited_view" model="ir.ui.view">
    <field name="name">Add To-Dos to Partner Form</field>
    <field name="model">res.partner</field>
    <field name="inherit_id" ref="base.view_partner_form"/>
    <field name="arch" type="xml">
      <field name="lang" position="after">
        <field name="todo_ids" />
      </field>
    </field>
  </record>
</odoo>
```

The `inherit_id` record field identifies the view to be extended by referring to its external identifier using the special `ref` attribute. External identifiers will be discussed in more detail in `Chapter 5`, *Access Control and Data Files*.

Usually, XPath is used to locate XML elements. Odoo also uses XPath for this, but it also has the simpler form we just used available. View extension and XPath are discussed further in `Chapter 9`, *Backend Views - Design the User Interface*.

The other view types, such as list and search views, also have an `arch` field and can be extended the same way as form views can.

The business logic layer

Now we will add the logic for our button. This is done with Python code, using the methods in the model's Python class.

Adding business logic

We should edit the `todo_task_model.py` Python file to add the methods called by the button. First, we need to import the new API, so add it to the import statement at the top of the Python file:

```
from odoo import api, fields, models
```

The logic for the **Clear Done** button is quite simple: just set the **Active?** flag to false. This takes advantage of an ORM built-in feature: records with an `active` flag set to `False` by default are filtered out and won't be presented to the user. You can think of it as a "soft delete."

In the `models/todo_task_model.py` file, add the following to the `TodoTask` class:

```
@api.multi
def do_clear_done(self):
    for task in self:
        task.active = False
    return True
```

For logic on records, we use the `@api.multi` decorator. Here, `self` will represent a recordset, and we should then loop through each record. In fact, this is the default for Model methods, so the `@api.multi` decorator can safely be omitted here. We prefer to keep it for clarity.

The code loops through all the To-Do task records and, for each one, assigns the `False` value on the `active` field.

The method does not need to return anything, but we should have it at least return a `True` value. The reason is that not all client implementations of the XML-RPC protocol support None/Null values, and may raise errors when such a value is returned by a method.

Extending Python methods

Python methods can also be extended for additional business logic. This is done by borrowing the mechanism Python already provides for inherited objects to extend their parent class behavior: `super()`.

As an example, we will have the `TodoTask` class extend the ORM `write()` method to add some logic to it: when writing on a non-active record, it will automatically reactivate it.

Add this additional method in the `models/todo_task_model.py` file:

```
@api.multi
def write(self, values):
    if 'active' not in values:
        values['active'] = True
    super().write(values)
```

The `write()` method expects an additional parameter, with a dictionary of values to write on the record. Unless a value is being explicitly set on the `active` field, we set it to `True` in case we are writing on an inactive record. We then use `super()` to call the parent `write()` method using the modified values.

> In previous Odoo versions using Python 2.7, `super()` needed two arguments, passing the class name and `self`. In that case, the last statement would be
> `super(TodoTask, self).write(values)`. This syntax also works with Python 3, so it should be preferred if keeping Python 2 compatibility is important.

We will have a chance to have a closer look at the ORM methods in Chapter 6, *The ORM - Handling Application Data*.

Adding automated tests

Programming best practices include having automated tests for your code. This is even more important for dynamic languages such as Python. Since there is no compilation step, you can't be sure there are no syntactic errors until the code is actually run by the interpreter. A good editor can help us spot these problems ahead of time, but can't help us ensure the code performs as intended like automated tests can.

Odoo supports two ways to describe tests: either using YAML data files or using Python code, based on the Unittest library. YAML tests are a legacy from older versions and are not recommended. We prefer using Python tests and will add a basic test case to our module.

The test code files should have a name starting with test_ and should be imported from tests/__init__.py. But the tests directory (also a Python submodule) should not be imported from the module's top __init__.py, since it will be automatically discovered and loaded only when tests are executed.

Tests must be placed in the tests/ subdirectory. Add a tests/__init__.py file with the following:

```
from . import test_todo
```

Now add the actual test code, available in the tests/test_todo.py file:

```
from odoo.tests.common import import TransactionCase

class TestTodo(TransactionCase):

    def test_create(self):
        "Create a simple Todo"
        Todo = self.env['todo.task']
        task = Todo.create({'name': 'Test Task'})
        self.assertEqual(task.is_done, False)
```

This adds a simple test case to create a new To-Do task and verifies that the **Is Done?** field has the correct default value.

Now we want to run our tests. This is done by adding the --test-enable option while installing or upgrading the module:

```
$ ./odoo-bin -d todo -u todo_app --test-enable
```

The Odoo server will look for a tests/ subdirectory in the upgraded modules and will run them. If any of the tests fail, the server log will show that.

Testing business logic

Now we should add tests for the business logic. Ideally, we want every line of code to be covered by at least one test case. In `tests/test_todo.py`, add a few more lines of code to the `test_create()` method:

```
def test_clear_done(self):
    "Clear Done sets Todo to not active"
    Todo = self.env['todo.task']
    task = Todo.create({'name': 'Test Task'})
    task.do_clear_done()
    self.assertFalse(task.active)
```

It is recommended to, as much as possible, write a different test case for each action to check. This test case begins in a similar way to the previous one: by creating a new To-Do task. This is needed because test cases are independent, and the data created or changed during one test case is rolled back when it ends. We then call the tested method on the created record, and then check the **Active?** flag is set to the intended value.

If we now run the tests and the model methods are correctly written, we should see no error messages in the server log.

Testing access security

In fact, our tests should be failing right now due to the missing access rules. They aren't because they are done with the Admin user. In databases with demo data enabled, we also make available a Demo user, with "typical" backend access. We should change the tests so that they are performed using the Demo user.

We can modify our tests to take this into account. Edit the `tests/test_todo.py` file to add a `setUp` method:

```
def setUp(self, *args, **kwargs):
    result = super(TestTodo, self).setUp(*args, **kwargs)
    user_demo = self.env.ref('base.user_demo')
    self.env= self.env(user=user_demo)
    return result
```

This first instruction calls the `setUp` code of the parent class. The next ones change the environment used to run the tests, `self.env`, to a new one using the Demo user. No further changes are needed for the tests we already wrote.

We should also add a test case to make sure that users can see only their own tasks. To do this, first add an additional import at the top:

```
from odoo.exceptions import AccessError
```

Next, add an additional method to the test class:

```
def test_record_rule(self):
    "Test per user record rules"
    Todo = self.env['todo.task']
    task = Todo.sudo().create({'name': 'Admin Task'})
    with self.assertRaises(AccessError):
        Todo.browse([task.id]).name
```

Since our `env` method is now using the Demo user, we use the `sudo()` method to change the context to the admin user. We then use it to create a task that should not be accessible to the Demo user.

When trying to access this task data, we expect an `AccessError` exception to be raised.

If we run the tests now, they should fail, so let's take care of that.

Setting up access security

You might have noticed that, upon loading, our module is getting a warning message in the server log:

```
The model todo.task has no access rules, consider adding one.
```

The message is pretty clear: our new model has no access rules, so it can't be used by anyone other than the admin superuser. As a superuser, the `admin` ignores data access rules, and that's why we were able to use the form without errors. But we must fix this before other users can use our model.

Another issue we have yet to address is that we want the To-Do tasks to be private to each user. Odoo supports row-level access rules, which we can use to implement that.

Adding access control security

To get a picture of what information is needed to add access rules to a model, use the web client and go to **Settings** | **Technical** | **Security** | **Access Controls List**:

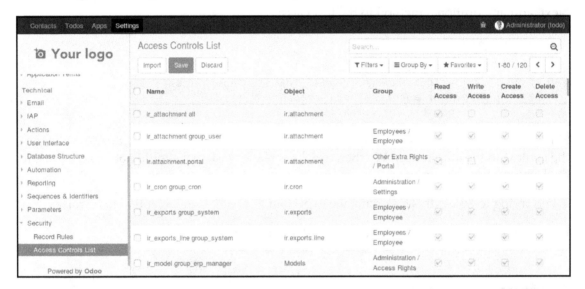

Here, we can see the ACL for some models. It indicates, per security group, what actions are allowed on records.

This information has to be provided by the module using a data file to load the lines into the `ir.model.access` model. We will add full access to the employee group on the model. Employee is the basic access group nearly everyone belongs to. The exceptions are external users, such as customers or website visitors.

This is done using a CSV file named `security/ir.model.access.csv`. Let's add it with the following content:

```
id,name,model_id:id,group_id:id,perm_read,perm_write,perm_create,perm_unlin
k
access_todo_task_group_user,todo.task.user,model_todo_task,base.group_user,
1,1,1,1
```

The filename corresponds to the model to load the data into, and the first line of the file has the column names. These are the columns provided in our CSV file:

- `id` is the record external identifier (also known as XML ID). It should be unique in our module.
- `name` is a description title. It is only informative and it's best if it's kept unique. Official modules usually use a dot-separated string with the model name and the group. Following this convention, we used `todo.task.user`.
- `model_id` is the external identifier for the model we are giving access to. Models have XML IDs automatically generated by the ORM; for `todo.task`, the identifier is `model_todo_task`.
- `group_id` identifies the security group to give permissions to. The most important ones are provided by the `base` module. The Employee group is such a case and has the `base.group_user` identifier.
- `perm` fields flag the access to grant `read`, `write`, `create`, or `unlink` (delete) access.

We must not forget to add the reference to this new file in the `__manifest__.py` descriptor's `data` attribute. It should look like this:

```
'data': [
    'security/ir.model.access.csv',
    'views/todo_menu.xml',
    'views/todo_view.xml',
    'views/res_partner_view.xml',
],
```

As before, upgrade the module for these additions to take effect. The warning message should be gone, and we can confirm that the permissions are OK by logging in with the user `demo` (password is also `demo`). If we run our tests now, they should only fail the `test_record_rule` test case.

Row-level access rules

We can find the **Record Rules** option in the **Technical** menu, alongside **Access Control List**.

Record rules are defined in the `ir.rule` model. As usual, we need to provide a distinctive name. We also need the model they operate on and the domain filter to use for the access restriction. The domain filter uses the usual list of tuples syntax used across Odoo. We will be explaining this **Domain Expression** syntax in Chapter 7, *Business Logic - Supporting Business Processes*.

Usually, rules apply to some particular security groups. In our case, we will make it apply to the Employees group. If it applies to no security group in particular, it is considered global (the `global` field is automatically set to `True`). Global rules are different because they impose restrictions that non-global rules can't override.

To add the record rule, we should create a `security/todo_access_rules.xml` file with the following content:

```xml
<?xml version="1.0" encoding="utf-8"?>
<odoo>
  <data noupdate="1">
    <record id="todo_task_user_rule" model="ir.rule">
      <field name="name">ToDo Tasks only for owner</field>
      <field name="model_id" ref="model_todo_task"/>
      <field name="domain_force">
          [('create_uid','=',user.id)]
      </field>
      <field name="groups" eval="
      [(4,ref('base.group_user'))]"/>
    </record>
  </data>
</odoo>
```

 Notice the `noupdate="1"` attribute. It means this data will not be updated in module upgrades. This will allow it to be customized later since module upgrades won't destroy user-made changes. But be aware that this will also be the case while developing, so you might want to set `noupdate="0"` during development until you're happy with the data file.

In the `groups` field, you will also find a special expression. It's a one-to-many relational field, and they have a special syntax to operate with. In this case, the `(4, x)` tuple indicates to append x to the records, and here x is a reference to the Employees group, identified by `base.group_user`. This one-to-many writing special syntax is discussed in more detail in Chapter 4, *Module Data*.

As before, we must add the file to `__manifest__.py` before it can be loaded into the module:

```
'data': [
  'security/ir.model.access.csv',
  'security/todo_access_rules.xml',
  'views/todo_menu.xml',
  'views/todo_view.xml',
  'views/res_partner_view.xml',
],
```

If we did everything right, we can run the module tests and now they should pass.

Web pages and controllers

Odoo also provides a web development framework, which can be used to develop website features closely integrated with our backend apps. We will take our first steps toward this by creating a simple web page to display the list of pending To-Do Tasks. It will respond at a URL with the format `http://my-server/todo`, so `/todo` is the URL endpoint we want to implement.

We will just have a short taste of what web development with Odoo looks like, and this topic is addressed in more depth in `Chapter 12`, *Creating Website Frontend Features*.

Web controllers are the components responsible for web page rendering. Controllers are methods defined in a `http.Controller` class, and they are bound to URL endpoints. When that URL endpoint is accessed, the controller code executes, producing the HTML to be presented to the user. To help with rendering the HTML, we have the QWeb templating engine available.

The convention is to place the code for controllers inside a `/controllers` subdirectory. First, edit the `todo_app/__init__.py` so that it also imports the `controllers` module directory:

```
from . import models
from . import controllers
```

We then need to add a `todo_app/controllers/__init__.py` file so that the directory can be Python imported, and add an import statement to it for the Python file we will add:

```
from . import main
```

Now add the actual file for the controller, `todo_app/controllers/main.py`, with the following code:

```
from odoo import http

class Todo(http.Controller):

    @http.route('/todo')
    def Main(self, **kwargs):
        TodoTask = http.request.env['todo.task']
        domain_todo = [('is_done', '=', False)]
        tasks =  TodoTask.search(domain_todo)
        return http.request.render(
            'todo_app.index_template', {'tasks': tasks})
```

The `odoo.http` module, imported here, is the core component providing web-related features. The `http.Controller` object is the class controller it should derive from. We use it for the main controller class.

The particular name we choose for the class and for their methods is not relevant. The `@http.route` decorator is the important part, since it declares the URL endpoint that will be bound to the class method, `/todo` in our case. By default, access to URL endpoints requires the user to be logged in. This can be changed, and anonymous access can be allowed by adding the `auth='public'` parameter to `@http.route`.

Inside the controller method, we access the environment using `http.request.env`. We use it to get a recordset with all not-done To-Do Tasks.

The final step is to use `http.request.render()` to process the `todo_app.index_template` QWeb template and generate the output HTML. We can make values available to the template through a dictionary. This is used to pass the `tasks` recordset.

If we try this now, we should get an error message in the server log:

```
ValueError: External ID not found in the system: todo_app.index_template
```

This is expected since we haven't defined that template yet. That should be our next step.

QWeb templates are a type of view, and should also go in the /views subdirectory. Let's create the views/index_template.xml file:

```xml
<?xml version="1.0" encoding="utf-8"?>
<odoo>

<template id="index_template" name="My Todo List">
  <div id="wrap" class="container">
    <h1>Todo Tasks</h1>
    <!-- List of Tasks -->
    <t t-foreach="tasks" t-as="task">
    <div class="row">
      <span t-field="task.name" />
    </div>
    </t>
  </div>
</template>

</odoo>
```

The <template> element is used to declare a QWeb template. In fact, it is a shortcut for a ir.ui.view record, and this is the base model where templates are stored. The template contains the HTML to use, and makes use of QWeb-specific attributes. t-foreach is used to loop through each item of the tasks variable, made available by the controller's http.request.render() call. The t-field takes care of properly rendering the content of a record field.

This is just a glimpse of the QWeb syntax. More details can be found in Chapter 12, *Creating Website Frontend Features*.

We still need to declare this file in the module manifest, like the other XML data files, so that it gets loaded and can be made available. After doing this and performing a module upgrade, our web page should be working. Open the http://<my-server>:8069/todo URL and you should see a simple list of To-Do Tasks.

Summary

We created a new module from the start, covering the most frequently used elements in a module: models, the three basic types of views (form, list, and search), business logic in model methods, and access security. We also learned about security access control, including record rules, and how to create web pages using web controllers and QWeb templates.

In the process, we got familiar with the module development process, which involves module upgrades and application server restarts to make the gradual changes effective in Odoo.

Always remember, when adding model fields, an upgrade is needed. When changing Python code, including the manifest file, a restart is needed. When changing XML or CSV files, an upgrade is needed; also, when in doubt, do both: restart the server and upgrade the modules.

In the next chapter, you will go deeper into models, and explore everything they have for us.

4
Models – Structuring the Application Data

In Chapter 3, *Your First Odoo Application - A Practical Overview*, we saw an overview of all the main components involved in building an application for Odoo. In these following chapters, it's time to explain the several layers that make up an application—models, views, and business logic—in more detail.

We will extend the To-Do app built in the previous chapter, and take it to another level. What if, instead of only a simple list of tasks, we also have a Kanban board showing the tasks as cards, and organize them into columns according to the stage they're at, such as To Do, Doing, and Done?

The following chapters will work toward this goal. Right now, in this chapter, we will learn how to use models to design the data structures that support applications in general, and our kanban extension in particular.

We will use that to explore the capabilities of models and fields, including defining model relations, adding computed fields, creating data constraints, and using the available extension (or inheritance) mechanisms to add them to models provided by already existing modules.

Let's get started then!

Organizing application features into modules

As before, we will use an example to help explain the concepts.

Odoo's inheritance features provide an effective extensibility mechanism. They allow you to extend existing third-party apps without changing them directly. This composability also enables a module-oriented development pattern, where large apps can be split into smaller features, rich enough to stand on their own.

This can be helpful to limit complexity, both at the technical level and the user experience level. From a technical perspective, splitting a large problem into smaller parts makes it easier to solve and is friendlier to incremental feature development. From the user experience perspective, we can choose to activate only the features that are really needed for them, for a simpler user interface. So, we will be improving our To-Do application through additional addon modules to finally form a fully featured application.

Introducing the todo_stage module

In the previous chapter, we created an app for personal To-Do items. Now we want to take our app to the next level by improving its user interface, including a kanban board. The kanban board is a simple workflow tool that organizes items into columns, where these items flow from the left-hand column to the right, until they are completed. We will organize our tasks into columns, according to their stages, such as **Waiting, Ready**, **Started**, or **Done**.

We will start by adding the data structures to enable this vision. We need to add stages, and it will be good to add support for tags as well, allowing the tasks to be categorized by subject. In this chapter, we will focus on the data models only. The user interface for these features will be discussed in Chapter 9, *Backend Views - Design the User Interface*, and Kanban views in Chapter 10, *Kanban Views and Client-Side Qweb*.

The first thing to figure out is how our data will be structured so that we can design the supporting models. We already have the central entity: the To-Do task. Each task will be at one stage at a time, and tasks can also have one or more tags on them. We will need to add these two additional models, and they will have these relationships:

- Each task has a stage, and there can be many tasks in each stage
- Each task can have many tags, and each tag can be attached to many tasks

This means that tasks have a many-to-one relationship with stages, and a many-to-many relationship with tags. On the other hand, the inverse relationships are that stages have a one-to-many relationship with tasks and tags have a many-to-many relationship with tasks.

We will start by creating the new `todo_stage` module and add the To-Do stage and To-Do tag models to it.

We've been using the `~/odoo-dev/custom-addons/` directory to host our modules. We should create a new `todo_stage` directory inside it for this new addon module. From the shell, we can use the following commands:

```
$ cd ~/odoo-dev/custom-addons
$ mkdir todo_stage
$ cd todo_stage
```

We begin by adding the `__manifest__.py` manifest file, with this content:

```
{
    'name': 'Add Stages and Tags to To-Dos',
    'description': 'Organize To-Do Tasks using Stages and Tags',
    'author': 'Daniel Reis',
    'depends': ['todo_app'],
}
```

We should also add an `__init__.py` file. It is perfectly fine for it to be empty for now.

Now we can install the module in our Odoo work database and get started with the models.

Creating models

For the To-Do tasks to have a kanban board, we need stages. Stages are board columns, and each task will fit into one of these columns:

1. Edit `todo_stage/__init__.py` to import the `models` submodule:

   ```
   from . import models
   ```

2. Create the `todo_stage/models` directory and add to it an `__init__.py` file with this:

   ```
   from . import todo_task_tag_model
   from . import todo_task_stage_model
   ```

3. Add the `todo_stage/models/todo_task_tag_model.py` Python code file:

```
from odoo import fields, models

class Tag(models.Model):
    _name = 'todo.task.tag'
    _description = 'To-do Tag'
    name = fields.Char('Name', translate=True)
```

4. Then, add the `todo_stage/models/todo_task_stage_model.py` Python code file:

```
from odoo import fields, models

class Stage(models.Model):
    _name = 'todo.task.stage'
    _description = 'To-do Stage'
    _order = 'sequence,name'

    name = fields.Char('Name', translate=True)
    sequence = fields.Integer('Sequence')
```

Here, we created the two new models that will be referenced in the To-Do tasks.

Focusing on the task stages, we have a Python class, `Stage`, based on the `models.Model` class, which defines a new Odoo model called `todo.task.stage`. We also have two fields: `name` and `sequence`. We can see some model attributes (prefixed with an underscore) that are new to us. Let's have a closer look at them.

Model attributes

Model classes can use additional attributes that control some of their behaviors. These are the most commonly used attributes:

- `_name` is the internal identifier for the Odoo model we are creating. Mandatory when creating a new model.
- `_description` is a user-friendly title for the model's records, shown when the model is viewed in the user interface. Optional but recommended.
- `_order` sets the default order to use when the model's records are browsed, or shown in a list view. It is a text string to be used as the SQL `order by` clause, so it can be anything you could use there, although it has smart behavior and supports translatable and many-to-one field names.

For completeness, there are a couple more attributes that can be used in advanced cases:

- _rec_name indicates the field to use as the record description when referenced from related fields, such as a many-to-one relationship. By default, it uses the name field, which is a common field in models. But this attribute allows us to use any other field for that purpose.
- _table is the name of the database table supporting the model. Usually, it is left to be calculated automatically, and is the model name with the dots replaced by underscores. But it's possible to set it to indicate a specific table name.

We can also have the _inherit and _inherits attributes, used to extend modules. We will look closer at them later in this chapter.

Models and Python classes

Odoo models are represented by Python classes. In the preceding code, we have a Python class, Stage, based on the models.Model class, which defines a new Odoo model called todo.task.stage.

Odoo models are kept in a central registry, also referred to as a pool in the old API. It is a dictionary that keeps references to all the model classes available in the instance, and it can be referenced by a model name. Specifically, the code in a model method can use self.env['x'] to get a reference to a class representing the model x.

You can see that model names are important since they are the keys used to access the registry. The convention for model names is to use a list of lowercase words joined with dots, such as todo.task.stage. Other examples from the core modules are project.project, project.task and project.task.type. We should use the singular form todo.task model instead of todo.tasks.

> For historical reasons, it is possible to find some core models that don't follow this, such as res.users, but this is not the rule.

Model names must be globally unique. Because of this, the first word should correspond to the main application the module relates to. In our example, it is todo. Other examples from the core modules are project, crm, and sale.

Python classes, on the other hand, are local to the Python file where they are declared. The identifier used for them is only significant for the code in that file. Because of this, class identifiers are not required to be prefixed by the main application they relate to. For example, there is no problem with naming our class `Stage` for the `todo.task.stage` model. There is no risk of collision with possible classes with the same name on other modules.

The convention for class identifiers is to use `CamelCase`. This follows the Python standard defined by the PEP8 coding conventions.

Transient and Abstract models

In the preceding code and in the vast majority of Odoo models, classes are based on the `models.Model` class. These types of model have permanent database persistence: database tables are created for them and their records are stored until explicitly deleted.

But Odoo also provides two other model types to be used: Transient and Abstract models.

Transient models are based on the `models.TransientModel` class and are used for wizard-style user interaction. Their data is still stored in the database, but it is expected to be temporary. A vacuum job periodically clears old data from these tables. For example, the **Load a Language** dialog window, found in the **Settings | Translations** menu, uses a Transient model to store user selections and implement wizard logic. An example of using a Transient model is discussed in `Chapter 7`, *Business Logic - Supporting Business Processes*.

Abstract models are based on the `models.AbstractModel` class and have no data storage attached to them. They act as reusable feature sets to be mixed in with other models, using the Odoo inheritance capabilities. For example, `mail.thread` is an Abstract model provided by the `Discuss` addon, used to add message and follower features to other models. This particular example is discussed later in this chapter.

Inspecting existing models

The models and fields created through the Python classes have their metadata available through the user interface. In the **Settings** top menu, navigate to the **Technical | Database Structure | Models** menu item. Here, you will find the list of all the models available in the database.

Clicking on a model in the list will open a form with its details:

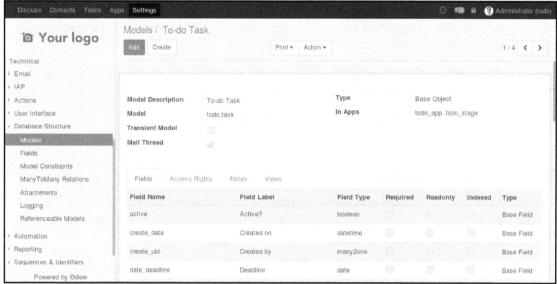

This is a good tool for inspecting the structure of a model, since in one place you can see the results of all the customization of different modules. In this case, as you can see in the top-right corner, in the **In Apps** field, the todo.task definitions for this model come from both the todo_app and todo_stage modules.

In the lower area, we have some tabs available with additional information: **Fields** with a quick reference for the model's fields, **Access Rights** with the access control rules granted to security groups, and **Views** with the list of views available for this model.

We can find the model's **External Identifier** using the **Developer menu** here, by accessing the **View Metadata** option. The model external identifiers, or XML IDs, are automatically generated by the ORM but fairly predictable: for the todo.task model, the external identifier is model_todo_task.

 As we have seen in Chapter 1, *Quick Start – the Odoo Developer Mode and Concepts*, the **Models** form is editable! It's possible to create and modify models, fields, and views from here. You can use this to build prototypes before persisting them in modules.

Creating fields

After creating a new model, the next step is to add fields to it. Odoo supports all the basic data types expected, such as text strings, integers, floating point numbers, Booleans, dates, date-times, and image/binary data.

Some field names are special, either because they are reserved by the ORM for special purposes, or because some built-in features make use of some default field names.

Let's explore the several types of field available in Odoo.

Basic field types

We now have a `Stage` model and we will expand it to add some additional fields. We should edit the `todo_stage/models/todo_task_stage_model.py` file and add extra field definitions to make it look like this:

```python
class Stage(models.Model):
    _name = 'todo.task.stage'
    _description = 'To-do Stage'
    _order = 'sequence,name'

    # String fields:
    name = fields.Char('Name')
    desc = fields.Text('Description')
    state = fields.Selection(
        [('draft','New'),
         ('open','Started'),
         ('done','Closed')],
        'State')
    docs = fields.Html('Documentation')

    # Numeric fields:
    sequence = fields.Integer('Sequence')
    perc_complete = fields.Float('% Complete', (3, 2))

    # Date fields:
    date_effective = fields.Date('Effective Date')
    date_created = fields.Datetime(
        'Create Date and Time',
        default=lambda self: fields.Datetime.now())

    # Other fields:
    fold = fields.Boolean('Folded?')
```

```
image = fields.Binary('Image')
```

Here, we have a sample of the non-relational field types available in Odoo with the positional arguments expected by each one.

For most non-relational fields, the first argument is the field title, corresponding to the `string` field argument. It is used as the default text for the user interface labels. It's optional and, if not provided, a title string will be automatically generated from the field name, replacing underscores with spaces and capitalizing the first letter in each word.

For the date field, the convention is to use `date` as a field name prefix. For example, we should use the `date_effective` field instead of `effective_date`. Similar conventions also apply to other fields, such as `amount_`, `price_`, or `qty_`.

These are the non-relational field types available, along with the positional arguments expected by each:

- `Char(string)` is a basic string field, presented as a single line. The only positional argument expected is the string title.
- `Text(string)` differs from `Char` in that it can hold multiline text content, but also one positional argument for the string title.
- `Selection(selection, string)` is a drop-down selection list. The first argument is the list of selectable options and the second is the string title. The selection item is a list of (`'value'`, `'Title'`) tuples, for the value stored in the database and the corresponding user interface description. When extending through inheritance, the `selection_add` argument is available to append new items to an existing selection list.
- `Html(string)` is stored as a text field, but has specific handling of the user interface for HTML content presentation. For security reasons, it is sanitized by default, but this behavior can be overridden.
- `Integer(string)` just expects a string argument for the field title.
- `Float(string, digits)` has a second optional argument, an (x, y) tuple with the field's precision. x is the total number of digits; of those, y are decimal digits.
- `Monetary(string, currency_field)` is similar to a float field, but has specific handling for currency. It needs a helper field to set the currency being used. By default, that field is expected to be named `currency_id`, but it has a different name we can use for the second positional argument to declare it.

- `Date(string)` and `Datetime(string)` fields expect only the string text as a positional argument. For historical reasons, the ORM handles their values in the UTC timezone represented as a string format. Helper functions should be used to convert them to actual date objects. This is discussed in more detail in `Chapter` 7, *Business Logic - Supporting Business Processes*.
- `Boolean(string)` holds `True` or `False` values, as you might expect, and only has one positional argument for the string text.
- `Binary(string)` stores file-like binary data, and also expects only the string argument. It can be handled by Python code using `base64` encoded strings.

Other than these, we also have the relational fields, which will be introduced later in this chapter. But for now, there is still more to learn about these field types and their attributes.

Common field attributes

Fields have additional attributes available for us to define their behavior. Some of these can be set positionally, without an argument keyword, as shown in the previous section.

For example, `perc_complete = fields.Float('% Complete', (3, 2))` is making use of positional arguments. Using the keyword arguments, it could be written as `perc_complete = fields.Float(string='% Complete', digits=(3,2))`. More information on keyword arguments can be found in the Python official documentation at `https://docs.python.org/3/tutorial/controlflow.html#keyword-arguments`.

These are the generally available attributes and the corresponding argument keywords:

- `string` is the field default label, to be used in the user interface. Except for Selection and Relational fields, it is the first positional argument, so most of the time it is not used as a keyword argument. If not provided, it is automatically generated from the field name.
- `default` sets a default value for the field. It can be a static value, such as a string, or a callable reference, either a named function or an anonymous function (a lambda expression). In the stage model, we can see an example of a default value on the `date_created` field that uses a lambda expression to set the current date and time when a new record is created.

- `size` applies only to `Char` fields, and can set a maximum size allowed. It's recommended to not use it unless there is a business requirement for it, for example, a social security number with a maximum length allowed.
- `translate` applies only to `Char`, `Text`, and `Html` fields, and makes the field contents translatable, holding different values for different languages.
- `help` provides the text for tooltips displayed to users.
- `readonly=True` makes the field not editable in the user interface by default. This is not enforced at the API level; code in model methods will still be capable of writing to it. It is only a user interface setting.
- `required=True` makes the field mandatory in the user interface by default. This is enforced at the database level by adding a `NOT NULL` constraint on the column.
- `index=True` adds a database index on the field, for faster search operations at the expense of slower write operations.
- `copy=False` has the field ignored when using the duplicate record feature - the `copy()` ORM method. The non-relational fields are copyable by default.
- `groups` allows limiting the field's access and visibility to only some groups. It expects a comma-separated list of XML IDs for security groups, such as `groups='base.group_user,base.group_system'`.
- `states` expects dictionary mapping values for UI attributes depending on values of the `state` field. The attributes that can be used are `readonly`, `required`, and `invisible`, for example: `states={'done':[('readonly',True)]}`.

Note that the `states` field attribute is equivalent to the `attrs` attribute in views. Also, note that views support a `states` attribute, but it has a different usage: it accepts a comma-separated list of states to control when the element should be visible.

For completeness, two other attributes are sometimes used when upgrading to Odoo major versions:

- `deprecated=True` logs a warning whenever the field is being used
- `oldname='field'` is used when a field is renamed in a newer version, enabling the data in the old field to be automatically copied into the new field

Special field names

A few field names are reserved for use by the ORM.

The `id` field is an automatic number uniquely identifying each record, and used as the database primary key. It's automatically added to every model.

The following fields are automatically created on new models, unless the `_log_access=False` model attribute is set:

- `create_uid` is for the user that created the record
- `create_date` is for the date and time when the record is created
- `write_uid` is for the last user to modify the record
- `write_date` is for the last date and time when the record was modified

The information in these fields is available in the web client, in the **Developer Mode** menu, by selecting the **View Metadata** option.

Some built-in API features expect specific field names by default. Our life would be easier if we could avoid using these field names for purposes other than the intended ones. Some of them are actually reserved and can't be used for other purposes at all:

- `name` is used by default as the display name for the record. Usually, it is a `Char`, but can also be a `Text` or a `Many2one` field type. We can choose another field to be used for the display name, using the `_rec_name` model attribute.
- `active`, of type `Boolean`, allows us to inactivate records. Records with `active==False` will automatically be excluded from queries. To access them, an `('active','=',False)` condition must be added to the search domain, or the `'active_test': False` key should be set on the current context.
- `sequence`, of type `Integer`, if present in a list view, allows us to manually drag records to define the order of the records. For it to work properly, you should not forget to include it in the model's `_order` attribute.
- `state`, of type `Selection`, represents basic states of the record's life cycle and can be used by the state's field attribute to dynamically modify the view; some form fields can be made `readonly`, `required`, or `invisible` in specific record states.
- `parent_id`, `parent_left`, and `parent_right`, of type `Integer`, have special meaning for parent/child hierarchical relations. We will discuss them in detail later in this chapter.

So far, we've discussed non-relational fields. But a good part of an application data structure is about describing the relationships between entities. Let's look at that now.

Extending models

To extend an existing model, we use a Python class with an _inherit attribute, identifying the model to be extended. The new class inherits all the features of the parent Odoo model, and we only need to declare the modifications we want to introduce. These modifications will also be available everywhere else this model is used. We can think about this type of inheritance as getting a reference for the existing model and making in-place changes to it.

Adding fields to a model

We will extend the todo.task model to add some fields to it. As an example, we will now add the effort_estimate field, to be used for the amount of time expected to be spent on the task.

We will do this in a models/todo_task_model.py file, so we should also import it in the todo_stage/models/__init__.py file to have this content:

```
from . import todo_task_tag_model
from . import todo_task_stage_model
from . import todo_task_model
```

Now, create the todo_stage/models/todo_task_model.py file, extending the original model:

```
from odoo import api, fields, models

class TodoTask(models.Model):
    _inherit = 'todo.task'
    effort_estimate = fields.Integer()
```

Here we declare a class, based on models.Model, just like when we create new models, but instead of a _name attribute, we used _inherit to declare the model being extended. Note that the name given to the class, TodoTask, is local to this Python file and, in general, is irrelevant for the Odoo ORM.

Next, we can declare the fields to add or modify the model being extended. In this case, we are adding the effort_estimate field.

Modifying existing fields

As you can see, adding new fields to an existing model is quite straightforward. Modifying the attributes on existing models is also as simple.

When extending a model, existing fields can be modified incrementally. This means that we just need to define the field attributes to change or add.

For example, to add a help tooltip to the `name` field, we would add this line to `todo_task_model.py`, described previously:

```
name = fields.Char(help="What needs to be done?")
```

This modifies the field with the specified attributes, leaving all the other attributes not explicitly used here unmodified. After this, when we upgrade the module, if we go to a To-Do task form and hover the mouse pointer over the **Description** field, the tooltip text will be displayed.

Relationships between models

Looking again at our module design, we have these relationships:

- Each task has a stage. That's a many-to-one relationship, also known as a foreign key. The inverse is a one-to-many relationship, meaning that each stage can have many tasks.
- Each task can have many tags. That's a many-to-many relationship. The inverse relationship, of course, is also a many-to-many, since each tag can be in many tasks.

The following entity relationship diagram can help visualize the relationships we are about to create in the model. The lines ending with a triangle represent the many sides of the relationships:

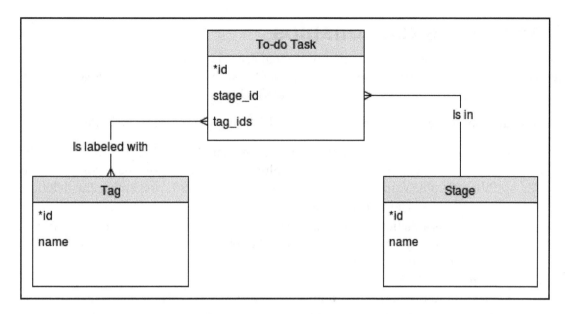

Let's add the corresponding relationship fields to the To-Do tasks in our
`todo_task_model.py` file:

```
class TodoTask(models.Model):
    _inherit = 'todo.task'
    stage_id = fields.Many2one('todo.task.stage', 'Stage')
    tag_ids = fields.Many2many('todo.task.tag', string='Tags')
```

The preceding code shows the basic syntax of these fields, setting the related model and the
field's title `string`. The convention for relational field names is to append `_id` or `_ids` to
the field names for to-one and to-many relationships, respectively.

As an exercise, you may try to also add the corresponding inverse relationships to the
related models:

- The inverse of the `Many2one` relationship is a `One2many` field for stages, since
  each stage can have many tasks. We should add this field to the Stage class.
- The inverse of the `Many2many` relationship is also a `Many2many` field on tags,
  since each tag can also be used on many tasks.

Let's have a closer look at relational field definitions.

Many-to-one relationships

The `Many2one` relationship accepts two positional arguments: the related model (corresponding to the `comodel` keyword argument) and the title `string`. It creates a field in the database table with a foreign key to the related table.

Some additional named arguments are also available to use with this type of field:

- `ondelete` defines what happens when the related record is deleted. Its default is `set null`, meaning that an empty value is set when the related record is deleted. Other possible values are `restricted`, raising an error preventing the deletion, and `cascade`, which also deletes this record.
- `context` is a dictionary of data, meaningful for the web client views, to carry information when navigating through the relationship, for example, to set default values. It will be better explained in `Chapter 7`, *Business Logic - Supporting business processes*.
- `domain` is a domain expression; a list of tuples used to filter the records made available for selection on the relation field. See `Chapter 7`, *Business Logic - Supporting Business Processes* for more details.
- `auto_join=True` allows the ORM to use SQL joins when doing searches using this relationship. If used, the access security rules will be bypassed, and the user could have access to related records the security rules wouldn't allow, but the SQL queries will be more efficient and run faster.

Many-to-many relationships

The `Many2many` minimal signature accepts one argument for the related model, and it is recommended to also provide the `string` argument with the field title.

At the database level, it does not add any columns to the existing tables. Instead, it automatically creates a new relationship table that has only two ID fields with foreign keys to the related tables. If not provided, the relationship table name and the field names are automatically generated. By default, the relationship table name is the two table names joined with an underscore and `_rel` appended at the end.

On some occasions, we may need to override these automatic defaults.

One such case is when the related models have long names, and the name for the automatically generated relationship table is too long, exceeding the 63-character PostgreSQL limit. In these cases, we need to manually choose a name for the relationship table to conform to the table name size limit.

Another case is when we need a second many-to-many relationship between the same models. In these cases, we need to manually provide a name for the relationship table so that it doesn't collide with the table name already being used for the first relationship.

There are two alternatives to manually override these values: either using positional arguments or keyword arguments.

Using positional arguments for the field definition, we have the following:

```
# Task <-> Tag relation (positional args)
tag_ids = fields.Many2many(
    'todo.task.tag',        # related model
    'todo_task_tag_rel',    # relation table name
    'task_id',              # field for "this" record
    'tag_id',               # field for "other" record
    'Tags')                 # string label text
```

Note that the additional arguments are optional. We could just set the name for the relationship table and let the field names use the automatic defaults.

We can instead use keyword arguments, which may be preferred for readability:

```
# Task <-> Tag relation (keyword args)
tag_ids = fields.Many2many(
    comodel_name='todo.task.tag',   # related model
    relation='todo_task_tag_rel',   # relation table name
    column1='task_id',              # field for "this" record
    column2='tag_id',               # field for "other" record
    string='Tags')
```

Just like many-to-one fields, many-to-many fields also support the `domain` and `context` keyword attributes.

There is a limitation in the ORM design regarding Abstract models. When you force the names of the relationship table and columns, they cannot be cleanly inherited anymore. So this should not be done in Abstract models.

The inverse of the `Many2many` relationship is also a `Many2many` field. If we also add a `Many2many` field to the `Tags` model, Odoo infers that this many-to-many relationship is the inverse of the one in the `Task` model.

The inverse relationship between tasks and tags can be implemented as follows:

```
class Tag(models.Model):
    _name = 'todo.task.tag'
    # Tag class relationship to Tasks
    task_ids = fields.Many2many(
        'todo.task',      # related model
        string='Tasks')
```

One-to-many inverse relationships

An inverse of a `Many2one` can be added to the other end of the relationship. This has no impact on the actual database structure, but allows us to easily browse from the **one** side of the **many** related records. A typical use case is the relationship between a document header and its lines.

In our example, a `One2many` inverse relationship on stages allows us to easily list all the tasks in that stage. The code to add this inverse relationship to stages is as follows:

```
class Stage(models.Model):
    _name = 'todo.task.stage'
    # Stage class relationship with Tasks
    task_ids = fields.One2many(
        'todo.task',   # related model
        'stage_id',    # field for "this" on related model
        'Tasks in this stage')
```

`One2many` accepts three positional arguments: the related model, the field name in that model referring to this record, and the title string. The first two positional arguments correspond to the `comodel_name` and `inverse_name` keyword arguments.

The additional keyword parameters available are the same as for `Many2one`: `context`, `domain`, and `ondelete` (here acting on the **many** side of the relationship).

Hierarchical relationships

Parent-child tree relationships are represented using a Many2one relationship with the same model, so that each record references its parent. The inverse One2many makes it easy for a parent to keep track of its children.

Odoo provides improved support for these hierarchical data structures, for faster browsing through tree siblings, and for easier searches using the additional child_of operator in domain expressions. To enable these features, we need to set the _parent_store flag attribute and add the helper fields parent_left and parent_right to the model.

Be aware that these additional operations come with storage and execution time penalties, so they are best used when you expect to read more frequently than write, such as in the case of category trees.

Revisiting the Tags model defined in the todo_model.py file, we should now edit it to look like this:

```
class Tags(models.Model):
    _name = 'todo.task.tag'
    _description = 'To-do Tag'
    _parent_store = True
    # _parent_name = 'parent_id'

    name = fields.Char('Name')
    parent_id = fields.Many2one(
        'todo.task.tag', 'Parent Tag', ondelete='restrict')
    parent_left = fields.Integer('Parent Left', index=True)
    parent_right = fields.Integer('Parent Right', index=True)
```

Here, we have a basic model with a parent_id field, to reference the parent record, and the additional _parent_store attribute, to add hierarchic search support. When doing this, the parent_left and parent_right fields must also be added.

The field referring to the parent is expected to be named parent_id, but any other field name can be used as long as we declare that in the _parent_name attribute.

Also, it is often convenient to add a field with the direct children:

```
child_ids = fields.One2many(
    'todo.task.tag', 'parent_id', 'Child Tags')
```

Dynamic relationships using Reference fields

Regular relational fields reference one fixed comodel. The Reference field type does not have this limitation and supports dynamic relationships, so that the same field is able to refer to more than one model.

For example, we can use it to add a `Refers to` field to To-Do tasks that can either refer to a `User` or a `Partner`:

```
# class TodoTask(models.Model):
    refers_to = fields.Reference(
        [('res.user', 'User'), ('res.partner', 'Partner')],
        'Refers to')
```

As you can see, the field definition is similar to a Selection field, but here the selection list holds the models that can be used. On the user interface, the user will first pick a model from the available list, and then pick a record from that model.

This can be taken to another level of flexibility: a **Referenceable Models** configuration table exists to configure the models that can be used in **Reference** fields. It is available in the **Settings | Technical | Database Structure** menu. A Reference field can make use of that list with the help of the `referenceable_models()` function in the `odoo.addons.res.res_request` module.

An improved version of the `Refers to` field, using the **Referenceable Models** configuration, looks like this:

```
from odoo.addons.base.res.res_request import referenceable_models
# class TodoTask(models.Model):
    refers_to = fields.Reference(
        referenceable_models, 'Refers to')
```

Computed fields

Fields can have their values automatically calculated by a function, instead of simply reading a database stored value. A computed field is declared just like a regular field, but has the additional `compute` argument to define the function used for its computation.

In most cases, computed fields involve writing some business logic. So, to take full advantage of this feature we need to learn the topics explained in Chapter 7, *Business Logic - Supporting business processes*. We can still explain computed fields here, but will keep the business logic as simple as possible.

Let's work on an example. Stages have a `fold` field. We will add a computed field with the **Folded?** flag for the corresponding stage to our To-Do tasks.

We should edit the `TodoTask` model in the `todo_task_model.py` file to add the following:

```python
# class TodoTask(models.Model):

    stage_fold = fields.Boolean(
        'Stage Folded?',
        compute='_compute_stage_fold')

    @api.depends('stage_id.fold')
    def _compute_stage_fold(self):
        for todo in self:
            todo.stage_fold = todo.stage_id.fold
```

The preceding code adds a new `stage_fold` field and the `_compute_stage_fold` method used to compute it. The function name was passed as a string, but it's also allowed to pass it as a callable reference (the function identifier, without the surrounding quotes). In that case, we need to make sure the function is defined in the Python file before the field is.

The `@api.depends` decorator is needed when the computation depends on other fields, as it usually does. It lets the server know when to recompute stored or cached values. One or more field names are accepted as arguments and dot-notation can be used to follow field relationships.

The computation function is expected to assign a value to the field or fields to compute. If it doesn't, it will produce an error. Since `self` is a recordset object, our computation here is simply to get the **Folded?** field using `stage_id.fold`. The result is achieved by assigning that value (writing it) on the field being computed, `stage_fold`.

We won't be working on the views for this module yet, but you can make a quick edit on the task form to confirm the computed field is working as expected by using the **Developer Mode**, picking the **Edit View** option, and adding the field directly in the form XML. Don't worry, it will be replaced by the clean module view on the next upgrade.

Searching and writing to computed fields

The computed field we just created can be read, but it can't be searched or written to. By default, computed field values are written on the fly, and are not stored in the database. That's why we can't search them like we can regular fields.

We can enable these search and write operations by implementing specialized functions for them. Along with the compute function, we can also set a search function, to implement the search logic, and the inverse function, to implement the write logic.

Using these, our computed field declaration looks as follows:

```
# class TodoTask(models.Model):
    stage_fold = fields.Boolean(
        string='Stage Folded?',
        compute='_compute_stage_fold',
        # store=False,   # the default
        search='_search_stage_fold',
        inverse='_write_stage_fold')
```

The supporting functions are as follows:

```
def _search_stage_fold(self, operator, value):
    return [('stage_id.fold', operator, value)]

def _write_stage_fold(self):
    for todo in self:
        todo.stage_id.fold = todo.stage_fold
```

When we perform a search on a model, a domain expression is used as an argument with the filter to perform. Domain expressions are explained in more detail in Chapter 7, *Business Logic - Supporting business processes,* but for now you should know that they are a list of (field, operator, value) conditions.

The search function is called whenever this computed field is found in conditions of a domain expression. It receives the operator and value for the search and is expected to translate the original search element into an alternative domain search expression. The **Fold** field is stored in the related **stages** model, so our search implementation just alters the original search expression to use the stage_id.fold field instead.

The inverse function performs the reverse logic of the calculation, to find the value to write in the computation's source fields. In our example, this means writing back to the stage_id.fold field. Notice that this modifies data in the shared stages model, so the change would also affect another To-Do task record using that stage. Regular access control also applies, so this action will only be successful if the user also has write access to the stages model.

Storing computed fields

Computed field values can also be stored in the database, by setting `store = True` in their definition. They will be recomputed when any of their dependencies change. Since the values are now stored, they can be searched just like regular fields, and a search function is not needed.

Related fields

The computed field we implemented in the previous section just copies a value from a related record into a model's own field. This is a common use case that can be automatically handled by Odoo using the **related field** feature.

Related fields make available, directly in a model, fields that belong to a related model and are accessible using a dot-notation chain. This makes them available in situations where dot-notation can't be used, such as UI form views.

To create a related field, we declare a field of the required type, just like with regular computed fields, but instead of `compute` we use the `related` attribute, setting it with the dot-notation field chain to reach the desired field.

We can use a reference field to get the exact same effect from the previous example, the `stage_fold` computed field:

```
# class TodoTask(models.Model):
    stage_fold = fields.Boolean(
        string='Stage Folded?',
        related='stage_id.fold')
```

Behind the scenes, related fields are just computed fields that conveniently implement `search` and `inverse` methods. This means that we can search and write to them out of the box, without having to write any additional code. It's also worth noting that these Related fields can also be stored in a database, using `store=True`, just like any other computed field.

To-Do tasks are organized in customizable stages, and these stages can be mapped into basic states. The `state` field supports special user interface logic, and we want to make use of that later, in `Chapter 9`, *Backend Views - Design the User Interface*.

Because of this, we want the state value to be available directly in the task model, and the easiest way to do that is to use a reference field. Similarly to `stage_fold`, we will add a computed field on the task model, but this time using the simpler related field:

```
# class TodoTask(models.Model):
    state = fields.Selection(
        related='stage_id.state',
        string='Stage State')
```

Model constraints

To enforce data integrity, models also support two types of constraints: SQL and Python.

SQL constraints are added to the database table definition and are enforced directly by PostgreSQL. They are defined using the `_sql_constraints` class attribute. It is a list of tuples with the constraint identifier name, the SQL for the constraint, and the error message to use.

A common use case is to add unique constraints to models. Suppose we don't want to allow two active tasks with the same title, as follows:

```
# class TodoTask(models.Model):
    _sql_constraints = [
        ('todo_task_name_uniq',  # Constraint unique identifier
         'UNIQUE (name, active)',  # Constraint SQL syntax
         'Task title must be unique!')  # Validation message
        ]
```

Python constraints can use a piece of arbitrary code to check the conditions. The checking function should be decorated with `@api.constrains` and the indication of the list of fields involved in the check. The validation is triggered when any of them is modified and will raise an exception if the condition fails.

For example, to ensure that a task name that is at least five characters long, we could add the following constraint:

```
from odoo.exceptions import ValidationError

# class TodoTask(models.Model):
    @api.constrains('name')
    def _check_name_size(self):
        for todo in self:
            if len(todo.name) < 5:
                raise ValidationError('Must have 5 chars!')
```

More model inheritance mechanisms

Previously, we saw the basic extension of models, called **classic inheritance** in the official documentation. This is the most frequent use of inheritance, and the easiest way to think about it is as an **in-place extension**. You take a model and extend it. As you add new features, they are added to the existing model. A new model isn't created.

We can also inherit from multiple parent models, setting a list of values to the _inherit attribute. Most of the time, this is done with **mixin classes.** Mixin classes are models that implement generic features to be reused. They are not expected to be used directly, and are like a container of features ready to be added to other models.

If, along with _inherit, we also use the _name attribute with a value different from the parent model, we get a new model reusing the features from the inherited one, with its own database table and data. The official documentation calls this **prototype inheritance**. Here, you take a model and create a brand new one that is a copy of the original one. As you add new features to it, they will be added only to the new model, and the original model isn't changed.

We also have the **delegation inheritance** method, available by using the _inherits attribute. It allows us to create a new model that contains and extends an existing model. When a new record is created for the new model, a new record in the original model is also created and linked, using a many-to-one field. Observers of the new model see all the fields, both from the original and new models, although behind the scenes each model handles its own data.

Let's explore these possibilities in more detail.

Copying features with prototype inheritance

The method we used to extend the model used only the _inherit attribute. We defined a class inheriting the todo.task model and added some features to it. The class attribute _name was not explicitly set; implicitly, it was todo.task. However, using the _name attribute allows us to create a new model by copying the features from the inherited ones.

For example, we can use this to add messaging features to our To-Do tasks.

The social network module (technically name `mail`) provides features for a message board, found at the bottom of many document forms, as well as the logic regarding messages and notifications. This is something we will often want to add to our models, so let's learn how to do that.

The social network messaging features are provided by the `mail.thread` model of the `mail` module. To add it to a custom model, we need to do the following:

1. Have the module depend on `mail`.
2. Have the class inherit from `mail.thread`.
3. Have the followers and thread widgets added to the form view.
4. Optionally, we need to set up record rules for followers.

Regarding the first point, our extension module will need the additional `mail` dependency on the module's `__manifest__.py` manifest file:

```
'depends': ['todo_app', 'mail'],
```

Regarding the second point, the inheritance from `mail.thread` is done using the `_inherit` attribute we used before. But our To-Do task extension class is already using the `_inherit` attribute. Fortunately, it can accept a list of models to inherit from, so we can use this to make it also include the inheritance for `mail.thread`:

```
class TodoTask(models.Model):
    _name = 'todo.task'
    _inherit = ['todo.task', 'mail.thread']
```

`mail.thread` is an abstract model. **Abstract models** are just like regular models, except that they don't have a database representation; no actual tables are created for them. Abstract models are not meant to be used directly. Instead, they are expected to be used as mixin classes, as we just did. We can think of them as templates with ready-to-use features. To create an abstract class, we just need it to use `models.AbstractModel` instead of `models.Model` as the class defining it.

This extends the `todo.task` model by copying into it the features from the `mail.thread` model. The `mail.thread` model implements the Odoo message and follower features and is reusable, so it's easy to add those features to any model.

Copying means that the inherited methods and fields will also be available in the inheriting model. The inherited fields will be created and stored in the target model's database tables. The data records of the original (inherited) and the new (inheriting) models are kept unrelated. Only the definitions are shared.

In practice, this type of inheritance is usually used with abstract mixin classes. It is rarely used to inherit from regular models because it duplicates data structures.

Odoo also has a delegation inheritance mechanism that avoids this data structure duplication, so it is usually preferred when inheriting from regular models. Let's look at it in more detail.

Embedding models using delegation inheritance

Delegation inheritance is less frequently used, but it can provide very convenient solutions. It is used through the _inherits attribute (note the additional "s") for dictionary mapping inherited models with fields linking to them.

A good example of this is the standard user's model, res.users; it has a partner model embedded in it:

```
from odoo import fields, models
class User(models.Model):
    _name = 'res.users'
    _inherits = {'res.partner': 'partner_id'}
    partner_id = fields.Many2one('res.partner')
```

With delegation inheritance, the res.users model embeds the inherited model, res.partner, so that when a new User class is created, a partner is also created and a reference to it is kept in the partner_id field of the User class. It has some similarities with the polymorphism concept in object-oriented programming.

Through the delegation mechanism, all fields from the inherited model and partner are available as if they were User fields. For example, the partner name and address fields are exposed as User fields, but in fact they are being stored in the linked partner model and no data duplication occurs.

The advantage of this, compared to prototype inheritance, is that there is no need to repeat data structures, such as addresses, across several tables. Any new model that needs to include an address can delegate that to an embedded partner model. If modifications are introduced in partner address fields, these are immediately available to all the models embedding them!

> Note that with delegation inheritance, fields are inherited but methods are not.

Summary

We went through a detailed explanation of models and fields, using them to extend the To-Do app with tags and stages for tasks. We learned how to define relationships between models, including hierarchical parent/child relationships. We also saw simple examples of computed fields and constraints when using Python code.

Several inheritance strategies were discussed, and we used them to add messaging features to our app.

In the next chapter, we will work on the user interface for these backend model features, making them available in the views used to interact with the application.

5
Import, Export, and Module Data

Most Odoo module definitions, such as user interfaces and security rules, are actually data records stored in specific database tables. The XML and CSV files found in modules are not used by Odoo applications at runtime. They are a means to load those definitions into the database tables.

Because of this, an important part of Odoo modules is about representing that data in files so that it can be loaded into a database upon module installation.

Modules can also have initial data and demonstration data. Data files allow us to add that to our modules. Additionally, understanding Odoo data representation formats is important in order to export and import business data within the context of a project implementation.

Before we go into practical cases, we will first explore the external identifier concept, which is the key to Odoo data representation.

Understanding external identifiers

An **external identifier**, also called **XML ID**, is a human-readable string identifier that uniquely identifies a particular record in Odoo. They are important when loading data into Odoo.

The actual database identifier for a record is an automatically assigned sequential number, and there is no way to know ahead of time what ID will be assigned for each record, during module installation. The external identifiers provide a way to reference a related record without the need to know the actual database ID assigned to it. The XML ID provides a convenient alias for the database ID so that we can use it whenever we need to reference a particular record.

Records defined in Odoo module data files use XML IDs. One reason for this is to avoid creating duplicate records when upgrading a module. The module upgrade will load the data files into the database again. We want it to detect the already existing records in order for them to be updated, instead of creating duplicate records.

Another reason to use XML IDs is to support interrelated data: data records that need to reference other data records. Since we can't know the actual database ID, we can use the XML ID, so the translation will be transparently handled by the Odoo framework.

Odoo takes care of translating the external identifier names into actual database IDs assigned to them. The mechanism behind this is quite simple: Odoo keeps a table with the mapping between the named external identifiers and their corresponding numeric database IDs: the `ir.model.data` model.

We must have **Developer mode** enabled to have the menu option available. Check whether you have the **Developer mode** bug icon in the upper-right, next to the user avatar icon. If not, you should enable it now, in the **Settings** top menu. You may refer to `Chapter 1`, *Quick Start – the Odoo Developer Mode and Concepts*, for more details.

We can inspect the existing mappings using the **Settings | Technical | External Identifiers | Sequences & Identifiers** menu item. For example, if we visit the **External Identifiers** list and filter it by the `todo_app` module, we will see the external identifiers generated by the module we created:

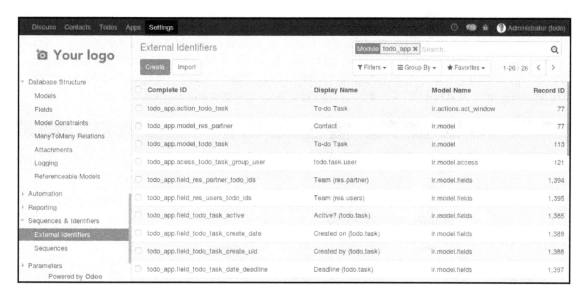

We can see that the external identifiers have a **Complete ID** label. Notice how it is composed of the module name and the identifier name, joined with a dot. For example: `todo_app.action_todo_task`.

External identifiers need to be unique only inside an Odoo module so that there is no risk of two modules conflicting because of accidentally choosing the same identifier name. The global unique identifier is built by joining together the module name with the actual external identifier name. This is what you can see in the **Complete ID** field.

When using an external identifier in a data file, we can choose to use either the complete identifier or just the external identifier name. Usually, it's simpler to just use the external identifier name, but the complete identifier enables us to reference data records from other modules. When doing so, make sure that those modules are included in the module dependencies, to ensure that those records are loaded before ours.

At the top of the list, we can see the `todo_app.action_todo_task` complete identifier. This is the menu action we created for the module, which is also referenced in the corresponding menu item. By clicking on it, we go to the form view with its details. There we can see that the `action_todo_task` external identifier in the `todo_app` module maps to a specific record ID in the `ir.actions.act_window` model, 77 in our case:

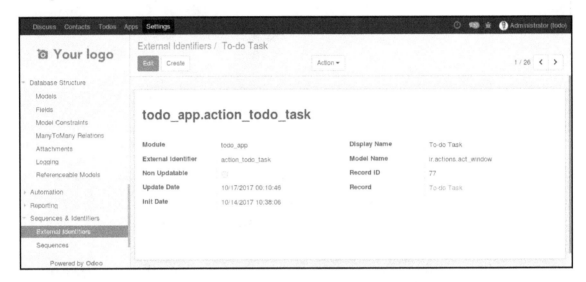

Besides providing a way for records to easily reference other records, external identifiers also allow you to avoid data duplication on repeated imports. If the external identifier is already present, the existing record will be updated, avoiding the creation of a new, duplicate record.

Finding external identifiers

When writing data records for our modules, we frequently need to look up the existing external identifiers to use for our reference.

One way to do this is to use the **Settings** | **Technical** | **External Identifiers** | **Sequences & Identifiers** menu shown earlier. We can also use the **Developer** menu for this. As you may recall from `Chapter 1`, *Quick Start – the Odoo Developer Mode and Concepts*, the **Developer** menu is activated in the **Settings** dashboard, in an option at the bottom-right.

To find the external identifier for a data record, we should open the corresponding form view, select the **Developer** menu, and then choose the **View Metadata** option. This displays a dialog with the record's database ID and external identifier (also known as XML ID).

For example, to look up the Demo user ID, we should navigate to the Users form view, at **Settings | Users**, select the **View Metadata** option, and the following will be shown:

To find the external identifier for view elements, such as form, tree, search, or action, the **Developer** menu is also a good source of help. For this, we can use the appropriate **Edit...** option, such as **Edit From View** or **Edit List View** to open a form with the details for the corresponding view. There we will find an **External ID** field providing the information we are looking for.

Exporting and importing data

We will now learn how to export and import data from Odoo's user interface. From there, we will move on to the technical details on how to use the data files in our addon modules.

Exporting data

Data exporting is a standard feature available in any list view. To use it, we must first pick the rows to export by selecting the corresponding checkboxes on the far left, and then select the **Export** option from the **Action** button at the top of the list:

We can also tick the checkbox in the header of the column. It will check all the records at once, and will export all the records that match the current search criteria.

In previous Odoo versions, only the records seen on the screen (the current page) would actually be exported. In Odoo 9, this was changed, so a ticked checkbox in the header will export all records that match the current filter, not just the ones currently displayed. This is very useful for exporting large sets of records that do not fit on the screen.

The **Export** option takes us to the **Export Data** dialog form, where we can choose what to export. At the top of the dialog form we have two selections available:

- For the **Export type** we now want to choose the **Import-Compatible Export** option so that data is exported in a format friendly to a later import.
- For the **Export formats**, we can choose between CSV or Excel. We will choose a CSV file to get a better understanding of the export format.

Next, we pick the columns we want to export. In this example we chose: **Description**, **Responsible**, **Deadline**, and **Done?**:

If we now click on the **Export To File** button, we will start the download of a file with the exported data. We should end up with a CSV text file similar to this:

```
"id","name","user_id/id","date_deadline"
"__export__.todo_task_11","Install Odoo","base.user_root","2017-10-31"
"__export__.todo_task_13","Create first app","base.user_demo","2017-11-15"
```

Notice that Odoo automatically exported an additional `id` column. This is an external identifier assigned to each record. If none exist, a new one is automatically generated using `__export__` in place of an actual module name. This makes it possible to edit the exported data, and, when it is re-imported, have the records updated with the changes we made.

Because of the automatically generated record identifiers, the export/import features can be used to mass edit Odoo data: export the data to CSV, use a spreadsheet software to mass edit it, and then import back to Odoo.

Importing data

First, we have to make sure the import feature is enabled. In Odoo 9 it is enabled by default. If not, the option is available in the **Settings** top menu, **General Settings** menu item. Under the **Users** section, the **Import & Export** option should be checked.

With this option enabled, list views show an **Import** option next to the **Create** button at the top of the list.

The **Import & Export** setting in fact installs the `base_import` module that is responsible for providing this feature.

Let's try a bulk edit on our To-Do data. Open the CSV file we just downloaded in a spreadsheet or a text editor and change a few values. We can also add some new rows, leaving the `id` column blank for them.

As mentioned before, the first column, `id`, provides a unique identifier for each row. This allows already existing records to be updated instead of duplicating them when we import the data back to Odoo. For new rows added to the CSV file, we can choose to either provide an external identifier of our choice or to leave the `id` column blank. Either way, a new record will be created for them.

After saving the changes to the CSV file, click on the **Import** option (next to the **Create** button) and we will be presented with the import assistant:

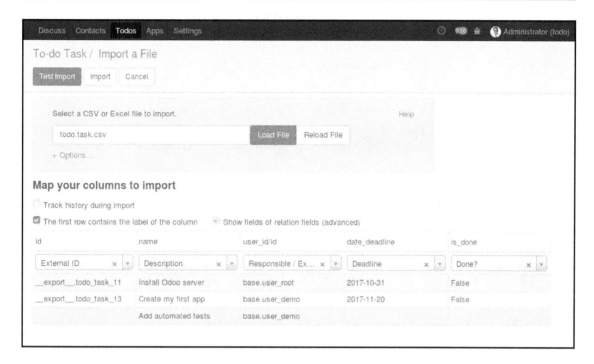

There, we should select the CSV file location on the disk and then click on the **Test Import** button, at the top right, to check it for correctness.

Since the file to import is based on an Odoo export, there is a good chance that it will be valid. Depending on the application used to edit the data file, you may have to play with separator and encoding options to get the best results.

Now we can click on **Import**, and there you go: our modifications and new records should have been loaded into Odoo.

Related records in CSV data files

In the preceding example, the person responsible for each task is a related record in the users model, with a many-to-one (or a foreign key) relation. The column name used for it in the CSV file was user_id/id, and the values for that field were external identifiers for the related records, such as base.user_root for the administrator user.

Relation columns should have /id appended to their name if we will be using external identifiers to reference the related records. It is possible to instead use /.id if we will be using actual database IDs (the real numeric identifier assigned).

 Unless you have good reason to do otherwise, always prefer to use external IDs instead of database IDs. Also remember that database IDs are specific to a particular Odoo database, and there is a good chance it won't work correctly if imported to a database other than the original.

Many-to-many fields can also be imported through CSV data files. It's as easy as providing a comma-separated list of external IDs, surrounded by double quotes. For example, To-Do tasks have the **Team** many-to-many fields, where we can have a list of the people working on a task. Here is an example of a data file with the team_ids many-to-many field:

```
id,team_ids/id
__export__.todo_task_11,"base.partner_root,base.partner_demo"
```

One-to-many fields often represent header/lines or parent/child relations, and there is special support to import these types of relations: for the same parent record, we can have several related lines.

We have an example of a one-to-many field in the partners model: a company partner can have several child contacts. If we export the data from the **Partner** model, and include the **Contacts/Name** field, we will see the structure that can be used to import this type of data:

id	name	child_ids/id	child_ids/name
base.res_partner_2	Agrolait	base.res_partner_address_31	Edward
		base.res_partner_address_22	Laith Jubair
		base.res_partner_address_4	Michel Fletcher
		base.res_partner_address_3	Thomas Passot

The id and name columns are for the parent records, and the child_ids columns are for the child records. Notice how the parent record columns are left blank for child records after the first one.

The preceding table, represented as a CSV file, looks as follows:

```
id,name,child_ids/id,child_ids/name
base.res_partner_2,Agrolait,base.res_partner_address_31,Edward
,,base.res_partner_address_22,Laith Jubair
,,base.res_partner_address_4,Michel Fletcher
,,base.res_partner_address_3,Thomas Passot
```

We can see that the first two columns, `id` and `name`, have values in the first line and are empty in the next three lines. They have data for the parent record, which is the company.

The other two columns are all prefixed with `child_ids/` and have values on all four lines. They have data for the contacts related to the parent company. The first line has data of both the company and the first contact, and the next three lines have data only for columns of the child contacts.

These are essential while working with export and import from the GUI. It is useful for setting up data in new Odoo instances, or for preparing data files to be included in Odoo modules. Next, we will learn more about using data files in modules.

Module data

Modules use data files to load their default data, demonstration data, user interface definitions, and other configurations into the database. This can be done using both CSV and XML files.

For completeness, the YAML file format can also be used, but it is seldom used to load data, and we won't discuss it. In fact, it is scheduled for deprecation in Odoo 12. Still, for a usage example you can look at the `110n_be` official module, and for information on the YAML format visit: `http://yaml.org/`.

CSV files used by modules are exactly the same as those we have seen and used for the import feature. When using them in modules, the filename must match the name of the model to which the data will be loaded. For example, a CSV file loading data into the `todo.task` model must be named `todo.task.csv`.

A common usage of data CSV files is for accessing security definitions loaded into the `ir.model.access` model. They usually use CSV files that are named `ir.model.access.csv`.

Demonstration data

Odoo addon modules may install demonstration data, and it is considered good practice to do so. This is useful for providing usage examples for a module and datasets to be used in tests. Demonstration data for a module is declared using the demo attribute of the __manifest__.py manifest file. Just like the data attribute, it is a list of filenames with the corresponding relative paths inside the module.

We should add some demonstration data to our todo_user module. An easy way to do that is to export some data from the To-Do tasks, as explained in the previous section. The convention is to place data files in a data/ subdirectory. So, we should save these data files in the todo_app addon module as data/todo.task.csv. Since this data will be owned by our module, we should edit the id values to remove the __export__ prefix in the identifiers.

As an example, our todo.task.csv data file may look as follows:

```
id,name,user_id/id,date_deadline
todo_task_a,"Install Odoo","base.user_root","2017-11-30"
todo_task_b","Create dev database","base.user_root",""
```

We must not forget to add this data file to the __manifest__.py manifest demo attribute:

```
'demo': ['data/todo.task.csv'],
```

Next time we update the module, as long as it is installed with demo data enabled, the content of the file will be imported.

 While data files are also re-imported on module upgrades, this is not the case for the demo data files: these are only imported upon module installation.

XML files are also used to load module data, and provide more features than plain CSV files. Let's learn more about what XML data files allow us to do that CSV files don't.

XML data files

While CSV files provide a simple and compact format to represent data, XML files are more powerful and give more control over the loading process. Their filenames are not required to match the model to be loaded. This is because the XML format is much richer and that information is provided by the XML elements inside the file.

We already used XML data files in the previous chapters. The user interface components, such as views and menu items, are in fact records stored in system models. The XML files in the modules are the means used to load these records into the instance database.

To showcase this, we will add a second data file to the todo_app module, data/todo_task.xml, with the following content:

```xml
<?xml version="1.0"?>
<odoo noupdate="1">
  <!-- Data to load -->
  <record model="todo.task" id="todo_task_c">
    <field name="name">Reinstall Odoo</field>
    <field name="user_id" ref="base.user_root" />
    <field name="date_deadline">2017-11-30</field>
    <field name="is_done" eval="False" />
  </record>
</odoo>
```

This XML is equivalent to the CSV data file we just saw in the previous section.

XML data files have an `<odoo>` top element, inside of which we can have several `<record>` elements that correspond to the CSV data rows.

> The `<odoo>` top element in data files was introduced in version 9.0 and replaces the former `<openerp>` tag. A `<data>` section inside the top element is still supported, but it's now optional. In fact, now `<odoo>` and `<data>` are equivalent, so we could use either one as top elements for our XML data files.

A `<record>` element has two mandatory attributes, `model` and `id` (the external identifier for the record), and contains `<field>` tags for each field to write on.

Note that the slash notation in field names is not available here; we can't use `<field name="user_id/id">`. Instead, the `ref` special attribute is used to reference external identifiers. We'll discuss the values of the relational to-many fields in a moment.

You may have noticed the `noupdate="1"` attribute in the top `<odoo>` element. This prevents the data records from being loaded on module upgrades, so that any later edits to them are not lost.

The noupdate data attribute

When a module is upgraded, the data file loading is repeated, and the module's records are rewritten. It is important to keep in mind that this means that upgrading a module will overwrite any manual changes that might have been made to the module's data.

 Notably, if views were manually modified to add customization, these changes will be lost with the next module upgrade. To avoid this, the correct approach is to instead create inherited views with the changes we want to introduce.

This rewrite behavior is the default, but it can be changed so that some of the data is only imported at install time, and is ignored in later module upgrades. This is done using the `noupdate="1"` attribute in the `<odoo>` or `<data>` elements.

This is useful for data that is to be used as initial configuration but is expected to be customized later, because these manually made customizations will be safe from module upgrades. For example, it is frequently used for record access rules, allowing them to be adapted to implementation-specific needs.

It is possible to have more than one `<data>` section in the same XML file. We can take advantage of this to separate data to import only once, with `noupdate="1"`, and data that can be re-imported on each upgrade, with `noupdate="0"`. The `noupdate="0"` is the default, so we can just omit it if we prefer.

The `noupdate` flag is stored in the **External Identifier** information for each record. It's possible to manually edit it directly using the **External Identifier** form, available in the **Technical** menu, using the **Non Updatable** checkbox.

 The `noupdate` attribute can be tricky when developing modules, because changes made to the data later will be ignored. One solution is to, instead of upgrading the module with the `-u` option, re-install it using the `-i` option. Reinstalling from the command line using the `-i` option ignores the `noupdate` flags on data records.

Defining records in XML

In an XML data file, each `<record>` element has two basic attributes, `id` and `model`, and contains `<field>` elements that assign values to each column. As mentioned before, the `id` attribute corresponds to the record's external identifier and the `model` attribute to the target model. The `<field>` elements have a few different ways to assign values. Let's look at them in detail.

Setting field values

The `<record>` element defines a data record and contains `<field>` elements to set values on each field.

The `name` attribute of the `field` element identifies the field to write on.

The value to write is the element content: the text between the field's opening and closing tag. For dates and datetimes, strings with `"YYYY-mm-dd"` and `"YYYY-mm-dd HH:MM:SS"` will be converted properly, but for Boolean fields any non-empty value will be converted as `True`, and the `"0"` and `"False"` values are converted to `False`.

> The way Boolean `False` values are read from data files is improved in Odoo 10. In previous versions, any non-empty values, including `"0"` and `"False"` were converted to `True`. For Booleans, using the `eval` attribute discussed in the next section is recommended.

Setting values using expressions

A more elaborate alternative for setting a field value is the `eval` attribute. It evaluates a Python expression and assigns the result to the field.

The expression is evaluated in a context that, besides Python built-ins, also has some additional identifiers available. Let's have a look at them.

To handle dates, the following Python modules are available: `time`, `datetime`, `timedelta`, and `relativedelta`. They allow you to calculate date values, something that is frequently used in demonstration and test data, so that the dates used are close to the module installation date. For more information about these Python modules see the documentation at `https://docs.python.org/3/library/datatypes.html`.

For example, to set a value to yesterday, we will use the following:

```
<field name="date_deadline"
    eval="(datetime.now() + timedelta(-1)).strftime('%Y-%m-%d')" />
```

Also available in the evaluation context is the `ref()` function, which is used to translate an external identifier into the corresponding database ID. This can be used to set values for relational fields. As an example, we have used it before to set the value for `user_id`:

```
<field name="user_id" eval="ref('base.group_user')" />
```

Setting values for relation fields

We have just seen how to set a value on a many-to-one relation field, such as `user_id`, using the `eval` attribute with a `ref()` function. But there is a simpler way.

The `<field>` element also has a `ref` attribute to set the value for a many-to-one field, using an external identifier. With this, we can set the value for `user_id` using just the following:

```
<field name="user_id" ref="base.user_demo" />
```

For one-to-many and many-to-many fields, a list of related IDs is expected, so a different syntax is needed; Odoo provides a special syntax to write to these types of fields.

The following example, taken from the official *Fleet* app, replaces the list of related records of a `tag_ids` field:

```
<field name="tag_ids"
        eval="[(6,0, [ref('vehicle_tag_leasing'),
                    ref('fleet.vehicle_tag_compact'),
                    ref('fleet.vehicle_tag_senior')]
            )]"
/>
```

To write to a to-many field, we use a list of triples. Each triple is a write command that does different things according to the code used:

- `(0, _ , {'field': value})` creates a new record and links it to this one
- `(1, id, {'field': value})` updates the values on an already linked record
- `(2, id, _)` unlinks and deletes a related record
- `(3, id, _)` unlinks but does not delete a related record
- `(4, id, _)` links an already existing record
- `(5, _, _)` unlinks but does not delete all the linked records
- `(6, _, [ids])` replaces the list of linked records with the provided list

The _ underscore symbol used in the preceding list represents irrelevant values, usually filled with 0 or `False`.

Shortcuts for frequently used models

If we go back to `Chapter 3`, *Your First Odoo Application - a practical overview*, we will find elements other than <record> in the XML files, such as <act_window> and <menuitem>.

These are convenient shortcuts for frequently used models that can also be loaded using regular <record> elements. They load data into base models supporting the user interface and will be explored in more detail later, specifically in `Chapter 9`, *Backend Views – Design the user interface*.

For reference, these are the shortcut elements available, along with the corresponding models they load data into:

- <act_window> is for the window action model, `ir.actions.act_window`
- <menuitem> is for the menu items model, `ir.ui.menu`
- <report> is for the report action model, `ir.actions.report.xml`
- <template> is for QWeb templates stored in the model `ir.ui.view`

In Odoo 11, the `<url>` tag was deprecated and removed. In previous versions it was used to load records for the URL action model, `ir.actions.act_url`.

It is worth noting that, if used to modify existing records, the shortcut elements overwrite all the fields. This differs from the `<record>` basic element, which only writes to the fields provided. So, for cases where we need to modify just a particular field of a user interface element, we should do it using a `<record>` element instead.

Other actions in XML data files

Until now, we have seen how to add or update data using XML files. But XML files also allow you to perform other types of actions that are sometimes needed to set up data. In particular, they can delete data and execute arbitrary model methods.

Deleting records

To delete a data record, we use the `<delete>` element, providing it with either an ID or a search domain to find the target records. For example, using a search domain to find the record to delete looks as follows:

```
<delete
  model="ir.rule"
  search="[('id','=',ref('todo_app.todo_task_user_rule'))]"
/>
```

If we know the specific ID to delete, we can use it with the `id` attribute instead. It was the case for the previous example, so it could also be written like this, for the same effect:

```
<delete model="ir.rule" id="todo_app.todo_task_user_rule" />
```

Triggering functions

An XML file can also execute arbitrary methods during its load process through the `<function>` element. This can be used to set up demo and test data. For example, the CRM app uses it to set up demonstration data:

```
<function
  model="todo.task"
  name="action_set_lost"
```

```
eval="[ref('crm_case_7'), ref('crm_case_9')
      , ref('crm_case_11'), ref('crm_case_12')]
      , {'install_mode': True}" />
```

This calls the `action_set_lost` method of the `crm.lead` model, passing two arguments through the `eval` attribute. The first is the list of IDs to work on, and the next is the context to use.

Modifying data

Unlike views, regular data records don't have an XML `arch` structure and can't be extended using XPath expressions. But they can still be modified by replacing the values in their fields.

The `<record id="x" model="y">` data loading elements actually perform an insert or update operation on model `y`: if record `x` does not exist, it is created; otherwise, it is updated/written over.

Since records in other modules can be accessed using a `<model>.<identifier>` global identifier, it's possible for our module to overwrite something that was written before by another module.

Note that since the dot is reserved to separate the module name from the object identifier, it can't be used in identifier names. Instead, you should use the underscore character.

As an example, we will make the To-Do menu option automatically filter only the tasks that have not been done.

The `todo_app` module already defined a search filter to show only the unfinished tasks, named `filter_not_done`. You can find it in the `todo_app/views/todo_view.xml` file. For the desired effect, we can have it enabled by default when selecting the To-Do menu option.

This can be done in the corresponding action, by adding a `default_search_` key to the action's context. For this, we will add the `todo_stage/views/todo_menu.xml` file with the following:

```
<odoo>
  <!-- Modify Window Action item -->
  <record id="todo_app.action_todo_task" model="ir.actions.act_window">
    <field name="context">
      {'search_default_filter_not_done': True}
    </field>
  </record>
</odoo>
```

Note that we used a `<record>` element, writing only to the `context` field. For this particular purpose, we can't use the `<act_window>`, because it resets all values in the record, and not just a particular one.

However, notice that the value of the field is overwritten. In this example, we are writing to the `context` field, containing a dictionary data structure. There may be an expectation that, in this case, the previous value is updated with the newly added key/values, but this is not the case: the previous value is erased and overwritten by the new value.

Working on data files with `<data noupdate="1">` at development time can be tricky because later edits on the XML definition will be ignored for module upgrades. To avoid this, you can instead re-install the module. This is more easily done through the command line using the `-i` option.

Summary

You have learned all the essentials about data serialization, and gained a better understanding of the XML aspects we saw in the previous chapters. We also spent some time understanding external identifiers, a central concept of data handling in general and module configurations in particular. XML data files were explained in detail. You learned about the several options available to set values on fields and also to perform actions, such as deleting records and calling model methods. CSV files and the data import/export features were also explained. These are valuable tools for Odoo's initial setup or for mass editing of data.

In the next chapter, we will explore the features provided by the ORM, and how they can be used to handle data.

6
The ORM API – Handling Application Data

In the previous chapters, we gave an overview of model creation, and how to load and export data from models. Now that we have our data model, and some data to work with, it's time to learn more about how we can programmatically interact with them.

The ORM supporting our models provides a few methods for this interaction, called the Application Programming Interface (API). These start with the basic CRUD (create, read, update, delete) operations, but also include other operations, such as data export and import, or utility functions to aid the user interface and experience. It also provides some decorators that we have already seen in the previous chapters. These allow us, when adding new methods, to let the ORM know how they should be handled.

In this chapter, we will learn how to use the most important API methods available for any Model, and the available API decorators to be used in our custom methods, depending on their purpose. We will also explore the API offered by the Discuss app, since it provides the message and notification features for Odoo.

We will start by having a closer look at the API decorators.

Understanding the ORM decorators

In the Odoo Python code encountered so far we can see that decorators, such as @api.multi, are frequently used in model methods. These are important for the ORM, and allow it to give those methods specific uses.

Let's see the ORM decorators we have available, and when each should be used.

Record handling decorators

Most of the time, we want a custom method to perform some actions on a recordset. For this, we should use @api.multi, and in that case, the self argument will be the recordset to work with. The method's logic will usually include a for loop iterating on it. This is surely the most frequently used decorator.

 If no decorator is used on a model method, it will default to @api.multi behavior.

In some cases, the method is prepared to work with a single record (a singleton). Here we could use the @api.one decorator, but this is not advised because for Version 9.0 it was announced it would be deprecated and may be removed in the future.

Instead, we should use @api.multi and add to the method code a line with self.ensure_one(), to ensure it is a singleton as expected. Despite being deprecated, the @api.one decorator is still supported. So it's worth knowing that it wraps the decorated method, doing the for-loop iteration to feed it one record at a time. So, in an @api.one decorated method, self is guaranteed to be a singleton. The return values of each individual method call are aggregated as a list and then returned.

 The return value of @api.one can be tricky: it returns a list, not the data structure returned by the actual method. For example, if the method code returns a dict, the actual return value is a list of dict values. This misleading behavior was the main reason the method was deprecated.

In some cases, the method is expected to work at the class level, and not on particular records. In some object-oriented languages this would be called a static method. These class-level static methods should be decorated with @api.model. In these cases, self should be used as a reference for the model, without expecting it to contain actual records.

 Methods decorated with @api.model cannot be used with user interface buttons. In those cases, @api.multi should be used instead.

Specific purpose decorators

A few other decorators have more specific purposes and are to be used together with the decorators described earlier:

- `@api.depends(fld1,...)` is used for computed field functions, to identify on what changes the (re)calculation should be triggered. It must set values on the computed fields, otherwise it will error.
- `@api.constrains(fld1,...)` is used for validation functions, and performs checks for when any of the mentioned fields are changed. It should not write changes in the data. If the checks fail, an exception should be raised.
- `@api.onchange(fld1,...)` is used in the user interface, to automatically change some field values when other fields are changed. The `self` argument is a singleton with the current form data, and the method should set values on it for the changes that should happen in the form. It doesn't actually write to database records, instead it provides information to change the data in the UI form.

When using the preceding decorators, no return value is needed. Except for `onchange` methods that can optionally return a `dict` with a warning message to display in the user interface.

As an example, we can use this to perform some automation in the To-Do form: when Responsible is set to an empty value, we will also empty the team list. For this, edit the `todo_stage/models/todo_task_model.py` file to add the following method:

```
@api.onchange('user_id')
def onchange_user_id(self):
    if not user_id:
        self.team_ids = None
        return {
            'warning': {
                'title': 'No Responsible',
                'message': 'Team was also reset.'
            }
        }
```

Here, we are using the `@api.onchange` decorator to attach some logic to any changes in the `user_id` field, when done through the user interface. Note that the actual method name is not relevant, but the convention is for its name to begin with `onchange_`.

Inside an `onchange` method, self represents a single virtual record containing all the fields currently set in the record being edited, and we can interact with them. Most of the time, this is what we want to do: to automatically fill values in other fields, depending on the value set to the changed field. In this case, we are setting the `team_ids` field to an empty value.

The `onchange` methods don't need to return anything, but they can return a dictionary containing a `warning` or a `domain` key:

- The `warning` key should describe a message to show in a dialogue window, such as: `{'title': 'Message Title', 'message': 'Message Body'}`.
- The `domain` key can set or change the `domain` attribute of other fields. This allows you to build more user-friendly interfaces, by having `to-many` fields list only the selection option that make sense for this case. The value for the domain key looks like this: `{'team_ids': [('is_author', '=', True)]}`

Using the ORM built-in methods

The decorators discussed in the previous section allow us to add certain features to our models, such as implementing validations and automatic computations.

We also have the basic methods provided by the ORM, used mainly to perform CRUD (create, read, update and delete) operations on our model data. To read data, the main methods provided are `search()` and `browse()`. We will discuss these in Chapter 7, *Business logic - supporting business processes*.

Now we will explore the write operations provided by the ORM, and how they can be extended to support custom logic.

Methods for writing model data

The ORM provides three methods for the three basic write operations:

- `<Model>.create(values)` creates a new record on the model. Returns the created record.
- `<Recordset>.write(values)` updates field values on the recordset. Returns nothing.
- `<Recordset>.unlink()` deletes the records from the database. Returns nothing.

The `values` argument is a dictionary, mapping field names to values to write.

In some cases, we need to extend these methods to add some business logic to be triggered whenever these actions are executed. By placing our logic in the appropriate section of the custom method, we can have the code run before or after the main operations are executed.

Using the `TodoTask` model as an example, we can make a custom `create()`, which would look like this:

```
@api.model
def create(self, vals):
    # Code before create: should use the `vals` dict
    new_record = super(TodoTask, self).create(vals)
    # Code after create: can use the `new_record` created
    return new_record
```

 Python 3 introduced a simplified way to use `super()` that could have been used in the preceding code samples. We chose to use the Python 2 compatible form. If we don't mind breaking Python 2 support for our code, we can use the simplified form, without the arguments referencing the class name and `self`. For example: `super().create(vals)`

A custom `write()` would follow this structure:

```
@api.multi
def write(self, vals):
    # Code before write: can use `self`, with the old values
    super(TodoTask, self).write(vals)
    # Code after write: can use `self`, with the updated values
    return True
```

While extending `create()` and `write()` opens up a lot of possibilities, remember in many cases we don't need to do that, since there are tools also available that may be better suited:

- For field values that are automatically calculated based on other fields, we should use computed fields. An example of this is to calculate a header total when the values of the lines are changed.
- To have field default values calculated dynamically, we can use a field default bound to a function instead of a fixed value.
- To have values set on other fields when a field is changed, we can use `onchange` functions. An example of this is when picking a customer, setting their currency as the document's currency that can later be manually changed by the user. Keep in mind that on change only works on form view interaction and not on direct `write` calls.
- For validations, we should use constraint functions decorated with `@api.constraints(fld1,fld2,...)`. These are like computed fields but, instead of computing values, they are expected to raise errors.

Consider carefully if you really need to use extensions to the `create` or `write` methods. In most cases, we just need to perform some validation or automatically compute some value, when the record is saved. But we have better tools for this: validations are best implemented with `@api.constrains` methods, and automatic calculations are better implemented as computed fields. In this case, we need to compute field values when saving. If, for some reason, computed fields are not a valid solution, the best approach is to have our logic at the top of the method, accumulating the changes needed into the `vals` dictionary that will be passed to the final `super()` call.

For the `write()` method, having further `write` operations on the same model will lead to a recursion loop and end with an error when the worker process resources are exhausted. Please consider if this is really needed. If it is, a technique to avoid the recursion loop is to set a flag in the `context`. For example, we could add code such as the following:

```
if not self.env.context.get('todo_task_writing'):
    self.with_context(todo_task_writing=True).write(
        some_values)
```

With this technique, our specific logic is guarded by an `if` statement, and runs only if a specific marker is not found in the context. Furthermore, our `self.write()` operations should use `with_context` to set that marker. This combination ensures that the custom login inside the `if` statement runs only once, and is not triggered on further `write()` calls, avoiding the infinite loop.

These are common extension examples, but of course any standard method available for a model can be inherited in a similar way to add our custom logic to it.

Methods for web client use over RPC

We have seen the most important model methods used to generate recordsets and how to write to them, but there are a few more model methods available for more specific actions, as shown here:

- `read([fields])` is similar to the `browse` method, but, instead of a recordset, it returns a list of rows of data with the fields given as its argument. Each row is a dictionary. It provides a serialized representation of the data that can be sent through RPC protocols and is intended to be used by client programs and not in server logic.

- `search_read([domain], [fields], offset=0, limit=None, order=None)` performs a search operation followed by a read on the resulting record list. It is intended to be used by RPC clients and saves them the extra round trip needed when doing a `search` followed by a `read` on the results.

Methods for data import and export

The import and export operations, discussed in `Chapter 5`, *Import Export and Module Data*, are also available from the ORM API, through the following methods:

- `load([fields], [data])` is used to import data acquired from a CSV file. The first argument is the list of fields to import, and it maps directly to a CSV top row. The second argument is a list of records, where each record is a list of string values to parse and import, and it maps directly to the CSV data rows and columns. It implements the features of CSV data import, such as the external identifiers support. It is used by the web client **Import** feature.

- `export_data([fields], raw_data=False)` is used by the web client **Export** function. It returns a dictionary with a data key containing the data: a list of rows. The field names can use the `.id` and `/id` suffixes used in CSV files, and the data is in a format compatible with an importable CSV file. The optional `raw_data` argument allows for data values to be exported with their Python types, instead of the string representation used in CSV.

Methods for the user interface

The following methods are mostly used by the web client to render the user interface and perform basic interaction:

- `name_get()` returns a list of (`ID`, `name`) tuples with the text representing each record. It is used by default for computing the `display_name` value, providing the text representation of relation fields. It can be extended to implement custom display representations, such as displaying the record code and name instead of only the name.
- `name_search(name='', args=None, operator='ilike', limit=100)` returns a list of (`ID`, `name`) tuples, where the display name matches the text in the `name` argument. It is used in the UI while typing in a relation field to produce the list with the suggested records matching the typed text. For example, it is used to implement product lookup both by name and by reference, while typing in a field to pick a product.
- `name_create(name)` creates a new record with only the title name to use for it. It is used in the UI for the "quick-create" feature, where you can quickly create a related record by just providing its name. It can be extended to provide specific defaults for the new records created through this feature.
- `default_get([fields])` returns a dictionary with the default values for a new record to be created. The default values may depend on variables such as the current user or the session context.
- `fields_get()` is used to describe the model's field definitions, as seen in the **View Fields** option of the developer menu.
- `fields_view_get()` is used by the web client to retrieve the structure of the UI view to render. It can be given the ID of the view as an argument or the type of view we want using `view_type='form'`. For example, you may try this: `self.fields_view_get(view_type='tree')`.

The Mail and Social features API

Odoo has available global messaging and activity planning features, provided by the Discuss app, with the technical name `mail`.

The `mail` module provides the `mail.thread` abstract class that makes it simple to add the messaging features to any model. This was done in `Chapter 4`, *Models – Structure The Application Data*, to explain how to inherit features from mixin abstract classes. To add the `mail.thread` features to the To-Do tasks, we just need to inherit from it:

```
class TodoTask(models.Model):
    _name = 'todo.task'
    _inherit = ['todo.task', 'mail.thread']
```

After this, among other things, our model will have two new fields available. For each record (sometimes also called a document) we have:

- `mail_follower_ids` stores the followers, and corresponding notification preferences
- `mail_message_ids` lists all the related messages

The followers can be either partners or channels. A partner represents a specific person or organization. A channel is not a particular person, and instead represents a subscription list.

Each follower also has a list of message types that they are subscribed to. Only the selected message types will generate notifications for them.

Message subtypes

Some types of messages are called subtypes. They are stored in the `mail.message.subtype` model and accessible in the **Technical | Email | Subtypes** menu.

By default, we have three message subtypes available:

- **Discussions**, with `mail.mt_comment` XMLID, used for the messages created with the **Send message** link. It is intended to send a notification.
- **Activities,** with `mail.mt_activities` XMLID, used for the messages created with the **Schedule activity** link. It is intended to send a notification.
- **Note**, with `mail.mt_note` XMLID, used for the messages created with the **Log note** link. It is not intended to send a notification.

Subtypes have the default notification settings described previously, but users are able to change them for specific documents, for example, to mute a discussion they are not interested in.

Other than the built-in subtypes, we can also add our own subtypes to customize the notifications for our apps. Subtypes can be generic or intended for a particular model. For the latter case, we should fill in the subtype's `res_model` field with the name of the model it should apply to.

Posting messages

Our business logic can make use of this messaging system to send notifications to users. To post a message we use the `message_post()` method. For example:

```
self.message_post('Hello!')
```

This adds a simple text message, but sends no notification to the followers. That is because by default the `mail.mt_note` subtype is used for the posted messages. But we can have the message posted with the particular subtype we want. To add a message and have it send notifications to the followers, we should use the following:

```
self.message_post('Hello again!', subtype='mail.mt_comment')
```

We can also add a subject line to the message by adding the `subject` parameter. The message body is HTML, so we can include markup for text effects, such as <b> for bold text or <i> for italics.

 The message body will be sanitized for security reasons, so some particular HTML elements may not make it to the final message.

Adding followers

Also interesting from a business logic viewpoint is the ability to automatically add followers to a document, so that they can then get the corresponding notifications. For this we have several methods available to add followers:

- `message_subscribe(partner_ids=<list of int IDs>)` adds Partners
- `message_subscribe(channel_ids=<list of int IDs>)` adds Channels
- `message_subscribe_users(user_ids=<list of int IDs>)` adds Users

The default subtypes will be used. To force subscribing a specific list of subtypes, just add the `subtype_ids=<list of int IDs>` with the specific subtypes you want to be subscribed.

Summary

We went through an explanation of the features the ORM API proposes, and how they can be used when creating our models. We also learned about the `mail` module and the global messaging features it provides. We explored how to use it to choose followers to be notified, and how to send messages to these followers.

In the next chapter, we will look further into the ORM, this time to have a deeper understanding on how recordsets work and can be manipulated. We will also learn how to implement wizards, requesting input from the user who will then perform some business logic based on it.

7

Business Logic – Supporting Business Processes

With the Odoo programming API, we can write complex logic and wizards to provide rich user interaction for our apps. In this chapter, we will see how to write code to support business logic in our models, and we will also learn how to activate it for events and user actions.

Additionally, we can also use wizards to implement more complex interactions with the user, allowing them to ask for input and provide feedback during the interaction.

We will start by building such a wizard for our To-Do app.

Creating a wizard

Suppose our To-Do app users regularly need to set the deadlines and person responsible for a large number of tasks. They could use an assistant to help with this. It should allow them to pick the tasks to be updated and then choose the deadline date and/or the responsible user to set for them.

Wizards are forms that get input from users, then use it for further processing. They can be used for simple tasks, such as asking for a few parameters and running a report, or for complex data manipulations, such as the use case we just described. Other more complex cases can involve several chained forms, where finishing a form opens up the next one where we can proceed a step further into the process.

For our case, this is what the wizard will look like:

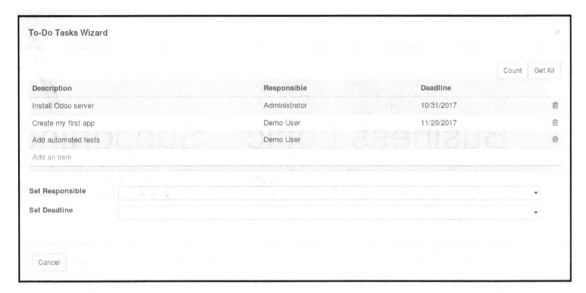

We will implement this feature in a new module, `todo_wizard`.

We should start by creating the corresponding directory, and the
`todo_wizard/__manifest__.py` description, with the following code:

```
{   'name': 'To-do Tasks Management Assistant',
    'description': 'Mass edit your To-Do backlog.',
    'author': 'Daniel Reis',
    'depends': ['todo_app'],
    'data': ['views/todo_wizard_view.xml'], }
```

As in previous addons, the `todo_wizard/__init__.py` file is just one line:

```
from . import models
```

Next, we need to describe the data model supporting our wizard.

The wizard model

A wizard displays a form view to the user, usually as a dialog window, with some fields to
be filled in. These will then be used for the wizard logic.

This is implemented using the same model/view architecture as for regular views, but the supporting model is based on `models.TransientModel` instead of the `models.Model`.

This type of model also has a database representation and stores state there, but the data is expected to be useful only until the wizard completes its work. A scheduled job regularly cleans up the old data from wizard database tables.

The `models/todo_wizard_model.py` file will define the fields we need to interact with the user: the list of tasks to be updated, the user responsible, and the deadline date to be set on them.

First add the `models/__init__.py` file with following line of code:

```
from . import todo_wizard_model
```

Then create the actual `models/todo_wizard_model.py` file:

```
from odoo import models, fields, api

class TodoWizard(models.TransientModel):
    _name = 'todo.wizard'
    _description = 'To-do Mass Assignment'
    task_ids = fields.Many2many(
        'todo.task',
        string='Tasks')
    new_deadline = fields.Date('Deadline to Set')
    new_user_id = fields.Many2one(
        'res.users',
        string='Responsible to Set')
```

It's worth noting that one-to-many relations for regular models should not be used in transient models. The reason for this is that it would require the regular model to have the inverse many-to-one relation with the transient model, but this is not allowed, since that could prevent old transient records from being cleaned up, because of the existing references in regular model records. An alternative to this is to use a many-to-many relation.

> Many-to-many relationships are stored in a dedicated table, and the rows in this table are automatically deleted when either side of the relationship gets deleted.

The wizard form

The wizard form views are the same as for regular models, except for two specific elements:

- A `<footer>` section can be used to place the action buttons
- A special `type= "cancel"` button is available to interrupt the wizard without performing any action

This is the content of our `views/todo_wizard_view.xml` file:

```xml
<odoo>
  <record id="To-do Task Wizard" model="ir.ui.view">
    <field name="name">To-do Task Wizard</field>
    <field name="model">todo.wizard</field>
    <field name="arch" type="xml">

      <form>
        <div class="oe_right">
          <button type="object"
            name="do_count_tasks"
            string="Count All" />
          <button type="object"
            name="do_populate_tasks"
            string="Get All" />
        </div>

        <field name="task_ids">
          <tree>
            <field name="name" />
            <field name="user_id" />
            <field name="date_deadline" />
          </tree>
        </field>

        <group>
          <group> <field name="new_user_id" /> </group>
          <group> <field name="new_deadline" /> </group>
        </group>

        <footer>
          <button type="object" name="do_mass_update"
            string="Mass Update" class="oe_highlight"
            attrs="{'invisible':
              [('new_deadline','=',False),
               ('new_user_id', '=',False)]
            }" />
```

```
            <button special="cancel" string="Cancel"/>
          </footer>
        </form>
      </field>
    </record>

    <!-- More button Action -->
    <act_window id="action_todo_wizard"
      name="To-do Tasks Wizard"
      src_model="todo.task"
      res_model="todo.wizard"
      view_mode="form"
      target="new"
      multi="True"
      />
  </odoo>
```

You may also have noticed that `attrs` is used in the **Mass Update** button, to add the nice touch of making it invisible until either a new deadline or responsible user is selected.

The `<act_window>` window action we see in the XML adds an option to the **Action** button of To-Do Tasks (using the `src_model` attribute). The `target="new"` attribute makes it open as a dialog window.

To open the wizard we should select one or more records from the To-Do list and then choose the **Todo Tasks Wizard** option from the **Action** menu, which shows up at the top of the list, next to the **Filters** menu.

Right now this opens the wizard form, but the records selected on the list are ignored. It would be nice for our wizard to show them preselected in the Tasks list. When a form is presented, the `default_get()` method is called to compute the default values to be presented. This is exactly what we want, so we should use that method. Note that at this point the `create()` method is yet to be invoked, so it can't be used for what we want.

Views add a few elements to the context dictionary, which are available when we click through an Action or jump to another view. These are:

- `active_model`, with the technical name of the view's model.
- `active_id`, with the ID of the form's active record (or the first record, if in a list).
- `active_ids`, with a list of the active records in a list (just one element, if in a form).

In our case the `active_ids` hold the IDs for the records selected in the Task list, and we can use them as the default values for the wizard's `task_ids` field:

```
@api.model
def default_get(self, field_names):
    defaults = super(TodoWizard, self
        ).default_get(field_names)
    defaults['task_ids'] = self.env.context['active_ids']
    return defaults
```

We first use `super()` to call the standard `default_get()` computation, and then add to the defaults the `task_ids`, with the `active_ids` value read from the environment context.

Next, we need to implement the actions to be performed on the form buttons.

The wizard business logic

Excluding the **Cancel** button, we have three action buttons to implement: **Count All**, **Get All**, and **Mass Update**. We will first focus on the **Mass Update** button.

The method called by the button is `do_mass_update` and it should be defined in the `models/todo_wizard_model.py` file, as shown in the following code:

```
from odoo import exceptions
import logging
_logger = logging.getLogger(__name__)

# ...
# class TodoWizard(models.TransientModel):
# ...

    @api.multi
    def do_mass_update(self):
        self.ensure_one()
        if not (self.new_deadline or self.new_user_id):
            raise exceptions.ValidationError('No data to update!')
        # Logging debug messages
        _logger.debug(
            'Mass update on Todo Tasks %s',
            self.task_ids.ids)
        vals = {}
        if self.new_deadline:
            vals['date_deadline'] = self.new_deadline
        if self.new_user_id:
            vals['user_id'] = self.new_user_id
```

```
# Mass write values on all selected tasks
if vals:
    self.task_ids.write(vals)
return True
```

Our code should handle one wizard instance at a time, so we used `self.ensure_one()` to make that clear. Here, `self` represents the browse record for the data on the wizard form.

The method begins by validating whether a new deadline date or responsible user was given, and raises an error if not. Next, we have an example of how to write a debug message to the server log.

Then the `vals` dictionary is built with the values to set with the mass update: a new date, new responsible user, or both. Afterwards, the `write` method is used on a recordset to perform the mass update. This is more efficient than a loop performing individual writes on each record.

It is good practice for methods to always return something. This is why it returns the `True` value at the end. The sole reason for this is that the XML-RPC protocol does not support `None` values, so those methods won't be usable using that protocol. In practice, you may not be aware of the issue because the web client uses JSON-RPC, not XML-RPC, but it is still a good practice to follow.

Next, we will have a closer look at logging, and then will work on the logic behind the two buttons at the top: **Count** and **Get All**.

Logging

These mass updates could be misused, so it may be a good idea to log some information when the updates happen. The preceding code initializes the `_logger` in the two lines before the `TodoWizard` class, using the Python `logging` standard library. The Python `__name__` internal variable is to identify the messages as coming from this module.

To write log messages in method code, we can use:

```
_logger.debug('A DEBUG message')
_logger.info('An INFO message')
_logger.warning('A WARNING message')
_logger.error('An ERROR message')
```

When passing values to use in the log message, instead of using string interpolation, we should provide them as additional parameters. For example, instead of `_logger.info('Hello %s' % 'World')` we should use `_logger.info('Hello %s', 'World')`. You may notice that we did so in the `do_mass_update()` method.

 An interesting thing to note about logging is that log entries always print the timestamp in UTC. This may come as a surprise to new administrators, but is due to the fact that the server internally handles all dates in UTC.

Raising exceptions

When something is not right, we will want to interrupt the program with an error message. This is done by raising an exception. Odoo provides a few additional exception classes in addition to the ones available in Python.

These are examples for the most useful ones:

```
from odoo import exceptions
raise exceptions.Warning('Warning message')
raise exceptions.ValidationError('Not valid message')
```

The `Warning` message also interrupts execution but can sound less severe than a `ValidationError`. All data manipulation done during the method execution is in a database transaction, which is rolled back when an exception occurs. This means that all these database operations will be canceled.

While it's not the best user interface, we take advantage of that on the **Count All** button to display a message to the user:

```
@api.multi
def do_count_tasks(self):
    Task = self.env['todo.task']
    count = Task.search_count([('is done', '=', False)])
    raise exceptions.Warning(
            'There are %d active tasks.' %count)
```

As a side note, it looks like we could have used the `@api.model` decorator, since this method does not operate on the `self` recordset. But in this case we can't because the method needs to be called from a button.

Helper actions in wizards

Now, suppose we want a button to automatically pick all the To-Do Tasks to spare the user from picking them one by one. That's the point of having the **Get All** button in the form. The code behind this button will get a recordset with all active tasks and assign it to the tasks in the many-to-many field.

But there is a catch here. In dialog windows, when a button is pressed, the wizard window is automatically closed. We didn't face this problem with the **Count** button because it uses an exception to display its message, so the action is not "successful" and the window is not closed.

Fortunately, we can work around this behavior by asking the client to re-open the same wizard. Model methods can return a window action to be performed by the web client, in the form of a dictionary object. This dictionary uses the same attributes used to define window actions in XML files.

We will define a helper function for the window action dictionary to reopen the wizard window, so that it can be easily reused in several buttons:

```python
@api.multi
def _reopen_form(self):
    self.ensure_one()
    return {
        'type': 'ir.actions.act_window',
        'res_model': self._name,  # this model
        'res_id': self.id,  # the current wizard record
        'view_type': 'form',
        'view_mode': 'form',
        'target': 'new'}
```

It is worth noting that the window action could be something else, such as jumping to a different wizard form to ask for additional user input, and that can be used to implement multi-page wizards.

Now the **Get All** button can do its job and still keep the user working on the same wizard:

```python
@api.multi
def do_populate_tasks(self):
    self.ensure_one()
    Task = self.env['todo.task']
    all_tasks = Task.search([('is_done', '=', False)])
    # Fill the wizard Task list with all tasks
    self.task_ids = all_tasks
```

```
# reopen wizard form on same wizard record
return self._reopen_form()
```

Here, we can see how to work with any other available model: we first use `self.env[]` to get a reference to the model, `todo.task` in this case, and can then perform actions on it, such as `search()` to retrieve records meeting some search criteria.

The transient model stores the values in the wizard form fields, and can be read or written just like any other model. The `all_tasks` variable is assigned to the model's `task_ids` one-to-many field. As you can see, this is done just like we would for any other field type.

Working with the ORM API

From the previous section, we already got a taste of what it is like to use the ORM API. Next we will look at what more we can do with it.

The shell command

Python has a command-line interface that is a great way to explore its syntax. Similarly, Odoo also has an equivalent feature, where we can interactively try out commands to see how they work. That is the `shell` command.

To use it, run Odoo with the `shell` command and the database to be used, as shown here:

```
$ ./odoo-bin shell -d todo
```

You should see the usual server start up sequence in the terminal until it stops on a >>> Python prompt waiting for your input. Here, `self` will represent the record for the `Administrator` user, as you can confirm by typing the following:

```
>>> self
res.users(1,)
>>> self._name
'res.users'
>>> self.name
'Administrator'
```

In the shell session here, we inspected our environment. The `self` represents a `res.users` recordset containing only the record with the ID 1. We can also confirm the recordset's model name by inspecting `self._name`, and get the value for the record's `name` field, confirming that it is the `Administrator` user.

As with Python, you can exit the prompt using *Ctrl + D*. This will also close the server process and return you to the system shell prompt.

> The shell feature was added in Version 9.0. For Version 8.0, there is a community back-ported module to add it. Once downloaded and included in the addons path, no further installation is necessary. It can be downloaded from `https://www.odoo.com/apps/modules/8.0/shell/`.

The server environment

The server shell provides a `self` reference identical to what you would find inside a method of the Users model, `res.users`.

As we have seen, `self` is a recordset. **Recordsets** carry with them environment information, including the user browsing the data and additional context information, such as the language and the time zone.

We can inspect the current environment with:

```
>>> self.env
<openerp.api.Environment object at 0xb3f4f52c>
```

The execution environment in `self.env` has the following attributes available:

- `env.cr` is the database cursor being used.
- `env.user` is the record for the current user.
- `env.uid` is the ID for the session user. It's the same as `env.user.id`.
- `env.context` is an immutable dictionary with a session context.

The environment also provides access to the registry where all the installed models are available. For example, `self.env['res.partner']` returns a reference to the Partners model. We can then use `search()` or `browse()` on it to retrieve recordsets:

```
>>> self.env['res.partner'].search([('name', 'like', 'Ag')])
res.partner(7, 51)
```

In this example, a recordset for the `res.partner` model contains two records, with IDs 7 and 51.

Modifying the execution environment

The environment is immutable, and so it can't be modified. But we can create a modified environment and then run actions using it.

To do so, we can make use of the following methods:

- `env.sudo(user)` is provided with a user record, and returns an environment with that user. If no user is provided, the Administrator superuser will be used, which allows for running specific operations, bypassing security rules.
- `env.with_context(dictionary)` replaces the context with a new one.
- `env.with_context(key=value,...)` modifies the current context setting values for some of its keys.

Additionally, we have the `env.ref()` function, taking a string with an external identifier and returning a record for it, as shown here:

```
>>> self.env.ref('base.user_root')
res.users(1,)
```

Transactions and low-level SQL

Database-writing operations are executed in the context of a database transaction. Usually, we don't have to worry about this as the server takes care of that while running model methods.

But, in some cases, we may need finer control over the transaction. This can be done through the database cursor `self.env.cr`, as shown here:

- `self.env.cr.commit()` commits the transaction's buffered write operations.
- `self.env.cr.savepoint()` sets a transaction savepoint to rollback to.
- `self.env.cr.rollback()` cancels the transaction's write operations since the last commit, or all if no commit was done.

In a shell session, your data manipulation won't be made effective in the database until you use `self.env.cr.commit()`.

With the cursor `execute()` method, we can run SQL directly in the database. It takes a string with the SQL statement to run and a second optional argument with a tuple or list of values to use as parameters for the SQL. These values will be used where `%s` placeholders are found.

Caution!
With `cr.execute()` we should not directly compose the SQL query string, used as the first parameter. This is a well-known security risk that can be exploited through SQL injection attacks. Always use `%s` placeholders and the second parameter to pass values.

If you're using a `SELECT` query, records should then be fetched. The `fetchall()` function retrieves all the rows as a list of `tuples`, and `dictfetchall()` retrieves them as a list of dictionaries, as shown in the following example:

```
>>> self.env.cr.execute("SELECT id, login FROM res_users WHERE login=%s OR
id=%s", ('demo', 1))
>>> self.env.cr.fetchall()
[(4, 'demo'), (1, 'admin')]
```

It's also possible to run **Data Manipulation Language** (**DML**) instructions, such as `UPDATE` and `INSERT`. Since the server keeps data caches, they may become inconsistent with the actual data in the database. Because of that, when using raw DML, the caches should be cleared afterward by using `self.env.invalidate_all()`.

Caution!
Executing SQL directly in the database can lead to inconsistent data. You should use it only if you are sure of what you are doing.

Before we go into more details on recordset handling, we should learn a little more about context and domain.

Context and domain

Context and domain are two widely used concepts which we have encountered several times in the previous chapters. We have seen them being used in the backend, in model fields and methods, and in the frontend, in windows actions and forms.

We will now take a closer look at them, to see when and how they should be used.

Context data

The **context** is dictionary-carrying session data that can be used on both the client-side user interface and the server-side ORM and business logic.

On the client side it can carry information from one view to the next, such as the ID of the record active on the previous view, after following a link or a button, or to provide default values to be used in the next view.

On the server side, some recordset field values can depend on the locale settings provided by the context. In particular, the `lang` key affects the value of translatable fields. Context can also provide signals for server-side code. For example, the `active_test` key, when set to `False`, changes the behavior of ORM's `search()` method so that it does not filter out inactive records.

An initial context from the web client looks like this:

```
{'lang': 'en_US', 'tz': 'Europe/Brussels', 'uid': 1}
```

You can see the `lang` key with the user language, `tz`, with the time zone information, and `uid` with the current user ID.

When opening a form from a link or a button in a previous view, an `active_id` key is added to the context, with the ID of the record we were positioned at, in the origin form. In the particular case of list views, we have an `active_ids` context key containing a list of the record IDs selected in the previous list.

On the client side, the context can be used to set default values or activate default filters on the target view, using keys with the `default_` or `default_search_` prefixes.

Here are some examples:

- To set the current user as a default value of the `user_id` field, we use `{'default_user_id': uid}`
- To have a `filter_my_tasks` filter activated by default on the target view, we use `{'default_search_filter_my_tasks': 1}`

Domain expressions

The **domain** is used to filter data records. They use a specific syntax that the Odoo ORM parses to produce the SQL WHERE expressions that will query the database.

A domain expression is a list of conditions. Each condition is a `('<field_name>', '<operator>', <value>')` tuple. For example, this is a valid domain expression, with only one condition: `[('is_done','=',False)]`.

The following is an explanation of each of these elements:

The `<field_name>` is the field being filtered, and can use dot-notation for fields in related models.

The `<value>` is evaluated as a Python expression. It can use literal values, such as numbers, Booleans, strings, or lists, and can use fields and identifiers available in the evaluation context. There are actually two possible evaluation contexts for domains:

- When used on the client side, such as in window actions or field attributes, the raw field values used to render the current view are available, but we can't use dot-notation on them.
- When used on the server side, such as in security record rules and in server Python code, dot-notation can be used on fields, since the current record is an object.

The `<operator>` can be:

- The usual comparison operators are `<`, `>`, `<=`, `>=`, `=`, and `!=`.
- `'=like'` matches against a pattern, where the underscore symbol, `_`, matches any single character and the percentage symbol, `%`, matches any sequence of characters.

- `'like'` matches against a `'%value%'` pattern. The `'ilike'` is similar but case insensitive. The `'not like'` and `'not ilike'` operators are also available.
- `'child of'` finds the children values in a hierarchical relation, for the models configured to support them.
- `'in'` and `'not in'` are used to check for inclusion in a given list, so the value should be a list of values. When used on a "to-many" relation field, the `in` operator behaves like a `contains` operator.

A domain expression is a list of items, and can contain several condition tuples. By default, these condition will implicitly be combined using the AND logical operator. This means that it will only return records meeting all these conditions.

Explicit logic operators can also be used: the ampersand symbol, `'&'`, for AND operations (the default), and the pipe symbol,`'|'`, for OR operations. These will operate on the next two items, working in a recursive way. We'll look at this in more detail in a moment.

The exclamation point, `'!'`, represents the NOT operator, and is also available and operates on the next item. So, it should be placed before the item to be negated. For example, the `['!', ('is_done','=',True)]` expression will filter all not-done records.

The "next item" can also be an operator item acting on its next items, defining nested conditions. An example may help us to better understand this.

In server-side record rules, we can find domain expressions similar to this one:

```
['|',
    ('message_follower_ids', 'in', [user.partner_id.id]),
    '|',
        ('user_id', '=', user.id),
        ('user_id', '=', False)
]
```

This domain filters all the records where the current user is in the follower list, is the responsible user, or does not have a responsible user set.

The first `'|'` (OR) operator acts on the follower's condition plus the result of the next condition. The next condition is again the union of two other conditions: records where either the user ID is the current session user or it is not set.

The following diagram illustrates this nested operators resolution:

Working with recordsets

We will now explore how the ORM works and learn about the most common operations performed with it. We will use the prompt provided by the `shell` command to interactively explore how recordsets work.

Querying models

Inside a method or a shell session, `self` represents the current model, and we can only access that model's records. To access other models, we should use `self.env`. For example, `self.env['res.partner']` returns a reference to the Partners model (which is actually an empty recordset). We can then use `search()` or `browse()` on it to generate recordsets.

The `search()` method takes a domain expression and returns a recordset with the records matching those conditions. An empty domain `[]` will return all records.

> If the model has the `active` special field, by default only the records with `active=True` will be considered.

A few optional keyword arguments are available, as shown here:

- `order` is a string to be used as the `ORDER BY` clause in the database query. This is usually a comma-separated list of field names. Each field name may be followed by the `DESC` keyword, to indicate a descending order.
- `limit` sets a maximum number of records to retrieve.
- `offset` ignores the first n results; it can be used with `limit` to query blocks of records at a time.

Sometimes, we just need to know the number of records meeting certain conditions. For that we can use `search_count()`, which returns the record count instead of a recordset. It saves the cost of retrieving a list of records just to count them, so it is much more efficient when we don't have a recordset yet and just want to count the number of records.

The `browse()` method takes a list of IDs or a single ID and returns a recordset with those records. This can be convenient in cases where we already know the IDs of the records we want.

Some usage examples of this are shown here:

```
>>> self.env['res.partner'].search([('name', 'like', 'Ag')])
res.partner(9, 31)
>>> self.env['res.partner'].browse([9, 31])
res.partner(9, 31)
```

Singletons

The special case of a recordset with only one record is called a **singleton**. Singletons are still a recordset, and can be used wherever a recordset is expected.

But unlike multi-element recordsets, singletons can access their fields using the dot notation, like this:

```
>>> print self.name
Administrator
```

In the next example, we can see the same `self` singleton recordset also behaves as a recordset, and we can iterate it. It has only one record, so only one name is printed out:

```
>>> for rec in self:
        print rec.name
Administrator
```

Trying to access field values on recordsets with more than one record will result in an error, so this can be an issue in the cases where we are not sure if we are working with a singleton recordset. For methods designed to work only with singleton, we can check this using `self.ensure_one()` at the beginning. It will raise an error if `self` is not a singleton.

> An empty record is also a singleton.

Writing on records

Recordsets implement the active record pattern. This means that we can assign values on them, and these changes will be made persistent in the database. This is an intuitive and convenient way to manipulate data, as shown here:

```
>>> admin = self.env['res.users'].browse(1)
>>> print admin.name
Administrator
>>> admin.name = 'Superuser'
>>> print admin.name
Superuser
```

Recordsets also have three methods to act on their data: `create()`, `write()`, and `unlink()`.

The `create()` method takes a dictionary to map fields to values and returns the created record. Default values are automatically applied as expected, which is shown here:

```
>>> Partner = self.env['res.partner']
>>> new = Partner.create({'name': 'ACME', 'is_company': True})
>>> print new
res.partner(45,)
```

The `unlink()` method deletes the records in the recordset, as shown here:

```
>>> rec = Partner.search([('name', '=', 'ACME')])
>>> rec.unlink()
True
```

Using the active record pattern has some limitations; it updates only one field at a time. The `write()` method can update several fields of several records at the same time by using a single database instruction. So it's usage should be considered in the cases where performance can be an issue.

The `write()` method takes a dictionary to map fields to values. These are updated on all elements of the recordset and nothing is returned, as shown here:

```
>>> recs = Partner.search(['name', 'ilike', 'Agro'])
>>> recs.write({'comment': 'Hello!'})
```

It is also worth mentioning `copy()` to duplicate an existing record; it takes that as an optional argument and a dictionary with the values to write on the new record. For example, to create a new user copying from the Demo User:

```
>>> demo = self.env.ref('base.user_demo')
>>> new = demo.copy({'name': 'Daniel', 'login': 'dr', 'email':''})
```

 Remember that model fields with the `copy=False` attribute won't be automatically copied.

Working with time and dates

For historical reasons, ORM recordsets handle `date` and `datetime` values using their strings representations, instead of actual Python `Date` and `Datetime` objects:

- `odoo.tools.DEFAULT_SERVER_DATE_FORMAT`
- `odoo.tools.DEFAULT_SERVER_DATETIME_FORMAT`

They map to `%Y-%m-%d` and `%Y-%m-%d %H:%M:%S` respectively. In the database, they are stored in date fields, but datetimes are stored without time zone, in UTC time.

To help handle dates, `fields.Date` and `fields.Datetime` provide a few functions, for example:

```
>>> from odoo import fields
>>> fields.Datetime.now()
'2017-11-21 23:11:55'
>>> fields.Datetime.from_string('2017-11-21 23:11:55')
    datetime.datetime(2017, 11, 21, 23, 11, 55)
```

Dates and times are handled and stored by the server in a naive UTC format, which is not time zone aware and may be different to the time zone that the user is working on. Because of this, we can make use of a few other functions to help us deal with this:

- `fields.Date.today()` returns a string with the current date in the format expected by the server and using UTC as a reference. This is adequate to compute default values.

- `fields.Datetime.now()` returns a string with the current datetime in the format, expected by the server using UTC as a reference. This is adequate to compute default values.

- `fields.Date.context_today(record, timestamp=None)` returns a string with the current date in the session's context. The time zone value is taken from the record's context. The optional parameter is a datetime object and will be used instead of the current time, if provided.

- `fields.Datetime.context_timestamp(record, timestamp)` converts a naive datetime (without time zone) into a time zone aware datetime. The time zone is extracted from the record's context, hence the name of the function.

To facilitate conversion between formats, both `fields.Date` and `fields.Datetime` objects provide these functions:

- `from_string(value)` converts a string into a date or datetime object
- `to_string(value)` converts a date or datetime object into a string in the format expected by the server

Operations on recordsets

Recordsets support some additional operations. We can check whether a record is included or not in a recordset. If x is a singleton recordset and `my_recordset` is a recordset containing many records, we can use:

- `x in my_recordset`
- `x not in my_recordset`

The following operations are also available:

- `recordset.ids` returns the list with the IDs of the recordset elements.
- `recordset.ensure_one()` checks if it is a single record (singleton); if it's not, a `ValueError` exception is raised.
- `recordset.filtered(func)` returns a filtered recordset. `func` can be a function or a dot-separated expression representing a path of fields to follow, as shown in the examples that follow.
- `recordset.mapped(func)` returns a list of mapped values.
- `recordset.sorted(func)` returns an ordered recordset.

Here are some usage examples for these functions:

```
>>> rs0 = self.env['res.partner'].search([])
>>> len(rs0)   # how many records?
40
>>> starts_A = lambda r: r.name.startswith('A')
>>> rs1 = rs0.filtered(starts_A)
>>> print rs1
res.partner(9, 8, 20, 31, 3)
>>> rs2 = rs1.filtered('is_company')
>>> print rs2
res.partner(9, 8)
>>> rs2.mapped('name')
['Agrolait', 'ASUSTeK']
>>> rs2.mapped(lambda r: (r.id, r.name))
[(9, 'Agrolait'), (8, 'ASUSTeK')]
>> rs2.sorted(key=lambda r: r.id, reverse=True)
res.partner(9, 8)
```

Manipulating recordsets

We will surely want to add, remove, or replace the elements in these related fields, and so this leads to the question: how can recordsets be manipulated?

Recordsets are immutable, meaning that their values can't be directly modified. Instead, modifying a recordset means composing a new recordset based on existing ones.

One way to do this is using the supported set operations:

- `rs1 | rs2` is the **union** set operation, and results in a recordset with all elements from both recordsets.
- `rs1 + rs2` is the **addition** set operation, to concatenate both recordsets into one. It may result in a set with duplicate records.
- `rs1 & rs2` is the **intersection** set operation, and results in a recordset with only the elements present in both recordsets.
- `rs1 - rs2` is the **difference** set operation, and results in a recordset with the `rs1` elements not present in `rs2`.

The slice notation can also be used, as shown in these examples:

- `rs[0]` and `rs[-1]` retrieve the first element and the last element, respectively.
- `rs[1:]` results in a copy of the recordset without the first element. This yields the same records as `rs - rs[0]` but preserves their order.

Since Odoo 10, recordset manipulation has preserved order. This is unlike previous Odoo versions, where recordset manipulation was not guaranteed to preserve the order, although addition and slicing were known to maintain record order.

We can use these operations to change a recordset by removing or adding elements. Here are some examples:

- `self.task_ids |= task1` adds the `task1` record, if not in the recordset
- `self.task_ids -= task1` removes the specific record `task1`, if present in the recordset
- `self.task_ids = self.task_ids[:-1]` removes the last record

The relational fields contain recordset values. Many-to-one fields can contain a singleton recordset, and to-many fields contain recordsets with any number of records. We set values on them using a regular assignment statement, or using the `create()` and `write()` methods with a dictionary of values. In this last case, a special syntax is used to modify to-many fields. It is the same syntax used in XML records to provide values for relational fields, and is described in `Chapter 5`, *Import, Export, and Module Data*.

As an example, the `write()` syntax equivalent to the three preceding assignment examples is:

- `self.write({'task_ids': [(4, task1.id)]})` adds the `task1` record.
- `self.write({'task_ids': [(3, task1.id)]})` removes `task1` from the recordset.
- `self.write({'task_ids': [(3, self.task_ids[-1].id)]})` removes the last record.

Using relational fields

As we saw earlier, models can have relational fields: **many-to-one**, **one-to-many**, and **many-to-many**. These field types have recordsets as values.

In the case of many-to-one, the value can be a singleton or an empty recordset. In both cases, we can directly access their field values. As an example, the following instructions are correct and safe:

```
>>> self.company_id
res.company(1,)
>>> self.company_id.name
'YourCompany'
>>> self.company_id.currency_id
res.currency(1,)
>>> self.company_id.currency_id.name
'EUR'
```

Conveniently, an empty recordset also behaves like singleton, and accessing its fields does not return an error but just returns `False`. Because of this, we can traverse records using dot notation without worrying about errors from empty values, as shown here:

```
>>> self.company_id.parent_id
res.company()
>>> self.company_id.parent_id.name
False
```

Working with relational fields

While using the active record pattern, relational fields can be assigned recordsets.

For many-to-one fields, the value assigned must be a single record (a singleton recordset).

For to-many fields, their value can also be assigned with a recordset, replacing the list of linked records, if any, with a new one. Here, a recordset with any size is allowed.

While using the `create()` or `write()` methods, where values are assigned using dictionaries, relational fields can't be assigned to recordset values. The corresponding ID or list of IDs should be used.

For example, instead of `self.write({'user_id': self.env.user})`, we should rather use `self.write({'user_id': self.env.user.id})`.

Summary

In the previous chapter, we saw how to build models. Here we went a little further, learning how to implement business logic and use recordsets to manipulate model data.

We also saw how the business logic can interact with the user interface and learn to create wizards that communicate with the user and serve as a platform to launch advanced processes.

Until now, our code was working inside the Odoo server. But the API can also be used from remote clients. In the next chapter, we will be learning how to interact with it through RPC calls.

8
External API – Integrating with Other Systems

The Odoo server also provides an external API, which is used by its web client and is also available for other client applications. In this chapter, we will learn how to use the Odoo external API from our own client programs, using Odoo's external API.

To avoid introducing additional languages the reader might not be familiar with, here we will focus on Python-based clients, although the techniques to handle the RPC calls also applies to other programming languages.

We will describe how to use the Odoo RPC calls, and then use that knowledge to build a simple To-Do desktop app using Python.

Finally, we will introduce the ERPpeek client. It is an Odoo client library that can be used as a convenient abstraction layer for the Odoo RPC calls, and is also a command-line client for Odoo, allowing you to remotely manage Odoo instances.

Setting up a Python client

The Odoo API can be accessed externally using two different protocols: XML-RPC and JSON-RPC. Any external program capable of implementing a client for one of these protocols will be able to interact with an Odoo server. To avoid introducing additional programming languages, we will keep using Python to explore the external API.

Until now, we have been running Python code only on the server. This time, we will use Python on the client side, so it's possible you might need to do some additional setup on your workstation.

To follow the examples in this chapter, you will need to be able to run Python files on your work computer. We will be using Python 3 for this. At this point you should make sure you have Python 3 installed in your workstation. If not, please refer the official website for your platform's installation package at `https://www.python.org/downloads/`.

For Ubuntu, at this point you probably already have Python 3 installed. If not, you can install it by running:

```
$ sudo apt-get install python3
```

If you are a Windows user and have Odoo installed on your machine, you may be wondering why you don't already have a Python interpreter and why additional installation is needed. The short answer is that the Odoo installation has an embedded Python interpreter that is not easily used outside.

Calling the Odoo API using XML-RPC

The simplest method to access the server is using XML-RPC. We can use the `xmlrpclib` library from Python's standard library for this. Remember that we are programming a client in order to connect to a server, so we need an Odoo server instance running to connect to. In our examples, we will assume that an Odoo server instance is running on the same machine (`localhost`), but you can use any reachable IP address or server name, if the server is running on a different machine.

Opening an XML-RPC connection

Let's make first contact with the Odoo external API. Start a Python 3 console and type in the following:

```
>>> from xmlrpc import client
>>> srv = 'http://localhost:8069'
>>> common = client.ServerProxy('%s/xmlrpc/2/common' % srv)
>>> common.version()
{'protocol_version': 1, 'server_serie': '11.0', 'server_version': '11.0',
'server_version_info': [11, 0, 0, 'final', 0, '']}
```

Here, we import the `xmlrpc.client` library and then set up a variable with the information for the server address and listening port. Feel free to adapt these to your specific setup.

Next, we set up access to the server's public services (not requiring a login), exposed at the `/xmlrpc/2/common` endpoint. One of the methods that is available is `version()`, which inspects the server version. We use it to confirm that we can communicate with the server.

Another public method is `authenticate()`. In fact, this does not create a session, as you might be led to believe. This method just confirms that the username and password are accepted and returns the user ID that should be used in requests instead of the username, as shown here:

```
>>> db = 'todo'
>>> user, pwd = 'admin', 'admin'
>>> uid = common.authenticate(db, user, pwd, {})
>>> print uid
```

If the login credentials are not correct, a `False` value is returned, instead of a user ID.

The `authenticate()` last argument, with an empty argument, is the user agent environment, used to provide the server with some metadata about the client. It can be kept empty here.

Reading data from the server

With XML-RPC, no session is maintained and the authentication credentials are sent with every request. This adds some overhead to the protocol, but makes it simpler to use.

Next, we set up access to the server methods that need a login to be accessed. These are exposed at the `/xmlrpc/2/object` endpoint, as shown in the following:

```
>>> api = client.ServerProxy('%s/xmlrpc/2/object' % srv)
>>> api.execute_kw(db, uid, pwd, 'res.partner', 'search_count', [[]])
40
```

Here, we are accessing the server API for the first time, performing a count on the **Partner** records. Methods are called using the `execute_kw()` method that takes the following arguments:

- The name of the database to connect to
- The connection user ID
- The user password

- The target model identifier name
- The method to call
- A list of positional arguments
- An optional dictionary with keyword arguments (not used in the example)

The preceding example calls the search_count method of the res.partner model with one positional argument, [], and no keyword arguments. The positional argument is a search domain; since we are providing an empty list, it counts all the Partners.

Frequent actions are search and read. When called from the RPC, the search method returns a list of IDs matching a domain. The browse method is not available from the RPC, and read should be used in its place to obtain a list of record IDs and retrieve their data, as shown in the following code:

```
>>> domain = [('country_id', '=', 'be'), ('parent_id', '!=', False)]
>>> api.execute_kw(db, uid, pwd, 'res.partner', 'search', [domain])
[19, 34, 24, 23]
>>> api.execute_kw(db, uid, pwd, 'res.partner', 'read', [[19]],
{'fields': ['id', 'name', 'parent_id']})
[{'id': 19, 'parent_id': [9, 'Agrolait'], 'name': 'Edward Foster'}]
```

Note that for the read method, we are using one positional argument for the list of IDs, [19], and one keyword argument, fields. We can also notice that many-to-one relational fields, such as parent_id, are retrieved as a pair, with the related record's ID and display name. That's something to keep in mind when processing the data in your code.

The search and read combination is so frequent that a search_read method is provided to perform both operations in a single step. The same result from the previous two steps can be obtained with the following:

```
>>> api.execute_kw(db, uid, pwd, 'res.partner', 'search_read', [domain],
{'fields': ['id', 'name', 'parent_id']})
```

The search_read method behaves like read, but expects a domain as a first positional argument instead of a list of IDs. It's worth mentioning that the fields argument on read and search_read is not mandatory. If not provided, all fields will be retrieved. This may cause expensive computations of function fields and a large amount of data to be retrieved but probably never used, so it is generally recommended to provide an explicit list of fields.

Calling other methods

All other model methods are exposed through RPC, except for the ones prefixed with an underscore, which are considered private. This means that we can use `create`, `write`, and `unlink` to modify data on the server as follows:

```
>>> api.execute_kw(db, uid, pwd, 'res.partner', 'create', [{'name': 'Packt
Pub'}])
46
>>> api.execute_kw(db, uid, pwd, 'res.partner', 'write', [[46], {'name':
'Packt Publishing'}])
True
>>> api.execute_kw(db, uid, pwd, 'res.partner', 'read', [[46], ['id',
'name']])
[{'id': 46, 'name': 'Packt Publishing'}]
>>> api.execute_kw(db, uid, pwd, 'res.partner', 'unlink', [[46]])
True
```

One limitation of the XML-RPC protocol is that it does not support `None` values. There is an XML-RPC extension that supports `None` values, but whether or not this is available will depend on the particular XML-RPC library being used on your client. Methods that don't return anything may not be usable through XML-RPC, since they are implicitly returning `None`. This is why methods should always finish with at least a `return True` statement.

It is worth repeating that the Odoo external API can be used by most programming languages. In the official documentation, we can find practical examples for Ruby, PHP, and Java. It is available at `https://www.odoo.com/documentation/10.0/api_integration.html`.

Writing a To-Do client application

Let's do something interesting with the Odoo RPC API. We built a simple app for tasks we need to perform. What if users could manage personal tasks directly from their computer's desktop? We will create a command-line (CLI) client application that connects directly to our Odoo server and lets us manage our tasks.

We will split it into two files: one dealing with interactions with the server backend, `todo_api.py`, and another dealing with the application's user interface, `todo.py`.

Communication layer with Odoo

We will create a class to set up the connection with an Odoo server, and read/write To-Do tasks data. It should expose the basic CRUD methods:

- `read()` to retrieve task data
- `write()` to create or update tasks
- `unlink()` to delete a task

Select a directory to host the application files and create the `todo_api.py` file. We can start by adding the class constructor, as follows:

```
from xmlrpc import client

class TodoAPI():
    def __init__(self, srv, port, db, user, pwd):
        common = client.ServerProxy(
            'http://%s:%d/xmlrpc/2/common' % (srv, port))
        self.api = client.ServerProxy(
            'http://%s:%d/xmlrpc/2/object' % (srv, port))
        self.uid = common.authenticate(db, user, pwd, {})
        self.pwd = pwd
        self.db = db
        self.model = 'todo.task'
```

Here, we store all the information needed in the created object to execute calls on a model: the API reference, `uid`, password, database name, and the model to use.

Next, we will define a helper method to execute the calls. It takes advantage of the object stored data to provide a smaller function signature, as shown next:

```
def execute(self, method, arg_list, kwarg_dict=None):
    return self.api.execute_kw(
        self.db, self.uid, self.pwd, self.model,
        method, arg_list, kwarg_dict or {})
```

Now we can use it to implement the higher-level methods.

The `read()` method will accept an optional list of IDs to retrieve. If none are listed, all records will be returned:

```
def read(self, ids=None):
    domain = [('id','in', ids)] if ids else []
    fields = ['id', 'name', 'is_done']
    return self.execute('search_read', [domain, fields])
```

The `write()` method will have the task text to write and an optional ID as arguments. If an ID is not provided, a new record will be created. It returns the ID of the record written or created, as shown here:

```
def write(self, text, id=None):
    if id:
        self.execute('write', [[id], {'name': text}])
    else:
        vals = {'name': text, 'user_id': self.uid}
        id = self.execute('create', [vals])
    return id
```

And next we have the `unlink()` method implementation, which is quite simple:

```
def unlink(self, id):
    return self.execute('unlink', [[id]])
```

Let's end the file with a small piece of test code that will be executed if we run the Python file:

```
if __name__ == '__main__':
    # Sample test configurations
    srv, db, port = 'localhost' , 8069, 'todo'
    user, pwd = 'admin', 'admin'
    api = TodoAPI(srv, db, user, pwd,)
    from pprint import pprint
    pprint(api.read())
```

If we run the Python script, we should see the content of our To-Do tasks printed out. Now that we have a simple wrapper around our Odoo backend, let's deal with the desktop user interface.

Creating the CLI

Our goal here was to learn to write the interface between an external application and the Odoo server, and this was done in the previous section. But it would be a shame not to go the extra step and actually make it available to the end user.

To keep the setup as simple as possible, we will use Python's built-in features to implement the command-line application. Since it is part of the standard library, it does not require any additional installation.

Now, alongside the `todo_api.py` file, create a new `todo.py` file. It will first import Python's command-line argument parser, and then the `TodoAPI` class, as shown in the following code:

```
from argparse import ArgumentParser
from todo_api import TodoAPI
```

Next, we describe the commands the argument parser will expect; there are four commands:

- List tasks
- Add tasks
- Delete tasks
- Set a task as done

This is the code for adding them to the command-line parser:

```
parser = ArgumentParser()
parser.add_argument(
    'command',
    choices=['list', 'add', 'del', 'done'])
parser.add_argument('text', nargs='?')   # optional arg
args = parser.parse_args()
```

At this point, `args` is an object containing the arguments given to the script, `args.command` is the command provided, and `args.text` will optionally hold additional text to use for the command. If no or incorrect commands are given, the argument parser will handle that for us and will show the user what input is expected. For a complete reference on `argparse` you can refer to the official documentation at `https://docs.python.org/3/library/argparse.html`.

The next step is to to perform the intended actions. We will first prepare the connection with the Odoo server:

```
srv, port, db = 'localhost', 8069, 'todo'
user, pwd = 'admin', 'admin'
api = TodoAPI(srv, port, db, user, pwd)
```

This has a hardcoded server address and plain text password, so it's far from being the best implementation. But we need to keep in mind that our goal here is to learn to work with the Odoo RPC, so consider this as proof of concept code, and not a finished product.

Now we will write the code to handle each of the supported commands, which will also make use of the `api` object.

We can start with the `list` command, providing a list of the To-Do tasks:

```
if args.command == 'list':
    todos = api.read()
    for todo in todos:
        todo['done'] = 'X' if todo['is_done'] else ' '
        print('%(id)d [%(done)s] %(name)s' % todo)
```

Here, we use the `TodoAPI.read()` method to retrieve the list of todo records from the server. We then iterate through each element in the list and print it out. We use Python's string formatting to present each `todo` record, a key-value dictionary, to the user.

Next, we have the add command. This will make use of the text additional argument for the task's description:

```
if args.command == 'add':
    todo_id = api.write(args.text)
    print('Todo %d created.' % todo_id)
```

Since the hard work was already done in the `TodoAPI` object, here we just need to call the `write()` method, and show the result to the end user.

Finally, we have the implementation for the `del` command, which should unlink a Todo record. At this point, this should be no challenge for us:

```
if args.command == 'del':
    api.unlink(int(args.text))
    print('Todo %s deleted.' % args.text)
```

This is a quite basic application, and you probably could think of a few ways to improve it while going through the code. But remember that the point here is to make an example of interesting ways to leverage the Odoo RPC API.

Introducing the ERPpeek client

ERPpeek is a versatile tool that can be used both as an interactive **Command-line Interface (CLI)** and as a **Python library**, with a more convenient API than the one provided by the `xmlrpc` library. It is available from the PyPi index and can be installed with the following:

```
$ pip3 install --user erppeek
```

More details about ERPpeek can be found at `https://github.com/tinyerp/erppeek`.

The ERPpeek API

The ERPpeek library provides a programming interface, which is similar to the programming interface we have for the server-side code. Our point here is to provide a glimpse into what the ERPpeek library has to offer, and not to provide a full explanation of all its features.

We can start by reproducing our first steps with the xmlrpc library using the erppeek. Start a Python 3 session and try the following:

```
>>> import erppeek
>>> api = erppeek.Client('http://localhost:8069', 'todo','admin', 'admin')
>>> api.common.version()
>>> api.count('res.partner', [])
>>> api.search('res.partner', [('country_id', '=', 'be'),
('parent_id', '!=', False)])
>>> api.read('res.partner', [19], ['id', 'name', 'parent_id'])
```

As you can see, the API calls use fewer arguments and are similar to the server-side counterparts.

But ERPpeek doesn't stop here, and also provides a representation for models. We have the following two alternative ways to get an instance for a model, either using the model() method or accessing it as a camel-case attribute name:

```
>>> m = api.model('res.partner')
>>> m = api.ResPartner
```

Now we can perform actions on that model as follows:

```
>>> m.count([('name', 'like', 'Agrolait%')])
1
>>> m.search([('name', 'like', 'Agrolait%')])
[9]
```

It also provides client-side object representation for records, as follows:

```
>>> recs = m.browse([('name', 'like', 'Agrolait')])
>>> recs
<RecordList 'res.partner,[9]'>
>>> recs.name
['Agrolait']
```

As you can see, the erppeek library goes further than plain xmlrpclib, and makes it possible to write code that can be reused server side with little or no modification.

The ERPpeek CLI

Not only can ERPpeek be used as a Python library, it is also a CLI that can be used to perform administrative actions on the server. Where the Odoo `shell` command provided a local interactive session on the host server, the `erppeek` library provides a remote interactive session for a client across the network.

Opening a command line, we can have a peek at the options available, as shown here:

```
$ erppeek --help
```

Let's see a sample session, as follows:

```
$ erppeek --server='http://localhost:8069' -d todo -u admin
Usage (some commands):
    models(name)                    # List models matching pattern
    model(name)                     # Return a Model instance
(...)
Password for 'admin':
Logged in as 'admin'
todo >>> model('res.users').count()
3
todo >>> rec = model('res.partner').browse(9)
todo >>> rec.name
'Agrolait'
```

As you can see, a connection was made to the server, and the execution context provided a reference to the `model()` method to get model instances and perform actions on them.

The `erppeek.Client` instance used for the connection is also available through the `client` variable.

Notably, it provides an alternative to the web client to manage the addon modules installed:

- `client.modules()` lists modules available or installed
- `client.install()` performs module installation
- `client.upgrade()` performs module upgrades
- `client.uninstall()` uninstalls modules

So, ERPpeek can also provide good service as a remote administration tool for Odoo servers.

Introducing the OdooRPC library

Another relevant client library to be considered is OdooRPC. It is a more modern client library that uses the JSON-RPC protocol instead of XML-RPC. The fact is that the Odoo official web client uses JSON-RPC, and the original XML-RPC is supported mostly for backward compatibility.

OdooRPC is now under the Odoo Community Association umbrella and is being actively maintained. You can learn more about it at https://github.com/OCA/odoorpc.

The way the Odoo API is used is not very different whether you are using JSON-RPC or XML-RPC. So, you will see that, while some details differ, the way these different client libraries are used is not very different.

OdooRPC sets up a server connection when a new odoorpc.ODOO object is created, and we should then use the ODOO.login() method to create a user session. Just like on the server side, the session has an env attribute with the session's environment, including the user ID, uid, and the context.

We can use OdooRPC to provide an alternate implementation to the todo_api.py interface with the server. It should provide the same features, but is implemented using JSON-RPC instead of XML-RPC.

Create a new todo_odoorpc.py file alongside it, with the following code:

```
from odoorpc import ODOO

class TodoAPI():

    def __init__(self, srv, port, db, user, pwd):
        self.api = ODOO(srv, port=port)
        self.api.login(db, user, pwd)
        self.uid = self.api.env.uid
        self.model = 'todo.task'
        self.Model = self.api.env[self.model]

    def execute(self, method, arg_list, kwarg_dict=None):
        return self.api.execute(
            self.model,
            method, *arg_list, **kwarg_dict)
```

OdooRPC implements Model and Recordset objects that mimic the behavior of the server-side counterparts. The goal is that programming the client should be about the same as programming in the server. The methods used by our client will make use of this, through the Todo Task Model stored in the `self.Model` attribute.

The `execute()` method implemented here won't be used by our client, and was included to allow for comparison to the other alternative implementations we discuss in this chapter.

Next, we look at the implementation for the `read()`, `write()` and `unlink()` client methods. Notice that the code is very similar to the server-side code:

```
def read(self, ids=None):
    domain = [('id','in', ids)] if ids else []
    fields = ['id', 'name', 'is_done']
    return self.Model.search_read(domain, fields)

def write(self, text, id=None):
    if id:
        self.Model.write(id, {'name': text})
    else:
        vals = {'name': text, 'user_id': 1}
        id = self.Model.create(vals)
    return id

def unlink(self, id):
    return self.Model.unlink(id)
```

Having done this, we can try it by editing the `todo.py` file, changing the `from` **todo_api** `import TodoAPI` line to `from` **todo_odoorpc** `import TodoAPI`. Now test drive the `todo.py` client application, and it should perform just like before.

Summary

Our goal for this chapter was to learn how the external API works and what it is capable of. We started exploring it using a simple Python XML-RPC client, but the external API can be used from any programming language. In fact, the official documentation provides code examples for Java, PHP, and Ruby.

There are a number of libraries to handle XML-RPC or JSON-RPC, some generic and some specific for use with Odoo. We showcased two particular libraries that can be helpful: ERPpeek and OdooRPC. These can not only act as client libraries, but can also be invaluable tools for remote server management and inspection.

With this, we finish the chapters dedicated to the programming API and business logic. Now it's time to enter into the views and user interface. In the next chapter, we will see in more detail the backend views and user experience that can be provided out of the box by the web client.

9
Backend Views – Design the User Interface

This chapter will help you learn how to build the graphical interface for users to interact with the To-Do application. You will discover the distinct types of views and widgets available, and learn how to use them to provide a good user experience.

We will continue working with the `todo_stage` module. It already has the Model layer ready, and now it needs the View layer for the user interface.

Defining the user interface with XML files

Each component of the user interface is stored in a database record, just like regular data records are. Modules provide these UI elements as data stored in XML files, which are loaded into the database when the module is installed.

This means that a new XML data file for our UI needs to be added to the `todo_stage` module. We can start by editing the `__manifest__.py` file to add the `views/todo_view.xml` data file:

```
{
    'name': 'Add Stages and Tags to To-Dos',
    'description': 'Organize To-Do Tasks using Stages and Tags',
    'author': 'Daniel Reis',
    'depends': ['todo_app', 'mail'],
    'data': [
        'security/ir.model.access.csv',
        'views/todo_menu.xml',
        'views/todo_view.xml',
```

```
  ]
'demo': [
  'data/todo.task.csv',
  'data/todo_task.xml',
],
}
```

 Remember that the data files are loaded in the order you specify. This is important because you can only reference XML IDs that were defined before they were being used.

Now we should create the subdirectory and the `views/todo_view.xml` file. A new XML file starts with this minimal structure:

```xml
<?xml version="1.0"?>
<odoo>
  <!-- Content will go here... -->
</odoo>
```

We need to also have a `views/todo_menu.xml` file. If you don't have it yet, no problem, just add it now like you did with the `views/todo_view.xml` file.

In `Chapter 3`, *Your First Odoo Application – A Practical Overview*, a basic menu was given to our application, but we now want to improve it. In the next section, we will be adding new menu items and the corresponding window actions.

Menu items

Menu items are stored in the `ir.ui.menu` model and can be browsed via the **Settings | Technical | User Interface | Menu Items** menu.

The `todo_app` addon created a top-level menu to open the To-Do Tasks. Now we want to modify it to a second-level menu and have other menu options alongside it.

To do this, we will modify the existing To-Do Task menu option, to remove the corresponding action and make it a parent menu item. Edit the `views/todo_menu.xml` to add:

```xml
<!-- Menu items -->
<!-- Overwrite the top menu item to remove Action -->
<menuitem id="todo_app.menu_todo_task"
    name="To-Do"
    action="" />
```

We used the more convenient `<menuitem>` shortcut element, instead of a `<record model="ir.ui.menu">` element, which provides an abbreviated way to define menu items.

This first menu item is for the To-Do app top-menu entry, with only the `name` attribute, and will be used as the parent for the next two options. Notice that it uses the existing XML ID `todo_app.menu_todo_task`, thus rewriting the menu item defined in the `todo_app` module, so that it does not have any action attached to it. This is to turn it into an intermediate menu item, to hold child menu items under it. We used an `action=""` attribute to emphasize this, but it is not strictly needed and could have been omitted.

Next, we add the second-level menu items:

```
<!-- Second level menu items -->
<menuitem id="menu_todo_task_view"
    name="Tasks"
    sequence="10"
    parent="todo_app.menu_todo_task"
    action="todo_app.action_todo_task" />

<menuitem id="menu_todo_config"
    name="Configuration"
    sequence="100"
    parent="todo_app.menu_todo_task"
    groups="base.group_system" />

<!-- Third level menu items -->
    <menuitem id="menu_todo_task_stage"
        name="Stages"
        parent="menu_todo_config"
        action="action_todo_stage" />
```

The second-level menu items are placed under the top-level item, using the `parent` attribute.

The first of these menus is the one opening the Task views, with the `action="todo_app.action_todo_task"` attribute. As you can see from the XML ID used, it is reusing an action already created by the `todo_app` module.

The next menu item adds the **Configuration** submenu for our app. We want it to be available only for super users, so we also use the `groups` attribute to make it visible only to the **Administration | Settings** security group.

Finally, under the **Configuration** menu, we add the option for the Task Stages. We will use it to maintain the Stages to be used by the kanban feature we will be adding to the To-Do Tasks.

We can also see the `sequence` attribute being used in the menu items. It allows us to control the order they are presented to the user: lower numbers come first, and larger numbers come later. Leaving room between menu items is good practice, to make it easier to later add additional menu items in the appropriate places.

At this point, if we try to upgrade the addon, we should get errors because we haven't defined the XML IDs used in the `action` attributes. We will be adding them in the next section.

Window actions

A **window action** gives instructions to the GUI client and is usually used by menu items or buttons in views. It tells the GUI what model to work on, and what views to make available. These actions can filter the records to be available, using a `domain` filter, and can set default values and filters through the `context` attribute.

We will add window actions to the `views/todo_menu.xml` data file, which will be used by the menu items created in the previous section. Edit the file, and make sure they are added before the menu items:

```xml
<!-- Actions for the menu items -->
<act_window id="action_todo_stage"
    name="To-Do Task Stages"
    res_model="todo.task.stage"
    view_mode="tree,form"
    target="current"
    context="{'default_state': 'open'}"
    domain="[]"
    limit="80" />

<!-- Modify the view_mode of the To-Do Task Action -->
<record id="todo_app.action_todo_task"
        model="ir.actions.act_window">
    <field name="view_mode"
    >tree,form,calendar,graph,pivot
    </field>
</record>
```

Window Actions can be defined in XML files using the `<act_window>` shortcut, used in the preceding code. It opens the Task Stages model and includes the most relevant attributes for window actions:

- `name` is the title that will be displayed on the views opened through this action.
- `res_model` is the identifier of the target model.
- `view_mode` declares the view types available and their order. The first is the one opened by default.
- `target`, if set to `new`, will open the view in a pop-up dialog window. By default it is `current`, opening the view inline in the main content area.
- `context` sets context information on the target views, which can set default values or activate filters, among other things.
- `domain` is a domain expression forcing a filter for the records that will be browsable in the opened views.
- `limit` is the number of records for each page, in the list view.

Window Actions are stored in the `ir.actions.act_window` model, used in the second element in the preceding code. It is replacing the original To-Do Tasks action of the `todo_app` addon so that it displays the other view types we will explore later in this chapter: calendar and graph.

After these changes are installed, you'll see additional buttons in the top-right corner, after the list and form buttons; however, these won't work until we create the corresponding views.

Window Actions can also be used from the Action menu button, available at the top of List and Form views. For this we just need to add two more attributes to the `<act_window>` element:

- `src_model` sets the Model where the Action will be made available. For example, `src_model="todo.task"`.
- `multi="true"` enables the Action on the List view also, so that it can work on multiple selected records. Otherwise, it is available only in the Form view, and can only be applied to one record at a time.

The form views

As we have seen in previous chapters, form views can either follow a simple layout or a business document layout, similar to a paper document.

We will now see how to design these business document views and how to use the elements and widgets available. We would normally do this by inheriting and extending the `todo_app` views. But, for the sake of clarity, we will instead create completely new views to override the original ones.

Dealing with several views of the same type

The same Model can have several Views of the same type, by default the view with the lowest Priority value, but an Action can set a specific view to be used, through its XML ID. Using this, we can have two different menu items opening the same model but use different views. This is achieved using the `view_id` attribute of the Window Action, with the XML ID of the view to use. For example, in the `todo_app.action_todo_task` Action, we could add to it the `view_id="view_form_todo_task_ui"` attribute.

To add a new View and have it as the new default we just have to set it with a lower Priority than the existing ones. Since the default value for the view priority is 16, any lower value would do, so a 15 priority will work. The final effect is that it looks like this new view is overriding the original one.

It's not the most commonly used route to help keep our examples as readable as possible. We will use the priority approach in our next examples.

Business document views

Business applications are often systems of record—for products in a warehouse, invoices in an accounting department, and many more. Most of the recorded data can be represented as a paper document. For a more intuitive user interface, form views can mimic these paper documents. For example, in our app, we can think of a To-Do Task as something that has a simple paper form to fill out. We will provide a form view that follows this design.

To add a view XML with the basic skeleton of a business document view, we should edit the `views/todo_views.xml` file and add it to the top:

```xml
<record id="view_form_todo_task_ui"
    model="ir.ui.view">
    <field name="model">todo.task</field>
    <field name="priority">15</field>
    <field name="arch" type="xml">
        <form>
            <header>
                <!-- To add buttons and status widget -->
            </header>
            <sheet>
                <!-- To add form content -->
            </sheet>
            <!-- Discuss widgets -->
            <div class="oe_chatter">
                <field name="message_follower_ids"
                        widget="mail_followers" />
                <field name="message_ids"
                        widget="mail_thread" />
            </div>
        </form>
    </field>
</record>
```

The view name is optional and automatically generated if missing. For simplicity, we took advantage of that and omitted the `<field name="name">` element from the view record.

We can see that business document views usually use three main areas: the **header** status bar, the **sheet** for the main content, and a bottom communication section, also known as **chatter**.

The communication section at the bottom uses the social network widgets provided by the `mail` addon module. To be able to use them, our model should inherit the `mail.thread` mixin model, as we saw in `Chapter 4`, *Models – Structuring the Application Data*.

The header

The header at the top usually features the life cycle or steps that the document will move through and the related action buttons. These action buttons are regular form buttons, and the most important next steps can be highlighted using `class="oe_highlight"`.

The document life cycle uses the `statusbar` widget on a field that represents the point in the life cycle where the document is currently at. This is usually a **State** selection field or a **Stage** many-to-one field. These two fields can be found across several Odoo core modules.

The Stage is a many-to-one field which uses a supporting model to set up the steps of the process. Because of this, it can be dynamically configured by end users to fit their specific business process and is perfect to support kanban boards.

The state is a selection list featuring a few rather stable steps in a process, such as **New**, **In Progress**, and **Done**. It is not configurable by end users but, since it is static, it is much easier to be used in business logic. View fields even have special support for States: the `states` field attribute allows it be made available to the user only when the record is in certain states.

Historically, Stages were introduced later than States. Both have coexisted, but the trend in Odoo core is for Stages to replace States. But, as seen in the preceding explanation, states still provide some features that stages don't.

It is still possible to benefit from the best of both worlds by mapping the stages into states. This was what we did previously for the To-Do app, by adding a state field in the task Stages model and making it available in the To-Do Task documents through a computed field, enabling the use of the `states` field attribute.

In the `views/todo_view.xml` file, we can now expand the basic header to add a status bar:

```xml
<header>
  <field name="state" invisible="True" />
  <button name="do_clear_done" type="object"
    string="Clear Done"
    attrs="{'invisible':[('state', 'in', ['draft'])]}"
    class="oe_highlight" />
  <field name="stage_id"
    widget="statusbar"
    clickable="True"
    options="{'fold_field': 'fold'}" />
</header>
```

Here, we add a **Clear Done** button to the status bar to let the user clear out a done Task (set the `active` flag to false). The `attrs` attribute is used to make this button visible only for Tasks in the `done` state. The condition to do this uses the `state` field, which will not be shown on the form. But, for the condition to work, we need all values it uses to be loaded in the web client. Since we are not planning to make the `state` field available to the end users, we need to add it as an invisible field.

The Fields used in a `domain` or `attrs` expression must be loaded into the view, and there must be a `<field>` element for them. If the field is not supposed to be seen by the users, we then have them loaded with an invisible field element.

In this particular case, the same effect can be achieved by the `states` field attribute, instead of `attrs`, using `states="open,done"`. While it's not as flexible as the `attrs` attribute, it is more concise.

The `attrs` and `states` element visibility features can be also used on other view elements, such as fields. We will explore them in more detail later in this chapter.

Next, a status bar widget is added to show the stage the document is in. Technically, it is a `<field>` element for the `stage_id` field using the `statusbar` widget.

The `clickable` attribute allows the user to change the document stage by clicking on the status bar. We usually want to enable this, but there are also cases where we don't, such as when we need more control over the workflow and require the users to progress through the stages using only the available action buttons. This approach allows for specific validations when moving between stages.

When using a status bar widget with Stages, we can have the seldom-used stages hidden (folded) in a **More** stage group. The corresponding Stages model must have a flag to configure the ones to hide, usually named `fold`. The `statusbar` widget should then use the `options` attribute, as shown in the preceding code, to provide this field name to the `fold_field` option.

The status bar can also work with States instead of Stages. In this case, to list the states to be made available in the status bar, we use the `statusbar_visible` attribute instead of the `fold_field` option. If we were to use it for the To-Do task form, it would look like this:

```
<field name="state"
  widget="statusbar"
  clickable="True"
  statusbar_visible="draft,open,done" />
```

The document sheet

The sheet canvas is the main area of the form where the actual data elements are placed. It is designed to look like an actual paper document, and it is common to see that the records in Odoo are referred to as **documents**.

Usually, a document sheet structure will have these areas:

- A document title and subtitle at the top left
- A button box at the top-right corner
- Other document header fields
- A notebook at the bottom, for additional fields organized into tabs or pages

Document lines usually go in the notebook's first page. After the sheet, we usually have the Chatter widget, with the discussion messages and document followers.

Let's go through each of these areas.

Title and subtitle

Fields outside a `<group>` element don't automatically have labels rendered for them. This will be the case for the title elements, so the `<label for="..."/>` element should be used to render it. At the expense of some extra work, this has the advantage of giving us more control over the label display.

Regular HTML, including CSS-style elements, can also be used to make the title shine. Usually, titles are placed inside a `<div>` with the `oe_title` class.

Here is the `<sheet>` element expanded to include the title plus some additional fields as subtitles:

```
<sheet>
  <div class="oe_title">
    <label for="name" class="oe_edit_only"/>
    <h1><field name="name"/></h1>
    <h3>
      <span class="oe_read_only">By</span>
      <label for="user_id" class="oe_edit_only"/>
      <field name="user_id" class="oe_inline" />
    </h3>
  </div>
  <!-- More elements will be added from here... -->
</sheet>
```

Here, we can see that we use regular HTML elements, such as div, span, h1, and h3.

The `<label>` element allows us to control when and where the field labels will be shown. The `for` attribute identifies the field we should get the label text from. Another possibility is to use the `string` attribute to provide a specific text to use for the label. Our example also uses the `class="oe_edit_only"` attribute so that it is visible only in edit mode.

In some cases, such as Partners or Products, a representative image is shown at the top-left corner. Supposing we had a `my_image` binary field, we could add it before the `<div class="oe_title">` line, using:

```
<field name="my_image" widget="image" class="oe_avatar"/>
```

Smart buttons area

Version 8.0 introduced smart buttons, shown as rectangles with a statistic indicator that can be followed through when clicked. The top-right area can have an invisible box where smart buttons can be placed.

This button box is usually added to the form just before the `<div class="oe_title">` element (and avatar image), with the following:

```
<div name="button_box" class="oe_button_box">
  <!-- Smart buttons will go here... -->
</div>
```

The container for the buttons is just a `div` with the `oe_button_box` class.

In Odoo versions before 11.0 you might need to also add the `oe_right` class, to ensure that the button box stays aligned to the right-hand side of the form.

We will be discussing buttons in more detail in a later section, so we will wait until then to add actual buttons in this box.

Grouping content in a form

The main content of the form should be organized using `<group>` tags.

The `<group>` tag inserts two columns in the canvas. Inside it, by default fields will be displayed along with their label, thus taking up these two columns. So, each field takes up a line, the next fields will take the next line, and they will be stacked up vertically.

A common pattern in Odoo forms is to have two columns of fields with labels, side by side. To achieve that we just need to add two `<group>` tags nested into the top one.

Try the **Toggle Form Layout Outline** option from the **Developer** menu: it draws lines around each group section, allowing for a better understanding of the current form layout.

Continuing with our form view, we will use this to add the main content, after the title DIV section:

```
<group name="group_top">
  <group name="group_left">
    <field name="date_deadline" />
    <separator string="Reference" />
    <field name="refers_to" />
  </group>
  <group name="group_right">
    <field name="tag_ids" widget="many2many_tags"/>
  </group>
</group>
```

It is a good practice to assign a `name` to group tags so that its easier for them to be referenced later when being extended by other modules.

The `string` attribute is also allowed, and, if set, is used to display a title for the section.

The `string` attribute cannot be used as an anchor for inheritance because it is translated before the inheritance is applied. The `name` attribute should be used as a workaround for this.

Inside a group, a `<newline>` element will force a new line and the next element will be rendered in the group's first column.

Additional section titles can be added inside a group using the `<separator>` element.

For better control over the elements layout, we can use the `col` and `colspan` attributes.

The `col` attribute can be used on `<group>` elements to customize the number of columns it will contain. As mentioned before, the default is two, but it can be changed to any other number. Even numbers work better, since by default each field added takes up two columns: the field label and the field value.

The elements placed inside the group, including `<field>` elements, can use a `colspan` attribute to set a specific number of columns they should take. By default, one column is taken up.

Tabbed notebooks

Another way to organize content is using the `notebook` element, containing multiple tabbed sections, called pages. These can be used to keep less used data out of sight until needed or to organize a large number of fields by topic.

We won't need to add this to our To-Do Task form, but here is an example that could be added to a Task Stages form:

```
<notebook>
  <page string="Team" name="team_page">
    <field name="team_ids" />
  </page>
  <page>
    <!-- Second page content -->
  </page>
</notebook>
```

View semantic components

We have seen how to organize the content in a form using structural components, such as header, group, and notebook. Now we can take a closer look at the semantic components, such as fields and buttons, and what we can do with them.

Fields

View fields have a few attributes available to them. Most of them have values taken from their definition in the model, but these can be overridden in the view.

Generic attributes, which do not depend on the field type, are:

- `name` identifies the field database name.
- `string` is the label text, to be used if we want to override the label text provided by the model definition.

- `help` is tooltip text shown when you hover the pointer over the field, and it allows you to override the help text provided by the model definition.
- `placeholder` is suggestion text to display inside the field.
- `widget` allows us to override the default widget used for the field. We will explore the available widgets in a moment.
- `options` is a JSON data structure with additional options for the widget. The values to use depend on what each widget supports.
- `class` are the CSS classes to use for the field HTML rendering.
- `nolabel="True"` prevents the automatic field label from being presented. It only makes sense for the fields inside a `<group>` element and is often used along with a `<label for="...">` element.
- `invisible="True"` makes the field not visible, but it's data is fetched from the server and is available on the form.
- `readonly="True"` makes the field non-editable on the form.
- `required="True"` makes the field mandatory on the form.

Attributes specific to some field types are:

- `password="True"` is used for text fields. It is displayed as a password field, masking the characters typed in.
- `filename` is used for binary fields, and it is the name of the model field to be used to store the name of the uploaded file.
- `mode` is used for one-to-many fields. It specifies the view type to use to display the records. By default, it is `tree`, but it can also be `form`, `kanban`, or `graph`.

Labels for fields

The `<label>` element can be used to better control the presentation of a field label. One case where this is used is to present the label only when the form is in edit mode:

```
<label for="name" class="oe_edit_only" />
```

When doing this, if the field is inside a `<group>` element, we usually want to also set `nolabel="True"` on it.

Relational fields

In relational fields, we can have some additional control as to what the user can do. By default, the user can create new records from these fields (also known as "quick create") and open the related record form. This can be disabled using the `options` field attribute:

```
options="{'no_open': True, 'no_create': True}"
```

The `context` and `domain` are also field attributes and are particularly useful on relational fields.

The `context` can define the default values for the related records, and the `domain` can limit the selectable records. A common example is for a field to have the selection options depend on the value of another field. A field's `domain` can be defined directly in the Model, but it can also be overridden in the View.

We also have the `mode` attribute to change the view type used to display the records. By default, it is `tree`, but other options are `form`, `kanban`, or `graph`.

Field widgets

Each field type is displayed in the form with the appropriate default widget. But additional alternative widgets are available to be used.

For text fields, we have the following widgets:

- `email` is used to make the email text an actionable "mail-to" address.
- `url` is used to format the text as a clickable URL.
- `html` is used to render the text as HTML content; in edit mode, it features a WYSIWYG editor to allow for the formatting of the content without the need for using the HTML syntax.

For numeric fields, we have the following widgets:

- `handle` is specifically designed for sequence fields in list views and displays a handle that allows you to drag lines to a custom order.
- `float_time` formats a float field with time quantities as hours and minutes.

- `monetary` displays a float field as the currency amount. It expects a `currency_id` companion field, but another field name can be provided with `options="{'currency_field': 'currency_id'}"`.
- `progressbar` presents a float as a progress percentage and can be useful for fields representing a completion rate.

For relational and selection fields, we have these additional widgets:

- `many2many_tags` displays values as a list of button-like labels.
- `selection` uses the selection field widget for a many-to-one field.
- `radio` displays the selection field options using radio buttons.
- `priority` represents the selection field as a list of clickable stars. The selection options are usually numeric digits.
- `state_selection` shows a semaphore light for the kanban state selection list. The normal state is represented in gray, done is represented in green, and any other state is represented in red.

The `state_selection` widget was introduced in Odoo 11, and replaces the former `kanban_state_selection`. The later one is deprecated, but for backward compatibility it is still supported.

Buttons

Buttons support these attributes:

- `string` is the button text label, or the HTML `alt` text when an icon is used.
- `type` is the type of the action to perform. Possible values are:
    - `object` is used for calling a Python method
    - `action` is used to run a window action
- `name` identifies the specific action to perform, according to the chosen type: either a model method name or the database ID of window action to run. The `%(xmlid)d` formula can be used to translate the XML ID into the required Database ID when the view is being loaded.
- `args` is used when the `type` is `object`, to pass additional parameters to the method, which must be purely static JSON parameters appended to the record ID to form the arguments of the method call.

- `context` adds values to the context, which can have an effect after the windows action is run, or in the Python code methods called.
- `confirm` displays a confirmation message box before running the related action, displaying the text assigned to this attribute.
- `special="cancel"` is used on wizard form, to add a **Cancel** button.
- `icon` is for the icon image to be shown in the button. The icons available are from the Font Awesome set and should be specified using the corresponding CSS class, such as `icon="fa-question"`. For more information, refer to `http://fontawesome.io`.

 Before Odoo 11.0, the button icons were images originating from the GTK client library, and were limited to the ones available in `addons/web/static/src/img/icons`.

 The workflow engine was deprecated and removed in Odoo 11. In previous versions, where workflows were supported, buttons could trigger workflow engine signals using the `type="workflow"`. In this case, the `name` attribute was supposed to have a workflow signal name.

Smart buttons

When designing the form structure, we included a top-right area to contain smart buttons. Let's now add a button inside it.

For our app, we will have a button displaying the total number of To-Do tasks for the owner of the current To-Do task, and clicking on it will navigate to the list of those items.

First, we need to add the corresponding computed field to `models/todo_task_model.py`. Add the following to the `TodoTask` class:

```
def _compute_user_todo_count(self):
    for task in self:
        task.user_todo_count = task.search_count(
            [('user_id', '=', task.user_id.id)])

user_todo_count = fields.Integer(
    'User To-Do Count',
    compute='_compute_user_todo_count')
```

Next, we add the button box and the button inside it. Right at the top of the `<sheet>` section, replace the button box placeholder we added before with the following:

```
<div name="button_box" class="oe_button_box">
  <button class="oe_stat_button"
    type="action" icon="fa-tasks"
    name="%(action_todo_task_button)d"
    context="{'default_user_id': user_id}"
    help="All to-dos for this user" >
    <field string="To-Dos" name="user_todo_count"
      widget="statinfo"/>
  </button>
</div>
```

This button displays the total number of To-Do Tasks for the person responsible for this To-Do task, computed by the `user_todo_count` field.

These are the attributes that we can use when adding smart buttons:

- `class="oe_stat_button"` renders a rectangle instead of a regular button.
- `icon` sets the icon to use, chosen from the Font Awesome set. Visit `http://fontawesome.io` to browse the available icons.
- `type` and `name` are the button type and the name of the action to trigger. For smart buttons, the type will usually be `action` for a window action, and `name` will be the ID of the action to execute. It expects an actual database ID, so we have to use a formula to convert an XML ID into a database ID: `"%(action-xmlid)d"`. This action should open a view with the related records.
- `string` adds label text to the button. We have not used it here because the contained field already provides a text for it.
- `context` should be used to set default values on the target view, to be used on new records created on the view after clicking on the button.
- `help` adds a help tooltip displayed when the mouse pointer is over the button.

The `button` element itself is a container, with fields displaying statistics. These statistics are regular fields using the widget `statinfo`. The field is usually a computed field defined in the underlying model. Other than fields, inside a button we can also use static text, such as `<div>User's To-dos</div>`.

When clicking on the button, we want to see a list with only the Tasks for the current responsible user. That will be done via the `action_todo_task_button` action, not yet implemented. But it needs to know the current responsible user to be able to perform the filtering. For that, we use the button's `context` attribute to store that value.

The Action used must be defined before the Form, so we should add it at the top of the XML file:

```
<act_window id="action_todo_task_button"
    name="To-Do Tasks"
    res_model="todo.task"
    view_mode="tree,form,calendar,graph,pivot"
    domain="[('user_id','=',default_user_id)]" />
```

Notice how we use the `default_user_id` context key for the domain filter. This particular key will also set the default value on the `user_id` field when creating new Tasks after following the button link.

Dynamic views

View elements also support a few dynamic attributes that allow views to dynamically change their appearance or behavior depending on field values. We may have on change events, able change values on other fields while editing data on a form, or have fields be mandatory or visible only when certain conditions are met.

On change events

The **on change** mechanism allows us to change values in other form fields when a particular field is changed. For example, the on change on a Product field can set the Price field to a default value whenever the product is changed.

In older versions, the on change events were defined at the view level, but since Version 8.0 they have been defined directly on the Model layer, without the need for any specific markup on the views. This is done by creating methods to perform the calculations, and by using `@api.onchange('field1', 'field2')` to bind it to fields. The on change methods are discussed in more detail in `Chapter 6`, *The ORM API – Handling Application Data*.

The on change mechanism also takes care of the automatic recomputation of computed fields to immediately react to the user input. Using the same example as before, if the Price field was changed when we changed the Product, a computed Total Amount field would also be automatically updated using the new price information.

Dynamic attributes

Some attributes allow us to dynamically change the display of view elements, depending on the record's values.

A couple of attributes provide an easy way to control the visibility of a particular user interface element:

- `groups` can make an element visible depending on the security groups the current user belongs to. Only the members of the specified groups will see it. It expects a comma-separated list of Group XML IDs.
- `states` can make an element visible depending on the record's State field. It expects a comma-separated list of State values, and only works on models with an actual `state` field.

Other than these, we also have a flexible method available to set element visibility depending on a client-side dynamically evaluated expression. This is the `attrs` special attribute, expecting as a value a dictionary that maps the value of the `invisible` attribute to the result of an expression.

For example, to have the `date_deadline` field visible in all states except draft, use the following code:

```
<field name="date_deadline"
      attrs="{'invisible':[('state', '=', ['draft'])]}"
/>
```

The `invisible` attribute is available in any element, not only fields. For example, we can use it on notebook pages and in `group` elements.

The `attrs` can also set values for two other attributes: `readonly` and `required`. These only make sense for data fields to make them not editable or mandatory. This allows us to implement some basic client-side logic, such as making a field mandatory depending on other record values, such as the State.

List views

At this point, list views should need little introduction, but we are still going to discuss the attributes that can be used with them. Here is an example of a list view for our To-Do Tasks:

```
<record id="view_tree_todo_task"
   model="ir.ui.view">
```

```xml
<field name="model">todo.task</field>
<field name="arch" type="xml">
  <tree decoration-muted="is_done"
    decoration-bf="state=='open'"
    delete="false">
    <field name="name"/>
    <field name="user_id"/>
    <field name="is_done"/>
    <field name="state" invisible="1"/>
  </tree>
</field>
</record>
```

The row text color and font can change dynamically depending on the results of a Python expression evaluation. This is done through decoration-NAME attributes, with the expression to evaluate based on field attributes. The NAME part can be bf or it, for bold and italic fonts, or any Bootstrap text contextual colors: danger, info, muted, primary, success, or warning. The Bootstrap documentation has examples of how these are presented: http://getbootstrap.com/css/#helper-classes-colors.

> The decoration-NAME attributes have been available since Odoo 9.0. In Odoo 8.0, instead we have the colors and fonts attributes.

Remember that fields used in expressions must be declared in a <field> element, so that the web client knows that that column needs to be retrieved from the server. If we don't want to have it displayed to the user, we should use the invisible="1" attribute on it.

Other relevant attributes of the tree element are:

- default_order allows us to override the model's default sort order, and its value follows the same format as an order attribute used in model definitions.
- create, delete, and edit, if set to false (in lowercase), disable the corresponding action on the list view.
- editable makes records editable directly on the list view. Possible values are top and bottom, the location where the new records will be added.

A list view can contain fields and buttons, and most of their attributes for forms are also valid here.

In list views, numeric fields can display summary values for their column. Add to the field one of the available aggregation attributes, `sum`, `avg`, `min`, or `max`, and assign to it the label text for the summary value, for example:

```
<field name="amount" sum="Total Amount" />
```

Search views

The search options available are defined through the `<search>` view type. We can choose the fields that can be automatically searched when typing in the search box. We can also provide predefined filters, activated with a click, and predefined grouping options to be used in list views.

Here is a possible search view for the To-Do Tasks:

```
<record id="view_filter_todo_task"
  model="ir.ui.view">
  <field name="model">todo.task</field>
  <field name="priority">15</field>
  <field name="arch" type="xml">
    <search>
      <field name="name"/>
      <field name="user_id"/>
      <filter name="filter_not_done" string="Not Done"
        domain="[('is_done','=',False)]"/>
      <filter name="filter_done" string="Done"
        domain="[('is_done','!=',False)]"/>

      <separator/>
      <filter name="group_user" string="By User"
        context="{'group_by': 'user_id'}"/>
    </search>
  </field>
</record>
```

We can see two fields to be searched on: `name` and `user_id`. When the user starts typing in the search box, a dropdown will suggest searching on any of these fields. If the user types ENTER the search will be performed on the first of the filter fields.

Then we have two predefined filters, filtering not-done and done tasks. These filters can be activated independently and will be joined by an OR operator. Blocks of filters separated with a `<separator/>` element will be joined by an AND operator.

The third filter only sets a group by context. This tells the view to group the records by that field, `user_id` in this case.

The field elements can use the following attributes:

- `name` identifies the field to use.
- `string` is label text which is used instead of the default.
- `operator` is used to change the operator from the default one (= for numeric fields and `ilike` for the other field types).
- `filter_domain` sets a specific domain expression to use for the search, providing one flexible alternative to the operator attribute. The searched text string is referred to in the expression as self. A trivial example is: `filter_domain="[('name', 'ilike', self)]"`.
- `groups` makes the search on the field available only for users belonging to some security groups and expects a comma-separated list of XML IDs.

For the filter elements, these are the attributes available:

- `name` is an identifier to be used for later inheritance/extension, or for being enabled through window actions. It is not mandatory, but it is good practice to always provide it.
- `string` is the label text to be displayed for the filter. Required.
- `domain` is the domain expression to be added to the current domain.
- `context` is a context dictionary to be added to the current context. Usually sets a `group_id` key with the name of the field to group records.
- `groups` makes the search on the field available only for a list of security groups (XML IDs).

Calendar views

As the name suggests, this view type presents the records in a calendar that can be viewed at different periods of time: per month, week, or day. A calendar view for the To-Do Tasks could look like this:

```
<record id="view_calendar_todo_task" model="ir.ui.view">
  <field name="model">todo.task</field>
  <field name="arch" type="xml">
    <calendar date_start="date_deadline" color="user_id">
      <!-- Fields used for the display text -->
```

```
        <field name="name" />
        <field name="stage_id" />
    </calendar>
  </field>
</record>
```

The calendar attributes are:

- `date_start` is the field for the start date. Mandatory.
- `date_end` is the field for the end date. Optional.
- `date_delay` is the field with the duration of days, which can be used instead of `date_end`.
- `all_day` provides the name of a Boolean field that is to be used to signal full day events. In these events, the duration is ignored.
- `color` is the field used to color a group of calendar entries. Each distinct value in this field will be assigned a color, and all its entries will have the same color.
- `mode` is the default display mode for the calendar, either `day`, `week`, or `month`.

> The `display` calendar attribute was removed in Odoo 11. In previous versions, it could be used to customize the format of the calendar entries title text, for example: `display="[name], Stage [stage_id]"`.

Graph and pivot views

Graph views provide a graphical view of the data, in the form of a chart. The current fields available in the To-Do Tasks are not good candidates for a chart, so we will add one to use on such a view.

In the `TodoTask` class, at the `todo_stage/models/todo_task_model.py` file, add:

```
effort_estimate = fields.Integer('Effort Estimate')
```

It also needs to be added to the To-Do Task form, so that we can add values for it on the existing records and are able to check this new view.

Now let's add the To-Do Tasks graph view:

```
<record id="view_graph_todo_task" model="ir.ui.view">
  <field name="model">todo.task</field>
  <field name="arch" type="xml">
    <graph type="bar">
```

```
      <field name="stage_id" />
      <field name="effort_estimate" type="measure" />
    </graph>
  </field>
</record>
```

The `graph` view element can have a `type` attribute that can be set to `bar` (the default), `pie`, or `line`. In the case of `bar`, the additional `stacked="True"` can be used to make it a stacked bar chart.

The data can also be seen in a pivot table, a dynamic analysis matrix. For this, we have the pivot view, introduced in Version 9.0. Pivot tables were already available in Version 8.0, but in 9.0, they moved into their own view type. Along with this, it improved the UI features of Pivot tables, and optimized the retrieval of pivot table data greatly.

To also add a pivot table to the To-Do Tasks, use this code:

```
<record id="view_pivot_todo_task" model="ir.ui.view">
  <field name="model">todo.task</field>
  <field name="arch" type="xml">
    <pivot>
      <field name="stage_id" type="col" />
      <field name="user_id" />
      <field name="date_deadline" interval="week" />
      <field name="effort_estimate" type="measure" />
    </pivot>
  </field>
</record>
```

The graph and pivot views should contain field elements describing the axes and measures to use. Most of the available attributes are common to both the view types:

- `name` identifies the field to use in the graph, just like in other views
- `type` is how the field will be used, as a `row` group (default), a `measure`, or as `col` (only for pivot tables, used for column groups)
- `interval` is meaningful for date fields, and is the time interval used to group time data by `day`, `week`, `month`, `quarter`, or `year`

By default, the aggregation used is the sum of the values. This can be changed by setting the `group_operator` attribute on the Python field definition. The values that can be used include `avg`, `max`, and `min`.

Other view types

It's worth noting that we didn't cover three other view types that are also available: kanban, gantt, and diagram.

Kanban views will be covered in detail in `Chapter 10`, *Kanban Views and Client Side QWeb*.

The gantt view was available until Version 8.0, but it was removed in Version 9.0 Community Edition because of license incompatibilities. An equivalent view is available in the Enterprise Edition. For a community open source alternative, you may want to have a look at the `web_timeline` module, hosted at `https://github.com/OCA/web`. At the time of writing, this module hasn't yet been ported to Odoo 11.

Finally, the diagram views are used in quite specific cases, and an addon module will need them rarely. Just in case, you might like to know that the reference material for the two view types can be found in the official documentation: `http://www.odoo.com/documentation/11.0/reference/views.html#diagram`.

Summary

In this chapter, we learned more about Odoo views in order to build the user interface. We explained form views in detail, and then provided an overview of the other view types, including list (or tree) and search view. We also learned how to add dynamic behavior to view elements.

In the next chapter, we will learn more about a specific view type not covered here: the Kanban view, and the templating syntax used by it, QWeb.

10
Kanban Views and Client-Side QWeb

QWeb is the template engine used by Odoo. It is XML-based and used to generate HTML fragments and pages. QWeb was first introduced in version 7.0 to enable richer Kanban views and, since version 8.0, used for report design and CMS website pages.

Here, you will learn about the QWeb syntax and how to use it to create your own Kanban views and custom reports. Let's get started by learning more about Kanban boards.

About Kanban boards

Kanban is a Japanese word literally meaning billboard, and is associated with lean manufacturing and just-in-time manufacturing, introduced by Taiichi Ohno, an industrial engineer working at Toyota. More recently, the concept of Kanban boards has been adopted in other areas, and has become popular in the software industry with the adoption of Agile methodologies.

The **Kanban board** allows you to visualize the work queue. The board is organized into columns representing the **stages** of the work process. Work items are represented by **cards** placed on the appropriate column of the board. New work items start from the leftmost column and travel through the board until they reach the rightmost column, representing completed work.

The simplicity and visual impact of Kanban boards make them excellent for supporting simple business processes. A basic example of a Kanban board can have three columns, as shown in the following diagram: **To Do**, **Doing**, and **Done**.

It can, of course, be extended to whatever specific process steps we may need:

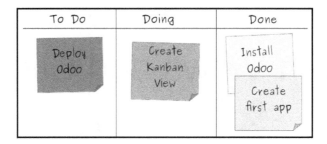

For many business use cases, a Kanban board can be a more effective way to manage the corresponding process, compared to a heavier workflow engine, such as the one featured in Odoo versions before 11.0. Odoo supports Kanban board views, along with the classic list and form views. This makes it easy to implement this type of view. Let's learn how to use them.

Kanban views

We will now add a Kanban view to our to-do model. Each to-do task will be a card, and the Kanban board will be organized into Stage columns. We already have a `stage_id` field to use for this, added in previous chapters.

Previously, in form views, we mostly used Odoo specific XML elements, such as `<field>` and `<group>`. HTML elements, such as `<h1>` or `<div>`, were also used, but less frequently. With Kanban views, it's quite the opposite: the presentation templates are HTML-based and support only two Odoo-specific elements, `<field>` and `<button>`.

The final HTML to be presented in the web client is dynamically generated from QWeb templates. The QWeb engine processes special XML tags and attributes to produce them. This brings a lot of control over how to render the content, but also makes the view design more complex.

The Kanban view design is quite flexible, so we'll do our best to prescribe a straightforward way for you to quickly build your Kanban views. A good approach is to find an existing Kanban view similar to what you need, and inspect it to for ideas on how to build yours.

We can see two different ways to use Kanban views. One is a card list. It is used in places such as contacts, products, employee directories, or apps.

Here is how the **Contacts** Kanban view looks:

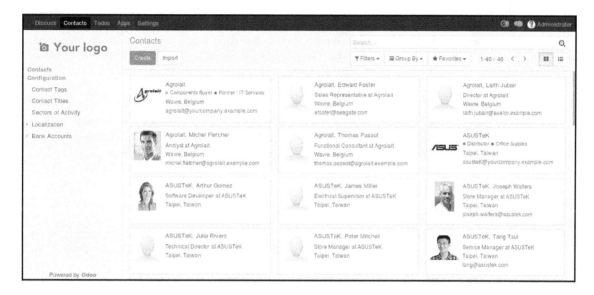

But this is not a true Kanban board. A Kanban board is expected to have the cards organized into columns, and of course, the Kanban view also supports that layout. We can see examples in the **CRM | Pipeline** or in **Project Tasks**.

Here is how the **CRM | Pipeline** looks:

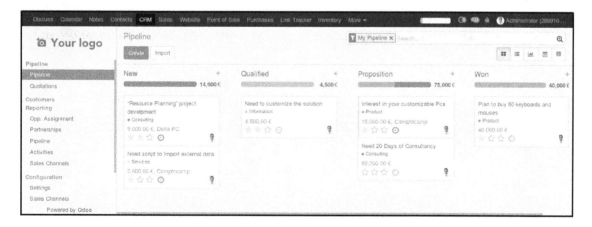

The most striking difference between the two is the card organization in columns. This is achieved by the **Group By** feature, similar to what List views can do. Usually, the grouping is done on a **Stage** field. One very useful feature of Kanban views is that they support dragging and dropping cards between columns, automatically assigning the corresponding value to the field the view is grouped by.

Looking at the cards in both examples, we can see some differences. In fact, their design is quite flexible, and there is not a single way to design a Kanban card. But these two examples provide a starting point for your designs.

The **Contact** cards basically have an image on the left-hand side, and a bold title in the main area followed by a list of values. The **CRM Pipeline** cards have a bit more structure. The main card area also has a title followed by a list of relevant information, as well as a footer area. In this footer area, we can see a priority widget on the left-hand side, followed by an Activities indicator, and at the right-hand side a small image of the the responsible user. It is not visible in the image, but the cards also have an options menu at the top-right, shown when hovering the mouse pointer over it. This menu allows us to, for example, change a color indicator for the card.

We will be using this more elaborate structure as a model for the cards on our to-do Kanban board.

Designing Kanban views

We will improve the `todo_stage` module we have been working with to add the Kanban view to the to-do tasks.

For this, we will use a new data file, `views/todo_kanban_view.xml`. We need to edit the `data` key in the descriptor file, `__manifest__.py`, to append this new data file at the end of the list.

Next, we can create the actual XML file where our shiny new Kanban view will go, at `todo_stage/views/todo_kanban_view.xml`:

```xml
<?xml version="1.0"?>
<odoo>

  <!-- Add Kanban view mode to the menu Action: -->
  <record id="todo_app.action_todo_task"
          model="ir.actions.act_window">
      <field name="view_mode"
      >kanban,tree,form,calendar,graph,pivot
```

```
      </field>
    </field>
    <!-- Add Kanban view -->
    <record id="todo_task_kanban" model="ir.ui.view">
      <field name="model">todo.task</field>
      <field name="arch" type="xml">
        <kanban>
          <!-- Empty for now, but the Kanban will go here! -->
        </kanban>
      </field>
    </record>
</odoo>
```

Here, we modify the menu Action to include `kanban` at the beginning of the `view_mode` list, so that it is the default view mode used. We then add the `kanban` view record. It is similar to the other views, except that inside the `arch` field we have a `<kanban>` top XML element.

Before starting with the kanban views, we need to add a couple of fields to the to-do tasks model.

Priority, kanban state, and color

Other than stages, a few more fields are useful and frequently used in kanban boards:

- `priority` lets users organize their work items, signaling what should be addressed first.
- `kanban_state` signals whether a task is ready to move to the next stage or is blocked for some reason. At the model definition layer, both are selection fields. At the view layer, they have specific widgets for them that can be used on form and Kanban views.
- `color` is used to store the color the Kanban card should display, and can be set using a color picker menu available on Kanban views.

To add these fields to our model, we should edit the `models/todo_task_model.py` file:

```
# class TodoTask (models.Model):
#     ...
    color = fields.Integer('Color Index')
    priority = fields.Selection(
        [('0', 'Low'),
         ('1', 'Normal'),
         ('2', 'High')],
```

```
        'Priority',
        default='1')
    kanban_state = fields.Selection(
        [('normal', 'In Progress'),
         ('blocked', 'Blocked'),
         ('done', 'Ready for next stage')],
        'Kanban State',
        default='normal')
```

We should also add these to the form view, using the special widgets available for them. The `kanban_stage` field should be added before the `<div oe_class="title">`, and after the button box, with `<field name="kanban_stage" widget="state_selection" />`. The `priority` should be added before the `name` field, inside the surrounding `<h1>` element, with `<field name="priority" widget="priority" />`. The `color` field is not usually represented in the form views.

Now that the to-do task model has all the fields we want to use, we can work on the Kanban view.

Kanban card elements

The Kanban view architecture has a `<kanban>` top element and the following basic structure:

```
<kanban default_group_by="stage_id" class="o_kanban_small_column" >
  <!-- Fields (to use in expressions)... -->
  <field name="stage_id" />
  <field name="color" />
  <field name="kanban_state" />
  <field name="priority" />
  <field name="is_done" />
  <field name="message_partner_ids" />
  <!-- Optional progress bar   -->
  <progressbar
      field="kanban_state"
      colors='{"done": "success", "blocked": "danger"}' />
  <!-- Templates with HTML snippets to use... -->
  <templates>
    <t t-name="kanban-box">
      <!-- HTML QWeb template... -->
    </t>
  </templates>
</kanban>
```

Notice the `default_group_by="stage_id"` attribute used in the `<kanban>` element. We used it so that, by default, the Kanban cards are grouped by Stage, like Kanban boards should be. In simple card list Kanbans, such as the one in **Contacts**, we don't need this and would instead just use a simple `<kanban>` opening tag.

The `<kanban>` top element supports a few interesting attributes:

- `default_group_by` sets the field to use for the default column groups.
- `default_order` sets a default order to use for the Kanban items.
- `quick_create="false"` disables the quick create option (the large *plus* sign) available at the top of each column, to create new items by providing just a title description. The false value is a JavaScript literal, and must be in lowercase.
- `class` adds a CSS class to the root element of the rendered Kanban view. A relevant class is `o_kanban_small_column`, making columns somewhat more compact than the default. Additional classes may be made available through additional CSS assets provided by our module.
- `group_create`, `group_edit`, and `group_delete` can be set to `false` to disable the corresponding action on the Kanban columns. For example, `group_create="false"` removes the vertical **Add new column** bar on the right.
- `on_create` can be used to create a custom, simplified, form view in a popup when the user clicks on the top-left **Create** button. It should be set with the `<module>.<xml_id>` value of the intended form view.

We then see a list of fields used in templates. To be exact, only fields used exclusively in QWeb expressions need to be declared here, to ensure that their data is fetched from the server.

The QWeb engine only looks for `<field name="...">` patterns in a view to find the fields to be fetched from the model before the template is processed. QWeb attributes often use `record.field` references that will not be detected. Because of this, they need to be included before the `<templates>` section, to make sure the corresponding field values are available when the template is processed.

In Odoo 11.0, a new Progress Bar widget was introduced. When used, a colored bar is shown at the top of each Kanban column, providing quick statistics on the status of that column's items. We can see an example in the previous screenshot, showing the **CRM Pipeline**.

The `<progressbar>` element has the following attributes:

- `field` is the field name used to color group the items in the column.
- `colors` is a dictionary mapping each value of the group field to one of the three available colors: `danger` (red), `warning` (yellow), or `success` (green).
- `sum_field` is optional, and can be used to choose the field name to use for the column total. If not set, the count of items in the column is used.

Next, we have a `<templates>` element, containing one or more QWeb templates to generate the used HTML fragments. We must have one template named `kanban-box`, which will render the Kanban cards. Additional templates can also be added, usually to define HTML fragments to be reused in the main template.

These templates use standard HTML and the QWeb templating language. QWeb provides special directives that are processed to dynamically generate the final HTML to be presented.

Odoo uses the Twitter Bootstrap 3 web style library, so those style classes are generally available wherever HTML can be rendered. You can learn more about Bootstrap at `https://getbootstrap.com`.

We will now have a closer look at the design of the QWeb templates to be used in Kanban views.

The Kanban card layout

The main content area of a Kanban card is defined inside the `kanban-box` template. This content area can also have a footer sub-container. A button opening an action menu may also be featured in the card's top-right corner.

For the footer area, we should use a `<div>` element at the bottom of the Kanban box with the `oe_kanban_bottom` CSS class. It can be further split into left and right footer areas, using the `oe_kanban_bottom_left` and `oe_kanban_bottom_right` CSS classes.

As an alternative, the Bootstrap provided classes `pull-left` and `pull-right` can be used to add left or right aligned elements anywhere in the card, including in the `oe_kanban_bottom` footer.

Here is our first iteration of the QWeb template for our Kanban card:

```
<!-- Define the kanban-box template -->
<t t-name="kanban-box">
  <!-- Set the Kanban Card color: -->
  <div t-attf-class="
    oe_kanban_color_#{kanban_getcolor(record.color.raw_value)}
    oe_kanban_global_click">
      <div class="o_dropdown_kanban dropdown">
          <!-- Top-right drop down menu here... -->
      </div>
      <div class="oe_kanban_body">
          <!-- Content elements and fields go here... -->
      </div>
      <div class="oe_kanban_footer">
        <div class="oe_kanban_footer_left">
            <!-- Left hand footer... -->
        </div>
        <div class="oe_kanban_footer_right">
            <!-- Right hand footer... -->
        </div>
      </div>
      <div class="oe_clear"/>
  </div> <!-- end of kanban color -->
</t>
```

This lays out the overall structure for the Kanban card. You may notice that the `color` field is being used in the top `<div>` element to dynamically set the card's color. We will explain the `t-attf` QWeb directive in more detail in one of the following sections.

Now let's work on the main content area, and choose what to place there:

```
<div class="oe_kanban_body">
  <!-- Content elements and fields go here... -->
  <div>
    <field name="tag_ids" />
  </div>

  <div>
    <strong>
      <a type="open"><field name="name" /></a>
    </strong>
  </div>

  <ul>
    <li><field name="user_id" /></li>
    <li><field name="date_deadline" /></li>
```

```
    </ul>

  </div>
```

Most of this template is regular HTML, but we also see the `<field>` element used to render field values, and the `type` attribute used in regular form view buttons, used here in an `<a>` anchor tag.

In the left-hand footer, we will insert the priority widget:

```
<div class="oe_kanban_footer_left">
  <!-- Left hand footer... -->
  <field name="priority" widget="priority"/>
</div>
```

Here, we can see the `priority` field added, just like we would do in a form view.

In the right-hand footer, we will place the Kanban state widget and the avatar for the owner of the to-do task:

```
<div class="oe_kanban_footer_right">
  <!-- Right hand footer... -->
  <field name="Kanban_state" widget="kanban_state_selection"/>
  <img t-att-src="kanban_image(
    'res.users', 'image_small', record.user_id.raw_value)"
    t-att-title="record.user_id.value"
    width="24" height="24"
    class="oe_kanban_avatar" />
</div>
```

The Kanban state is added using a `<field>` element, just like in regular form views. The user avatar image is inserted using the HTML `<img>` tag. The image content is dynamically generated using the QWeb `t-att-` directive, which will be explained in more detail later on. It makes use of the `kanban_image()` Odoo helper function to get the value for the `src` attribute.

Sometimes, we may want to have a small representative image to be shown on the card, such as in the **Contacts** example. For reference, this can be done by adding the following as the first content element:

```
<img t-att-src="kanban_image(
    'res.partner', 'image_medium', record.id.value)"
    class="o_kanban_image"/>
```

Adding a Kanban card option menu

Kanban cards can have an option menu, placed in the top-right. Usual actions are to edit or delete the record, but it's possible to have any action that can be called from a button. We also have a widget to set the card's color.

The following is baseline HTML code for the option menu to be added at the top of the `oe_kanban_content` element:

```
<div class="o_dropdown_kanban dropdown">
  <!-- Top-right drop down menu here... -->
  <a class="dropdown-toggle btn" data-toggle="dropdown" href="#">
    <span class="fa fa-ellipsis-v" aria-hidden="true"/>
  </a>
  <ul class="dropdown-menu" role="menu" aria-labelledby="dLabel">
    <!-- Edit and Delete actions, if available: -->
    <t t-if="widget.editable">
      <li><a type="edit">Edit</a></li>
    </t>
    <t t-if="widget.deletable">
      <li><a type="delete">Delete</a></li>
    </t>
    <!-- Call a server-side Model method: -->
    <t t-if="!record.is_done.value">
      <li><a name="do_toggle_done" type="object">Set as Done</a>
      </li>
    </t>
    <!-- Color picker option: -->
    <li class="divider"/>
    <li class="dropdown-header">Color</li>
    <li>
      <ul class="oe_kanban_colorpicker" data-field="color"/>
    </li>
  </ul>
</div>
```

Notice that the previous code won't work unless we have `<field name="is_done" />` somewhere in the view, because it is used in one of the expressions. If we don't need to use it inside the template, we can declare it before the `<templates>` element as we did when defining the `<kanban>` view.

The drop-down menu is basically composed of `<li>` HTML list elements containing an `<a>` element. Some options, such as **Edit** and **Delete**, are made available only if certain conditions are met. This is done with the `t-if` QWeb directive. Later in this chapter, we explain this and other QWeb directives in more detail.

The `widget` global variable represents a `KanbanRecord()` JavaScript object, which is responsible for the rendering of the current Kanban card. Two particularly useful properties are `widget.editable` and `widget.deletable`, which allow us to check whether the corresponding actions are available.

We can also see how to show or hide an option depending on the record field values. The **Set as Done** option will only be displayed if the `is_done` field is not set.

The last option adds the color picker special widget using the `color` data field to select and change the card's background color.

Actions in Kanban views

In QWeb templates, the `<a>` tag for links can have a `type` attribute. It sets the type of action the link will perform so that links can act just like buttons in regular forms. So in addition to the `<button>` elements, the `<a>` tags can also be used to run Odoo actions.

As in form views, the action type can be `action` or `object`, and it should be accompanied by a `name` attribute, identifying the specific action to execute. Additionally, the following action types are also available:

- `open` opens the corresponding form view
- `edit` opens the corresponding form view directly in edit mode
- `delete` deletes the record and removes the item from the Kanban view

The QWeb templating language

The QWeb parser looks for special directives in the templates and replaces them with dynamically generated HTML. These directives are XML element attributes, and can be used in any valid tag or element, such as `<div>`, `<span>`, or `<field>`.

Sometimes, we may want to use a QWeb directive but we don't want to place it in any of the XML elements in our template. For those cases, we have a `<t>` special element that can have QWeb directives, such as a `t-if` or a `t-foreach`, but is silent, and won't have any output on the final XML/HTML produced.

The QWeb directives will frequently make use of evaluated expressions to produce different results depending on the current record values. There are two different QWeb implementations: client-side JavaScript and server-side Python.

The reports and website pages use the server-side Python implementation of QWeb.

Kanban views use the client-side JavaScript implementation. This means that the QWeb expression used in Kanban views should be written using the JavaScript syntax, not Python.

When displaying a Kanban view, the internal steps are roughly as follows:

1. Get the XML for the templates to render
2. Call the server `read()` method to get the data for the fields mentioned in the templates
3. Locate the `kanban-box` template and parse it using QWeb to output the final HTML fragments
4. Inject the HTML in the browser's display (the DOM)

This is not meant to be technically exact. It is just a mind map that can be useful to understand how things work in Kanban views.

Next, we will learn about QWeb expression evaluation and explore the available QWeb directives, using examples that enhance our to-do task Kanban card.

The QWeb JavaScript evaluation context

Many of the QWeb directives use expressions that are evaluated to produce some result. When used from the client side, as is the case for Kanban views, these expressions are written in JavaScript. They are evaluated in a context that has a few useful variables available.

A `record` object is available, representing the current record, with the fields requested from the server. The field values can be accessed using either the `raw_value` or the `value` attributes:

- `raw_value` is the value returned by the `read()` server method, so it's more suitable for use in condition expressions.
- `value` is formatted according to the user settings, and is meant to be used for display in the user interface. This is typically relevant for date/datetime, float/monetary fields, and also relational fields.

The QWeb evaluation context also has references available for the JavaScript web client instance. To make use of them, a good understanding of the web client architecture is needed, but we won't be able to go into that in detail. For reference purposes, the following identifiers are available in QWeb expression evaluation:

- `widget` is a reference to the current `KanbanRecord()` widget object, responsible for the rendering of the current record into a Kanban card. It exposes some useful helper functions we can use.
- `record` is a shortcut for `widget.record` and provides access to the fields available, using dot notation.
- `read_only_mode` indicates whether the current view is in read mode (and not in edit mode). It is a shortcut for `widget.view.options.read_only_mode`.
- `instance` is a reference to the full web client instance.

It is also noteworthy that some characters are not allowed inside expressions. The lower than sign (<) is such a case. This is because of the XML standard, where such characters have special meaning and shouldn't be used on the XML content. A negated >= is a valid alternative, but the common practice is to use the following alternative symbols that are available for inequality operations:

- `lt` is for less than
- `lte` is for less than or equal to
- `gt` is for greater than
- `gte` is for greater than or equal to

 The preceding comparison symbols are specific to Odoo, and were introduced to overcome limitations in the XML format. They are not part of the XML standard.

Dynamic attributes by string substitution – t-attf

Our Kanban card is using the `t-attf` QWeb directive to dynamically set a class on the top `<div>` element so that the card is colored depending on the `color` field value. For this, the `t-attf-` QWeb directive was used.

The `t-attf-` directive dynamically generates tag attributes using string substitution. This allows for parts of larger strings generated dynamically, such as a URL address or CSS class names.

The directive looks for expression blocks that will be evaluated and replaced by the result. These are delimited either by `{{` and `}}` or by `#{` and `}`. The content of the blocks can be any valid JavaScript expression and can use any of the variables available for QWeb expressions, such as `record` and `widget`.

In our case, we also used the `kanban_color()` JavaScript function, specially provided to map color index numbers into the CSS class color names.

As a more elaborate example, we can use this directive to dynamically change the color of the **Deadline Date**, so that overdue dates are shown in red.

For this, replace `<field name="date_deadline"/>` in our Kanban card with the following:

```
<li t-attf-class="oe_kanban_text_{{
  record.date_deadline.raw_value and
  record.date_deadline.raw_value lt (new Date())
  ? 'red' : 'black' }}">
  <field name="date_deadline"/>
</li>
```

This results in either `class="oe_kanban_text_red"` or `class="oe_kanban_text_black"`, depending on the deadline date. Please note that, while the `oe_kanban_text_red` CSS class is available in Kanban views, the `oe_kanban_text_black` CSS class does not exist and was used to better explain the point.

 Notice the `lt` symbols used in the JavaScript expression. It is an escape expression for the < sign, not allowed in XML.

Dynamic attributes by expressions – t-att

The `t-att-` QWeb directive dynamically generates an attribute value by evaluating an expression. Our Kanban card uses it to dynamically set some attributes on the `<img>` tag.

The `title` element is dynamically rendered using the following:

```
t-att-title="record.user_id.value"
```

The field `.value` returns its value representation as it should be shown on the screen. For many-to-one fields, this is usually the related record's `name` value. For users, this is the username. As a result, when hovering the mouse pointer over the image, you will see the corresponding username.

When the expression evaluates to a false equivalent value, the attribute is not rendered at all. This is important for special HTML attributes such as the input field `checked`, which can have an effect even without attribute value.

In our example, the `src` tag is also dynamically generated to provide the image corresponding to the responsible user. The image data is provided by the helper JavaScript function `kanban_image()`:

```
t-att-src="kanban_image('res.users', 'image_small',
    record.user_id.raw_value)"
```

The function parameters are the model to read the image from, the field name to read, and the ID of the record. Here, we used `.raw_value` to get the user's database ID instead of its representation text. The `kanban_image()` function returns a URL to call a special controller that will serve an image based on the `model`, `field`, and `record_id` values.

It doesn't stop there. `t-att-NAME` and `t-attf-NAME` can be made to render any attribute, as the name of the generated attribute is taken from the NAME suffix used.

Loops – t-foreach

A block of HTML can be repeated by iterating through a loop. We can use it to add the avatars of the task followers to the task's Kanban card.

Let's start by rendering just the partner IDs of the task, as follows:

```
<t t-foreach="record.message_partner_ids.raw_value" t-as="rec">
  <t t-esc="rec" />;
</t>
```

The `t-foreach` directive accepts a JavaScript expression evaluating to a collection to iterate. In most cases, this will be just the name of a *to-many* relation field. It is used with a `t-as` directive to set the name to be used to refer to each item in the iteration.

The `t-esc` directive used next evaluates the provided expression, just the `rec` variable name in this case, and renders it as safely escaped HTML.

In the previous example, we loop through the task followers stored in the `message_parter_ids` field. Since there is limited space on the Kanban card, we could have used the `slice()` JavaScript function to limit the number of followers to display, as shown in the following:

```
t-foreach="record.message_partner_ids.raw_value.slice(0, 3)"
```

The `rec` variable holds each iteration's value, a partner ID in this case. With this, we can rewrite the follower's loop as follows:

```
<t t-foreach="record.message_parter_ids.raw_value.slice(0, 3)"
  t-as="rec">
  <img t-att-src="kanban_image('res.partner', 'image_small', rec)"
    class="oe_avatar" width="24" height="24" />
</t>
```

For example, this could be added next to the responsible user image, in the right-hand footer.

A few helper variables are also available. Their name has the variable name defined in `t-as` as a prefix. In our example, we used `rec`, so the helper variables available are as follows:

- `rec_index` is the iteration index, starting from zero
- `rec_size` is the number of elements of the collection
- `rec_first` is true on the first element of the iteration
- `rec_last` is true on the last element of the iteration
- `rec_even` is true on even indexes
- `rec_odd` is true on odd indexes
- `rec_parity` is either `odd` or `even`, depending on the current index
- `rec_all` represents the object being iterated over
- `rec_value` when iterating through a dictionary, `{key: value}`, holds the value (`rec` holds the key name)

For example, we could make use of the following to avoid a trailing comma on our ID list:

```
<t t-foreach="record.message_parter_ids.raw_value.slice(0, 3)"
  t-as="rec">
  <t t-esc="rec" />
  <t t-if="!rec_last">;</t>
</t>
```

Conditionals – t-if

Our Kanban view used the `t-if` directive in the card option menu to make some options available depending on some conditions. The `t-if` directive expects an expression to be evaluated in JavaScript when rendering Kanban views on the client side. The tag and its content will be rendered only if the condition evaluates to true.

As an example, to display the task effort estimate in the Kanban card only if it has a value, add the following after the `date_deadline` field:

```
<t t-if="record.effort_estimate.raw_value gt 0">
  <li>Estimate <field name="effort_estimate"/></li>
</t>
```

We used a `<t t-if="...">` element so that if the condition is false, the element produces no output. If it is true, only the contained `<li>` element is rendered to the output. Notice that the condition expression used the `gt` symbol instead of `>` to represent the *greater than* operator.

The `else if` and `else` conditions are also supported, with the `t-elif` and `t-else` directives. Here is an example of their usage:

```
<t t-if="record.effort_estimate.raw_value == 0">
  <li>No estimate"/></li>
</t>
<t t-elif="record.effort_estimate.raw_value gt 1000">
  <li>Estimate 999/></li>
</t>
<t t-else="">
  <li>Estimate <field name="effort_estimate"/></li>
</t>
```

Rendering values – t-esc and t-raw

We used the `<field>` element to render the field content. But field values can also be presented directly without a `<field>` tag.

The `t-esc` directive evaluates an expression and renders it as an HTML-escaped value, as shown in the following:

```
<t t-esc="record.message_parter_ids.raw_value" />
```

In some cases, and if the source data is guaranteed to be safe, `t-raw` can be used to render the field raw value without any escaping, as shown in the following example:

```
<t t-raw="record.message_parter_ids.raw_value" />
```

> For security reasons, it is important to avoid using `t-raw` as much as possible. Its usage should be strictly reserved for outputting HTML data that was specifically prepared without any user data in it, or where any user data was escaped explicitly for HTML special characters.

Set values on variables – t-set

For more complex logic, we can store the result of an expression into a variable to use it later in the template. This is to be done using the `t-set` directive, naming the variable to set followed by the `t-value` directive with the expression calculating the value to assign.

As an example, the following code renders missed deadlines in red, just as in the previous section, but uses a `red_or_black` variable for the CSS class to use, as shown in the following:

```
<t t-set="red_or_black"
   t-value="
     record.date_deadline.raw_value and
     record.date_deadline.raw_value lte (new Date())
     ? 'oe_kanban_text_red' : ''" />
<li t-att-class="red_or_black">
  <field name="date_deadline" />
</li>
```

Variables can also be assigned HTML content, as in the following example:

```
<t t-set="calendar_sign">
  <i class="fa fa-calendar"/>
</t>
<t t-raw="calendar_sign" />
```

Odoo bundles the **Font Awesome** icon set, and we used it here for the calendar icon. Many more icons are available. Check `http://fontawesome.io` for reference.

Call and reuse other templates – t-call

QWeb templates can be reusable HTML snippets that can be inserted into other templates. Instead of repeating the same HTML blocks over and over again, we can design building blocks to compose more complex user interface views.

Reusable templates are defined inside the `<templates>` tag and identified by a top element with a `t-name` other than `kanban-box`. These other templates can then be included using the `t-call` directive. This is true for the templates declared in the same Kanban view, somewhere else in the same add-on module, or in a different add-on.

The follower avatar list is something that could be isolated in a reusable snippet. Let's rework it to use a sub-template. We should start by adding another template to our XML file, inside the `<templates>` element, after the `<t t-name="kanban-box">` node, as shown in the following:

```
<t t-name="follower_avatars">
  <div>
    <t t-foreach="record.message_parter_ids.raw_value.slice(0, 3)"
      t-as="rec">
      <img t-att-src="kanban_image(
        'res.partner', 'image_small', rec)"
        class="oe_avatar" width="24" height="24" />
    </t>
  </div>
</t>
```

Calling it from the `kanban-box` main template is quite straightforward. Instead of the `<div>` element containing the `for each` directive, we should use the following:

```
<t t-call="follower_avatars" />
```

To call templates defined in other add-on modules, we need to use the `module.name` full identifier, as we do with the other views. For instance, this snippet can be referred using the full identifier `todo_kanban.follower_avatars`.

The called template runs in the same context as the caller, so any variable names available in the caller are also available when processing the called template.

A more elegant alternative is to pass arguments to the called template. This is done by setting variables inside the `t-call` tag. These will be evaluated and made available in the sub-template context only, and won't exist in the caller's context.

We could use this to have the maximum number of follower avatars set by the caller instead of being hardcoded in the sub-template. First, we need to replace the fixed value, 3, with a variable, `arg_max` for example:

```
<t t-name="follower_avatars">
  <div>
    <t t-foreach="record.message_parter_ids.raw_value.slice(0, arg_max)"
      t-as="rec">
      <img t-att-src="kanban_image('res.partner', 'image_small', rec)"
        class="oe_avatar" width="24" height="24" />
    </t>
  </div>
</t>
```

Then, define that variable's value when performing the sub-template call as follows:

```
<t t-call="follower_avatars">
  <t t-set="arg_max" t-value="3" />
</t>
```

The entire content inside the `t-call` element is also available to the sub-template through the magic variable 0. Instead of argument variables, we can define an HTML code fragment that can be used in the sub-template with `<t t-raw="0" />`. This is especially useful for building layouts and combining/nesting QWeb templates in a modular way.

Dynamic attributes using dicts and lists

We have gone through the most important QWeb directives, but there are a few more we should be aware of. Let's look at a short explanation of them.

We have seen the `t-att-NAME` and `t-attf-NAME` style dynamic tag attributes. Additionally, the fixed `t-att` directive can be used. It accepts either a key-value dictionary mapping or a pair (a two-element list).

Use the following mapping:

```
<p t-att="{'class': 'oe_bold', 'name': 'test1'}" />
```

This results in the following:

```
<p class="oe_bold" name="test1" />
```

Use the following pair:

```
<p t-att="['class', 'oe_bold']" />
```

This results in the following:

```
<p class="oe_bold" />
```

Inheritance on Kanban views

The templates used in Kanban views and reports are extended using the regular techniques used for other views, for example using XPath expressions. See `Chapter 3`, *Inheritance – Extending Existing Applications*, for more details.

A common case is to use the `<field>` elements as selectors, then add other elements before or after them. In the case of Kanban views, the same field can be declared more than once, for example, once before the templates, and again inside the templates. Here, the selector will match the first field element and won't add our modification inside the template as intended.

To work around this, we need to use XPath expressions to make sure that the field inside the template is the one matched. For example:

```
<record id="res_partner_kanban_inherit" model="ir.ui.view">
  <field name="name">Contact Kanban modification</field>
  <field name="model">res.partner</field>
  <field name="inherit_id" ref="base.res_partner_kanban_view" />
  <field name="arch" type="xml">
    <xpath expr="//t[@t-name='kanban-box']//field[@name='display_name']"
      position="before">
      <span>Name:</span>
    </xpath>
  </field>
</record>
```

In the previous example, the XPath looks for a `<field name="display_name">` element inside a `<t t-name="kanban-box">` element. This rules out the same field element outside of the `<templates>` section.

For these more complex XPath expressions, we can explore the correct syntax using some command-line tools. The `xmllint` command-line utility is probably already available on your Linux system, and has an `--xpath` option to perform queries on XML files.

Another option, providing nicer outputs, is the xpath command from the libxml-xpath-perl Debian/Ubuntu package:

```
$ sudo apt-get install libxml-xpath-perl
$ xpath -e "//record[@id='res_partner_kanban_view']" -e
"//field[@name='display_name']]" /path/to/myfile.xml
```

Custom CSS and JavaScript assets

As we have seen, Kanban views are mostly HTML and make heavy use of CSS classes. We have introduced some frequently used CSS classes provided by the standard product, but for best results, modules can also add their own CSS.

We won't go into detail here on how to write CSS code, but it's relevant to explain how a module can add its own CSS (and JavaScript) web assets. Odoo assets for the backend are declared in the assets_backend template. To add our module assets, we should extend that template. The XML file for this is usually placed inside a views/ module subdirectory.

The following is a sample XML file to add a CSS and a JavaScript file to the todo_kanban module, and it could be at todo_kanban/views/todo_kanban_assets.xml:

```xml
&amp;lt;?xml version="1.0" encoding="utf-8"?>
<odoo>
  <template id="assets_backend" inherit_id="web.assets_backend"
    name="Todo Kanban Assets" >
    <xpath expr="." position="inside">
      <link rel="stylesheet"
        href="/todo_stage/static/src/css/todo_kanban.css"/>
      <script type="text/javascript"
       src="/todo_stage/static/src/js/todo_kanban.js">
      </script>
    </xpath>
  </template>
</odoo>
```

As usual, it should be referenced in the __manifest__.py descriptor file. Notice that the assets are located inside a /static/src subdirectory. While this is not required, it is a generally used convention.

Summary

You learned about Kanban boards and how to build Kanban views to implement them. We also introduced QWeb templating and how it can be used to design Kanban cards. QWeb is also the rendering engine powering the website CMS, so it's growing in importance in the Odoo toolset. In the next chapter, we will keep using QWeb, but on the server side, to create our custom reports.

11
Reports and Server-Side QWeb

Reports are an invaluable feature for business apps. The built-in QWeb reports engine, available since version 8.0, is the default report engine. Reports are designed using QWeb templates to produce HTML documents that can then be converted to PDF form.

The Odoo built-in report engines have undergone significant changes. Before version 7.0, reports were based on the ReportLab library and used a specific markup syntax, RML. In version 7.0, the Webkit report engine was included in the core, allowing for reports to be designed using regular HTML instead. Finally, in version 8.0 this concept was taken a little further, and the QWeb templates became the main concept behind the built-in reporting engine.

This means we can conveniently leverage what we have learned about QWeb and apply it to create business reports. In this chapter, we will be adding a report to our to-do app, and will review the most important techniques to use with QWeb reports, including report computations, such as totals, translation, and print paper formats.

Before we start, we must make sure that we have installed the recommended version of the utility used to convert HTML into PDF documents.

Installing wkhtmltopdf

To correctly generate reports, the recommended version of the `wkhtmltopdf` utility needs to be installed. It's name stands for **Webkit HTML to PDF**. Odoo uses it to convert a rendered HTML page into a PDF document.

Some versions of the `wkhtmltopdf` library are known to have issues, such as not printing page headers and footers, so we need to be picky about the version to use. Since Odoo 9.0, the officially recommended version to use has been 0.12.1, and this is still true for Odoo 11.0. Version 0.12.2 is known to have some issues, and later versions are also reported to not work correctly in some cases.

 The official Odoo project keeps a wiki page with information and recommendations about `wkhtmltopdf` usage. It can be found at: `https:/ /github.com/odoo/odoo/wiki/Wkhtmltopdf`.

Unfortunately, the odds are that the packaged version provided for your host system, Debian/Ubuntu or any other, is not adequate. So, we should download and install the package recommended for our OS and CPU architecture. The download links can be found at `https://wkhtmltopdf.org`.

We should first make sure that we don't have an incorrect version already installed on our system:

```
$ wkhtmltopdf --version
```

If the preceding command reports a version other than the one we want, we should uninstall it. On a Debian/Ubuntu system, this is done with the following command:

```
$ sudo apt-get remove --purge wkhtmltopdf
```

Next, we need to download the appropriate package for our system and install it. Check the correct download link at https://wkhtmltopdf.org/downloads.html. For version 0.12.1, the latest Ubuntu build is for "trusty," Ubuntu 14.04 LTS, but it should still work with later Ubuntu versions. We installed it on a recent Ubuntu 64-bit system. The download command used was as follows:

```
$ wget "https://github.com/wkhtmltopdf/wkhtmltopdf/releases"\
"/download/0.12.1/wkhtmltox-0.12.1_linux-trusty-amd64.deb" -O \
/tmp/wkhtml.deb
```

Next, we should install it. Installing a local deb file does not automatically install dependencies, so a second step will be needed to do that and complete the installation:

```
$ sudo dpkg -i /tmp/wkhtml.deb
```

In case you find missing dependency errors, the following command may be able to fix them for you:

```
$ sudo apt-get -f install
```

Now we can check the wkhtmltopdf library is correctly installed, and confirm its version number is the one we want:

```
$ wkhtmltopdf --version
wkhtmltopdf 0.12.1 (with patched qt)
```

After this, the Odoo server start sequence won't display the **You need Wkhtmltopdf to print a pdf version of the report's** info message.

Creating business reports

We will continue using the todo_stage module that has been used in previous chapters, and add to it the files implementing the reports.

The report we are going to create will look like this:

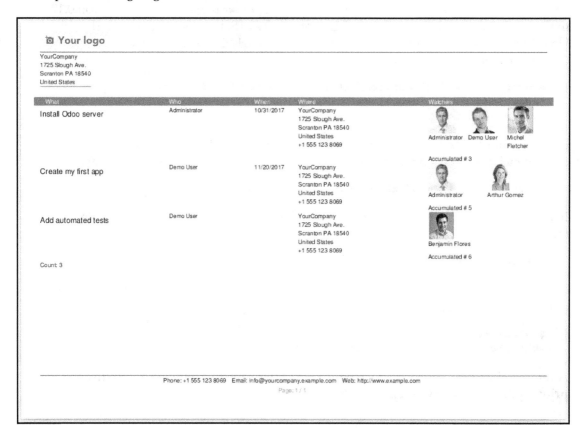

The report files should be placed inside a `/reports` module subdirectory. We will start by adding a `reports/todo_report.xml` data file. As usual when adding data files, remember to add it to the `data` key in the `__manifest__.py` file.

The `reports/todo_report.xml` file can start off by declaring the new report as follows:

```xml
<?xml version="1.0"?>
<odoo>
  <report id="action_todo_task_report"
    string="To-do Tasks"
    model="todo.task"
    report_type="qweb-pdf"
    name="todo_stage.report_todo_task_template"
  />
</odoo>
```

The `<report>` tag is a shortcut to write data to the `ir.actions.report.xml` model, which is a particular type of client action. Its data is available in the **Settings** | **Technical** | **Reports** menu option.

> During the design of the report, you might prefer to leave `report_type="qweb-html"` and change it back to a `qweb-pdf` file once finished. This will make it quicker to generate and easier to inspect the HTML result from the QWeb template.

After upgrading the module with this addition, the to-do task form view will display a **Print** button at the top, to the left of the **Actions** button, containing this option to run the report.

It won't work right now since we haven't defined the report yet. This will be a QWeb report, so it will use a QWeb template. The `name` attribute identifies the template to be used. Unlike other identifier references, the module prefix in the `name` attribute is required. We must use the full reference, `<module_name>.<identifier_name>`.

QWeb report templates

The reports will usually follow a basic skeleton, as shown in the following code. This can be added to the `reports/todo_report.xml` file, just after the `<report>` element:

```
<template id="report_todo_task_template">
  <t t-call="web.html_container">
    <t t-call="web.external_layout">
      <div class="page">

        <!-- Report header content -->
        <t t-foreach="docs" t-as="o">
          <!-- Report row content -->
        </t>
        <!-- Report footer content -->

      </div>
    </t>
  </t>
</template>
```

The most important elements here are the `t-call` directives using standard report structures. The `web.html_container` template does the basic setup to support an HTML document. The `web.external_layout` template handles the report header and footer, using the corresponding setup from the appropriate company. As an alternative, we can use the `web.internal_layout` template instead, which uses only a basic header.

 Odoo 11 introduces a few alternatives for the `external_layout` template. This selection can be done in the ;**Settings | General Settings** menu, **Business Documents | Document Template** section.

 In Odoo 11.0, the support layouts for reports moved from the `report` module to the `web` module. This means that, whereas in previous Odoo versions the `report.external_layout` or `report.internal_layout` references were used, in version 11.0 they should be replaced with `web.<...>` references.

This report skeleton is appropriate for the case of a list report, where each record is a line in the report. The report header area usually presents a title, and the report footer area usually presents the grand totals.

An alternative format is the document report, where each record is a page, such as a mailing letter. In this case, the appropriate report skeleton would be as follows:

```
<template id="report_todo_task_template">
  <t t-call="web.html_container">
    <t t-call="web.external_layout">

      <t t-foreach="docs" t-as="o">
        <div class="page">
          <!-- Report content -->
        </div>
      </t>

    </t>
  </t>
</template>
```

We will be creating a list report, so we will be using the first skeleton, rather than the previous example.

Now, we have the basic skeleton for our report in place. Notice that, since reports are just QWeb templates, inheritance can be applied, just like in the other views. QWeb templates used in reports can be extended using the regular inherited views with **XPATH** expressions.

Presenting data in reports

Unlike Kanban views, the QWeb templates in reports are rendered on the server side and use a Python QWeb implementation. We can see this as two implementations of the same specification, and there are some differences that we need to be aware of.

To start with, QWeb expressions are evaluated using Python syntax, not JavaScript. For the simplest expressions, there may be little or no difference, but more complex operations will probably be different.

The context where expressions are evaluated is also different. For reports, we have the following variables available:

- `docs` is an iterable collection with the records to print
- `doc_ids` is a list of the IDs of the records to print
- `doc_model` identifies the model of the records, `todo.task` for example
- `time` is a reference to Python's time library
- `user` is the record for the user running the report
- `res_company` is the record for the current user's company

Field values can be referenced using the `t-field` attribute, and can be complemented with the `t-options` attribute to use a specific widget to render the field content.

In previous Odoo versions, the `t-field-options` attribute was used, but in Odoo 11 it was deprecated in favor of the `t-options` attribute.

For example, assuming that `doc` represents a particular record, it would look as follows:

```
<t t-field="doc.date_deadline"
   t-options="{'widget': 'date'}" />
```

Unfortunately, the QWeb-supported widgets and their options are not covered by the official documentation. So, at the moment the only way to learn more about them is to read the corresponding code. You can find it at: https://github.com/odoo/odoo/blob/11.0/odoo/addons/base/ir/ir_qweb/fields.py.

Now, we can start designing the page content for our report. The report content is written in HTML, and makes use of Twitter Bootstrap to help design the report layout.

Here is the XML we will use to render the report content:

```
<!-- Report header content -->
<div class="row bg-primary">
  <div class="col-xs-3">
    <span class="glyphicon glyphicon-pushpin" />
    What
  </div>
  <div class="col-xs-2">Who</div>
  <div class="col-xs-1">When</div>
  <div class="col-xs-3">Where</div>
  <div class="col-xs-3">Watchers</div>
</div>

<t t-foreach="docs" t-as="o">
  <div class="row">
    <!-- Report Row Content -->
  </div>
</t>
<!-- Report footer content -->
```

The layout of the content uses the Twitter Bootstrap HTML grid system. In a nutshell, Bootstrap has a grid layout with 12 columns. A new row can be added using `<div class="row">`. Inside a row, we have cells, each spanning a certain number of columns, that should take up the 12 columns. Each cell can be defined with the row `<div class="col-xs-N">`, where N is the number of columns it spans.

 A complete reference for Bootstrap, describing these and other style elements, can be found at `http://getbootstrap.com`. Take note that the latest release is Bootstrap 4, but Odoo uses Bootstrap 3.

Here we are adding a header row with titles, and then we have a `t-foreach` loop iterating through each record and rendering a row for each one.

Since the rendering is done on the server side, records are objects and we can use dot notation to access fields from related data records. This makes it easy to follow through relational fields to access their data. Notice that this is not possible in client-side rendered QWeb views, such as web client kanban views.

This is the XML for the content of the record rows inside the `<div class="row">` element:

```
<div class="col-xs-3">
  <h4><span t-field="o.name" /></h4>
</div>
<div class="col-xs-2">
  <span t-field="o.user_id" />
</div>
<div class="col-xs-1">
  <span t-field="o.date_deadline"
        t-options="{'widget': 'date'}" />
</div>
<div class="col-xs-3">
  <div t-field="res_company.partner_id"
        t-options='{
          "widget": "contact",
          "fields": ["address", "name", "phone", "fax"],
          "no_marker": true}' />
</div>
<div class="col-xs-3">
  <!-- Render followers -->
</div>
```

As we can see, fields can be provided additional options through the `t-options` attribute containing a JSON dictionary. It is very similar to the `options` attribute used on form views, as seen in `Chapter 9`, *Backend Views – Design the User Interface*, along with an additional `widget` to render the field. An example of this is the monetary widget used previously, next to the deadline date.

A more sophisticated example is the `contact` widget, used to format addresses. We used the company address, `res_company.partner_id`, since it has some default data and we can immediately see the rendered address. But it would make more sense to use the assigned user's address, `o.user_id.partner_id`. By default, the `contact` widget displays addresses with some pictograms, such as a phone icon. The `no_marker="true"` option we used disables them.

Rendering images

The last column of our report will feature the list of followers with their avatars. We will use the `media-list` Bootstrap component and a loop through the followers to render each one of them:

```
<!-- Render followers -->
<ul class="media-list">
  <t t-foreach="o.message_follower_ids" t-as="f">

    <li t-if="f.partner_id.image_small"
        class="media-left">
      <span t-field="f.partner_id.image_small"
            t-options="{'widget': 'image'}"
            class="media-object" />
      <span class="media-body"
            t-field="f.partner_id.name" />
    </li>

  </t>
</ul>
```

Using the `image` widget takes care of generating the `<img>` tag with the proper `src` attribute, and expects a `base64` image as the value of the `t-field`.

Report totals

A common need in reports is to provide totals. This can be done using Python expressions to compute those totals.

After the closing tag of `<t t-foreach>`, we will add a final row with the totals:

```
<!-- Report footer content -->
<div class="row">
  <div class="col-xs-3">
    Count: <t t-esc="len(docs)" />
  </div>
  <div class="col-xs-2" />
  <div class="col-xs-1" />
  <div class="col-xs-3" />
  <div class="col-xs-3" />
</div>
```

The `len()` Python statement is used to count the number of elements in a collection. Similarly, totals can also be computed using `sum()` over a list of values. For example, if we had an `amount_cost` field, we could have used the following list comprehension to compute the corresponding total:

```
<t t-esc="sum([o.amount_cost for o in docs])" />
```

You can think of list comprehensions as embedded `for` loops.

Sometimes, we want to perform some computations as we go along with the report, for example, a running total, with the total up to the current record. This can be implemented with `t-set` to define an accumulating variable and then update it on each row.

To illustrate this, we can compute the accumulated number of followers. We should start by initializing the variable, just before the `t-foreach` loop on the `docs` recordset, using the following:

```
<!-- Running total: initialize variable -->
<t t-set="follower_count" t-value="0" />
```

Then, inside the loop, add the record's number of followers to the variable. We will choose to do this right after presenting the list of followers, and will also print out the current total on every line:

```
<!-- Running total: increment and present -->
<t t-set="follower_count"
   t-value="follower_count + len(o.message_follower_ids)" />
Accumulated #
<t t-esc="follower_count" />
```

Defining paper formats

At this point, our report looks good in HTML, but it doesn't print out nicely on a PDF page. We might get some better results using a landscape page. So we need to add this paper format.

At the top of the XML file, add this record:

```
<record id="paperformat_euro_landscape"
        model="report.paperformat">
  <field name="name">European A4 Landscape</field>
  <field name="default" eval="True" />
  <field name="format">A4</field>
  <field name="page_height">0</field>
```

```
    <field name="page_width">0</field>
    <field name="orientation">Landscape</field>
    <field name="margin_top">40</field>
    <field name="margin_bottom">23</field>
    <field name="margin_left">7</field>
    <field name="margin_right">7</field>
    <field name="header_line" eval="False" />
    <field name="header_spacing">35</field>
    <field name="dpi">90</field>
</record>
```

It is a copy of the European A4 format, defined in the `addons/report/data`, `report_paperformat.xml` file, but changing the orientation from portrait to landscape. The defined paper formats can be seen from the web client through the menu **Settings** | **Technical** | **Reports** | **Paper Format**.

Now, we can use it in our report. The default paper format is defined in the company setup, but we can also specify the paper format to be used by a specific report. That is done using a `paperfomat` attribute in the report action.

Let's edit the action used to open our report, to add this attribute:

```
<report  id="action_todo_task_report"
         string="To-do Tasks"
         model="todo.task"
         report_type="qweb-pdf"
         name="todo_stage.report_todo_task_template"
         paperformat="paperformat_euro_landscape"
/>
```

> The `paperformat` attribute on the `<report>` tag was added in version 9.0. For 8.0, we need to use a `<record>` element to add a report action with a `paperformat` value.

Enabling language translation in reports

To enable translations for a report, they need to be called from a template, using a `<t t-call>` element with a `t-lang` attribute.

The `t-lang` attribute should evaluate to a language code, such as `es` or `en_US`. It needs the name of the field where the language to use can be found.

One way to do this is by using the current user's language. For this, we define an outer translation report that calls a report to translate, setting the source for the language in the t-lang attribute:

```
<report id="action_todo_task_report_translated"
        string="Translated To-do Tasks"
        model="todo.task"
        report_type="qweb-pdf"
        name="todo_stage.report_todo_task_translated"
        paperformat="paperformat_euro_landscape"
/>

<template id="report_todo_task_translated">
  <t t-call="todo_stage.report_todo_task_template"
     t-lang="user.lang" />
</template>
```

In some cases, we may need each record to be rendered in a specific language. For example, we might want each sales order to be printed in the corresponding partner's preferred language. In our case, we might want each task to be rendered in the user's language, user_id.lang.

The QWeb template for this case would look something like this:

```
<template id="report_todo_task_translated">
  <t t-foreach="docs" t-as="o">
    <t t-call="todo_stage.report_todo_task_template"
       t-lang="docs.user_id.lang" >
      <t t-set="docs" t-value="o" />
    </t>
  </t>
</template>
```

Here we iterate through the records, and then for each one call the report template using the appropriate language, depending on the data in that record, in this case the user's language, user_id.lang.

Reports based on custom SQL

The report we built was based on a regular recordset. However, in some cases we need to transform or aggregate data in ways that are not easy or desirable to process in a QWeb template.

One approach for this is to write a SQL query to build the dataset we need, expose those results through a special model, and have our report work based on a recordset.

To showcase this, we will create a `reports/todo_task_report.py` file with the following code:

```python
from odoo import models, fields

class TodoReport(models.Model):
    _name = 'todo.task.report'
    _description = 'To-do Report'
    _auto = False

    name = fields.Char('Description')
    is_done = fields.Boolean('Done?')
    active = fields.Boolean('Active?')
    user_id = fields.Many2one('res.users', 'Responsible')
    date_deadline = fields.Date('Deadline')

    def init(self):
        self.env.cr.execute("""
            CREATE OR REPLACE VIEW todo_task_report AS
            (SELECT *
            FROM todo_task
            WHERE active = True)
        """)
```

For this file to be loaded, we need to add a `from . import reports` line to the module's top `__init__.py` file, and `from . import todo_task_report` to the `reports/__init__.py` file.

The `_auto` attribute is used to disable the database table's automatic creation. We provide the alternative SQL for that in the model's `init()` method. It creates a database view providing the data needed for the report. Our SQL query is quite simple, but the point is that we could use any valid SQL query for our view, possibly performing aggregations or computing additional data.

We still need to declare the model fields so that Odoo knows how to properly handle the data in each one.

Remember to also add the security access to this new model, otherwise only the admin user will be able to see it. As usual, this is done by adding a line to the `security/ir.model.access.csv`, such as:

```
access_todo_task_report,access_todo_task_report,model_todo_task_report,base
.group_user,1,0,0,0
```

It is also worth noting that this is a new, different model, and does not not have the same record access rules as the to-do task model. As is, users accessing the report will be able to see everyone's tasks. To have them see only their own to-do tasks, we would need to add the record rules that were added to the to-do tasks model, to the report model.

Next, we can add a new report based on this model, `reports/todo_task_report.xml`:

```
<odoo>

<report id="action_todo_model_report"
        string="To-do Special Report"
        model="todo.task"
        report_type="qweb-html"
        name="todo_stage.report_todo_task_special"
/>

<template id="report_todo_task_special">
  <t t-call="web.html_container">
    <t t-call="web.external_layout">
      <div class="page">

        <!-- Report page content -->
        <table class="table table-striped">
          <tr>
            <th>Title</th>
            <th>Owner</th>
            <th>Deadline</th>
          </tr>
          <t t-foreach="docs" t-as="o">
            <tr>
              <td class="col-xs-6">
                <span t-field="o.name" />
              </td>
              <td class="col-xs-3">
                <span t-field="o.user_id" />
              </td>
              <td class="col-xs-3">
                <span t-field="o.date_deadline"
                      t-options="{'widget': 'date'}" />
              </td>
```

```
          </tr>
        </t>
      </table>

    </div>
  </t>
</t>
</template>

</odoo>
```

For even more complex cases, we can use a different solution: a wizard. For this, we should create a transient model to hold the report parameters introduced by the user. This model should have related lines, generated by a model method, to be used by the report. Since they are generated by our code, we can implement whatever logic we may need.

It is strongly recommended to get inspiration from an existing, similar report. A good example is the **Leaves by Department**, in the **Leaves** menu option. The corresponding transient model definition can be found at `addons/hr_holidays/wizard/hr_holidays_summary_employees.py`.

Summary

In the previous chapter, we learned about QWeb and how to use it to design a `kanban` view. In this chapter, we learned about the QWeb report engine and the most important techniques when building reports with the QWeb templating language.

In the next chapter, we will keep working with QWeb, this time to build website pages. We will also learn to write web controllers, providing richer features for our web pages.

12
Creating Website Frontend Features

Odoo began as a backend system, but the need for a frontend interface was soon felt. The early portal features, based on the same interface as the backend, were not very flexible or mobile device-friendly.

To solve this gap, Odoo 8 introduced new website features, adding a **Content Management System** (**CMS**) to the product. This allows us to build beautiful and effective frontends without the need to integrate a third-party CMS.

Here, we will learn how to develop our own frontend-oriented addon modules, leveraging the website features provided by Odoo.

Roadmap

We will create a website page listing our To-Do Tasks, allowing us to navigate to a detailed page for each existing task. We also want to be able to propose new To-Do Tasks through a web form.

With this, we will be able to cover the essential techniques for website development: creating dynamic pages, passing parameters between pages, creating forms, and handling form data validation.

But first, we will introduce the basic website concepts with a very simple **Hello World** web page.

Our first web page

We will create an addon module for our website features, which we will call `todo_website`. To introduce the basics of Odoo web development, we will implement a simple **Hello World** web page. Imaginative, right?

As usual, we will start by creating its manifest file. Create the `todo_website/__manifest__.py` file with:

```
{
    'name': 'To-Do Website',
    'description': 'To-Do Tasks Website',
    'author': 'Daniel Reis',
    'depends': ['todo_stage'],
}
```

We are building on top of the `todo_stage` addon module so that we have all the features available added to the To-Do Tasks model throughout the book.

Notice that right now, we are not depending on the `website` addon module. While `website` provides a useful framework to build full-featured websites, the basic web capabilities are built into the core framework. Let's explore them.

Hello World!

To provide our first web page, we will add a controller object. We will begin by having this file imported with the module:

1. First, add a `todo_website/__init__.py` file with the following line:

   ```
   from . import controllers
   ```

2. Then, add a `todo_website/controllers/__init__.py` file with the following line:

   ```
   from . import main
   ```

3. Now, add the actual file for the controller, `todo_website/controllers/main.py`, with the following code:

   ```
   from odoo import http

   class Todo(http.Controller):
   ```

```
@http.route('/helloworld', auth='public')
def hello_world(self):
    return('<h1>Hello World!</h1>')
```

The `odoo.http` module provides the Odoo web-related features. Our controllers, responsible for page rendering, should be objects inheriting from the `odoo.http.Controller` class. The actual name used for the class is not important; here, we chose to use `Todo`. Another popular choice is to use `Main`.

Inside the controller class, we have methods that match URL routes. These are expected to do some processing and then return a result, which is usually the HTML page to show to the user.

The `odoo.http.route` decorator is what binds a method to a URL route. Our example uses the `/helloworld` route.

Once we install the new `todo_website` module, we can use our web browser to open `http://localhost:8069/helloworld` and you will be greeted with a **Hello World** message. In this example, the processing performed by the method is quite trivial: it just returns a text string with the HTML markup for the **Hello World** message.

 Accessing the controller with the simple URL used here, not specifying a target database, can fail if there are multiple databases available on the same Odoo instance. This can be avoided by making sure the `-d` or the `--db-filter` startup configurations are set, as advised in `Chapter 2`, *Installing and Organizing the Development Environment*.

You probably noticed that we added the `auth='public'` argument to the route. This is needed for the page to be available to non-authenticated users. If we remove it, only authenticated users can see the page. If no session is active, the login screen will be shown instead.

 The `auth='public'` parameter actually means that the request will use the special `public` user to run the web controller for any visitor that is not already authenticated. If they are, the logged in user is used, instead of `public`.

Hello World! with a QWeb template

Using Python strings to build HTML will get boring very fast. QWeb templates does a much better job. So, let's write an improved version of our **Hello World** web page, using a template.

QWeb templates are added through XML data files, and technically they are just a type of view, alongside form or tree views. They are even stored in the same technical Model, `ir.ui.view`.

As usual, data files to be loaded must be declared in the manifest file, so edit the `todo_website/__manifest__.py` file to add the key:

```
'data': ['views/todo_web.xml'],
```

Then, add the actual data file, `views/todo_web.xml`, with the following content:

```
<odoo>
  <template id="hello" name="Hello Template">
    <h1>Hello World !</h1>
  </template>
</odoo>
```

The `<template>` element is actually a shortcut for declaring a `<record>` for the `ir.ui.view` model, using `type="qweb"`.

Now, we need to have our controller method to use this template:

```
from odoo.http import request
# ...
@http.route('/hello', auth='public')
def hello(self, **kwargs):
    return request.render('todo_website.hello')
```

Template rendering is provided by `request`, through its `render()` function.

Notice that we added `**kwargs` to the method arguments. With this, any additional parameters provided by the HTTP request, such as query string or POST parameters, can be captured by the `kwargs` dictionary. This makes our method more robust, since providing unexpected parameters will not cause it to produce errors.

Extending web features

Extensibility is something we expect in all features of Odoo, and the web features are no exception. We can even extend existing controllers and templates. As an example, we will extend our **Hello World** web page so that it takes a parameter with the name to greet. For example, using the URL /hello?name=Brian would return a **Hello Brian!** greeting.

Extending is usually done from a different addon module, but it works just as well inside the same addon. To keep things concise and simple, we'll do it without creating a new addon module.

Let's add a new todo_website/controllers/extend.py file with the following code:

```
from odoo import http
from odoo.addons.todo_website.controllers.main import Todo

class TodoExtended(Todo):
    @http.route()
    def hello(self, name=None, **kwargs):
        response = super(TodoExtended, self).hello()
        response.qcontext['name'] = name
        return response
```

Here, we can see how to extend a controller.

First, we use a Python import to get a reference to the controller class we want to extend. This is different from Models, where there is a central registry accessible through the env object that can be used to reference any model class, without the need to know the particular module and file implementing it. With controllers, we don't have that, and we need to know the module and file implementing the controller we want to extend.

Next, we need to (re)define the method from the controller being extended. It needs to be decorated with at least the simple @http.route() for its route to be kept active. If used like this, with no arguments, it will preserve the routes defined by the parent class. Of course, we can also provide parameters to the route() decorator. If so, it will redefine and replace the class routes.

The extended hello() method now has a name parameter. The parameters can get their values from segments of the route URL, from query string parameters, or from POST parameters. In this case, since we are handling GET requests, not POST, the value for the name parameter will be extracted from the URL query string. An example URL could be http://localhost:8069/hello?name=Brian.

Inside the `hello()` method, we begin by calling the inherited method to get its response, and then get to modify it according to our needs. The common pattern for controller methods is to end with a statement performing the template rendering, in our case:

```
return request.render('todo_website.hello')
```

The preceding instruction generates a `http.Response` object, but the actual rendering is delayed until the end of dispatching.

This means that the inheriting method can still change the QWeb template and context to use for rendering. We could change the template modifying `response.template`, but we won't need that. Rather, we want to modify `response.qcontext` to add the `name` key to the rendering context.

For the `extend.py` code to be used by our module, don't forget to add the new Python file to `todo_website/controllers/__init__.py`:

```
from . import main
from . import extend
```

Now, we need to modify the QWeb template, so that it makes use of this additional piece of information. Add a `todo/website/views/todo_extend.xml`:

```
<odoo>
  <template id="hello_extended"
    name="Extended Hello World"
    inherit_id="todo_website.hello">
      <xpath expr="//h1" position="replace">
        <h1>
          Hello <t t-esc="name or 'Someone'" />!
        </h1>
      </xpath>
  </template>
</odoo>
```

Web page templates are XML documents, just like the other Odoo view types, and we can use `xpath` to locate elements and then manipulate them, just like we could with the other view types. The inherited template is identified in the `<template>` element by the `inherit_id` attribute.

We should not forget to declare this additional data file in our addon manifest, `todo_website/__manifest__.py`:

```
'data': [
  'views/todo_web.xml',
  'views/todo_extend.xml'],
```

After this, accessing `http://localhost:8069/hello?name=Brian` should show us a **Hello Brian!** message, as intended.

It is also possible to provide parameters through URL segments. For example, we could get the exact same result from the `http://localhost:8069/hello/Brian` URL, using this alternative implementation:

```
class TodoExtended(Todo):
    @http.route(['/hello', '/hello/<name>'])
    def hello(self, name=None, **kwargs):
        response = super(TodoExtended, self).hello()
        response.qcontext['name'] = name
        return response
```

As you can see, routes can contain placeholders that can extract values that are passed as arguments to the method. In the preceding example, the `<name>` route placeholder extracts a value passed on to the method through the `name` argument.

These placeholders can also specify a converter to implement a specific type mapping. For example, `<int:user_id>` would extract the `user_id` parameter as an integer value. Converters are a feature provided by the `werkzeug` library, used by Odoo, and most of the ones available can be found in the `werkzeug` library's documentation at `http://werkzeug.pocoo.org/docs/routing/`.

Odoo adds a specific and particularly helpful converter: extracting a Model record. For example, `@http.route('/hello/<model("res.users"):user>)` extracts the `user` parameter as a record object for the `res.users` model. The `http://localhost:8069/hello/1` URL would set the controller's `user` parameter value to the browsed record for the User with ID 1.

HelloCMS!

Let's make this even more interesting, and create our own simple CMS. For this, we can have the route expect a template name (a page) in the URL and then just render it. We could then dynamically create web pages and have them served by our CMS.

It turns out that this is quite easy to do:

```
@http.route('/hellocms/<page>', auth='public')
def hello(self, page, **kwargs):
    return http.request.render(page)
```

The `page` argument should match a Template External ID. If you open `http://localhost:8069/hellocms/todo_website.hello` in your web browser, you should see our **Hello World** web page!

In fact, the built-in `website` module provides CMS features, including a more robust implementation of this, at the `/page` endpoint route.

 In werkzeug jargon, the endpoint is an alias of the route, and is represented by its static part (without the placeholders). For example, for our simple CMS example, the endpoint is `/hellocms`.

Most of the time, we want our pages to be integrated into the Odoo website. So, from here on all of our examples will be working with the `website` addon module.

Building websites

The pages given by the previous examples are not integrated into the Odoo website; we have no page footer, menu, and so on. The Odoo `website` addon module conveniently provides all these features so that we don't have to worry about them ourselves.

To use it, we should start by installing the `website` addon module in our work instance and then add it as a dependency to our module. The `__manifest__.py` key `depends` should look like this:

```
'depends': ['todo_stage', 'website'],
```

To use the website, we also need to modify the controller and the template.

The controller can have an additional `website=True` argument on the route:

```
@http.route('/hello', auth='public', website=True)
def hello(self, **kwargs):
    return request.render('todo_website.hello')
```

This `website=True` parameter is not strictly required for integration with the website module. We can use the website layout in our template views without adding it. However, it does make a few features available that can then be used by our web controller:

- The route will automatically become multilingual and attempt to auto-detect the closest language to use from the website's installed languages. It's worth noting that this can cause rerouting and redirections.
- Any exceptions thrown by the controller will be handled by the website code, and a friendlier error page will be shown to the visitors, instead of the default error code.
- The `request.website` variable, with a browse record of the current Website record, will become available on the request.
- The `public` user for any `auth=public` route will be the Public User selected on the Website configurations in the backend. This might be relevant for matters of localization, timezones, and so on.

If none of the preceding features are relevant for the web controller, the `website=True` parameter can be omitted.

To add the website's general layout to our templates, we should wrap our QWeb/HTML with a `t-call="website.layout"` directive, like this:

```
<template id="hello" name="Hello World">
  <t t-call="website.layout">
    <h1>Hello World!</h1>
  </t>
</template>
```

The `t-call` runs the XML inside the `website.layout` template and passes the full content inside the tag to it. The `website.layout` is designed to render the full website page, with menus, headers, footers, and so on, and place that content in the appropriate main area.

With this, the **Hello World!** example we used before should now be shown inside an Odoo website page.

Adding CSS and JavaScript assets

Our website pages might need some additional CSS or JavaScript assets. This aspect of the web pages is managed by the website, so we need a way to tell it to also use our files.

We will add some CSS to add a simple strikeout effect for completed tasks. For that, create the `todo_website/static/src/css/index.css` file with the following content:

```css
.todo-app-done {
    text-decoration: line-through;
}
```

Next, we need to have it included in the website pages. This is done by adding them in the `website.assets_frontend` template, responsible for loading website-specific assets. Edit the `todo_website/views/todo_templates.xml` data file to extend that template:

```xml
<odoo>
  <template id="assets_frontend"
    name="todo_website_assets"
    inherit_id="website.assets_frontend">
      <xpath expr="." position="inside">
        <link rel="stylesheet" type="text/css"
              href="/todo_website/static/src/css/index.css"/>
      </xpath>
  </template>
</odoo>
```

We will soon be using this new `todo-app-done` style class. Of course, JavaScript assets can also be added using a similar approach.

The to-do list controller

Now that we have gone through the basics, let's work on our Todo Task list. We want to have a `/todos` URL showing us a web page with a list of Todo Tasks.

For that, we need a controller method to prepare the data to present, and a QWeb template to present it to the user.

Edit the `todo_website/controllers/main.py` file to add this method:

```python
#class Todo(http.Controller):
#...
    @http.route('/todos', auth='user', website=True)
    def index(self, **kwargs):
        TodoTask = request.env['todo.task']
        tasks = TodoTask.search([])
        return request.render(
            'todo_website.index',
            {'tasks': tasks})
```

The controller retrieves the data to be used and makes it available to the rendered template. In this case, the controller requires an authenticated session, since the route has the auth='user' attribute. This is the default behavior, and it's a good practice to explicitly state that a user session is required. A user having logged in, the Todo Task search() statement will run in that context and return the appropriate records.

For controllers that don't require an authenticated access, the data that can be read is very limited. In those cases, we will often need to run part of the code in an elevated access context. For this, we can use the sudo() Model method; it changes the security context to the **Admin** user, removing most restrictions.

While this gives us power, it also brings security risks and should be used with care. Particular attention should be given to the validation of input parameters, and to the actions performed with the elevated access made. It is a good idea to keep the use of the sudo() recordset strictly limited to the minimum operations needed.

Going back to our code, it ends with the request.render() method. As before, we pass the identifier for the QWeb template to render, and additionally a dictionary with the context available for template evaluation. In this case, we make the tasks variable available in the template, containing the recordset with the To-Do Tasks to render.

The to-do list template

The QWeb template is added using a data file. We can use the existing todo_website/views/todo_templates.xml data file for that, and add the following:

```
<template id="index" name="Todo List">
  <t t-call="website.layout">
    <div id="wrap" class="container">
      <h1>Todo Tasks</h1>

      <!-- List of Tasks -->
      <t t-foreach="tasks" t-as="task">
        <div class="row">
          <input type="checkbox" disabled="True"
            t-att-checked=" 'checked' if task.is_done else None" />
          <a t-attf-href="/todo/{{slug(task)}}">
            <span t-field="task.name"
              t-att-class="'todo-app-done' if task.is_done
                          else ''" />
          </a>
        </div>
      </t>
```

```
            <!-- Add a new Task -->
            <div class="row">
              <a href="/todo/add" class="btn btn-primary btn-lg">
                  Add
              </a>
            </div>

          </div>
        </t>
      </template>
```

The preceding code uses the `t-foreach` directive to iterate through the task recordset.

We have a checkbox input, and want it to be checked if the task is done. In HTML, a checkbox is checked depending on it having or not having a `checked` attribute. For this, we use the `t-att-NAME` directive to dynamically render the `checked` attribute depending on an expression. When the the expression evaluates to `None` (or any other false value), QWeb will omit the attribute, which is convenient in this case.

When rendering the task name, the `t-attf` directive is used to dynamically create the URL to open the detail form for each specific task. We used the special function `slug()` to generate a human-readable URL for each record. The link won't work for now, since we haven't created the corresponding controller yet.

On each task, we also use the `t-att` directive to set the `todo-app-done` style only for the tasks that are done.

Finally, we have an **Add** button to open a page with a form to create a new To-Do Task. We implement that in a later section, and with it introduce web form handling.

The To-Do Task detail page

Each item in the Todo list has a link to the corresponding detail page. We should implement a controller for those links and a QWeb template for their presentation. At this point, this should be a straightforward exercise.

In the `todo_website/controllers/main.py` file, add the method:

```
#class Todo(http.Controller):
#...
    @http.route('/todo/<model("todo.task"):task>',
                auth="user",  # default, but made explicit here
                website=True)
    def detail(self, task, **kwargs):
```

```
return http.request.render(
    'todo_website.detail',
    {'task': task})
```

Notice that the route is using a placeholder with the `model("todo.task")` converter, which will be mapped to the method's `task` argument. It captures a Task identifier from the URL, either a simple ID number or a slug representation, and converts it into the corresponding browse record object.

For the QWeb template, we should add the following code to the `todo_website/views/todo_web.xml` data file:

```
<template id="detail" name="Todo Task Detail">
<t t-call="website.layout">
  <div id="wrap" class="container">
    <h1 t-field="task.name" />
    <p>Responsible: <span t-field="task.user_id" /></p>
    <p>Deadline: <span t-field="task.date_deadline" /></p>
  </div>
</t>
</template>
```

Noteworthy here is the usage of the `<t t-field>` element. It handles the proper representation of the field value, just like in the backend. It correctly presents date values and many-to-one values, for example.

Website forms

Forms are a common feature found on websites. We already have all the tools needed to implement one: a QWeb template can provide the HTML for the form, the corresponding submit action can be a URL, processed by a controller that can run all the validation logic, and it can finally store the data in the proper model.

But for non-trivial forms, this can be a demanding task. It's not that simple to perform all the necessary validations and provide feedback to the user about what is wrong.

Since this is a common need, a `website_form` addon is available to aid us with this. Let's see how to use it.

Looking back at the **Add** button in the Todo Task list, we can see that it opens the `/todo/add` URL. This should present a form to submit a new Todo Task, and the fields available will be the task name, a person (user) responsible for the task, and a file attachment.

We should start by adding the `website_form` dependency to our addon module. We can replace `website`, since keeping it explicitly would be redundant. In the `todo_website/__manifest__.py` file, edit the `depends` keyword to:

```
'depends': ['todo_kanban', 'website_form'],
```

Now, we will add the page with the form.

The form page

We can start by implementing the controller method to support the form rendering, in the `todo_website/controllers/main.py` file:

```python
@http.route('/todo/add', auth="user", website=True)
def add(self, **kwargs):
    users = request.env['res.users'].search([])
    return request.render(
        'todo_website.add', {'users': users})
```

This is a simple controller, rendering the `todo_website.add` template, and provides it with a list of users so that they can be used to build a selection box.

The corresponding QWeb template can be added to the `todo_website/views/todo_web.xml` data file:

```xml
<template id="add" name="Add Todo Task">
  <t t-call="website.layout">
    <t t-set="additional_title">Add Todo</t>
    <div id="wrap" class="container">
      <div class="row">
        <section id="forms">

          <form method="post"
            class="s_website_form
                   container-fluid form-horizontal"
            action="/website_form/"
            data-model_name="todo.task"
            data-success_page="/todos"
            enctype="multipart/form-data" >

          <!-- Form fields will go here! -->

            <!-- Submit button -->
            <div class="form-group">
              <div class="col-md-offset-3 col-md-7
```

```
                  col-sm-offset-4 col-sm-8">
                <a class="o_website_form_send
                          btn btn-primary btn-lg">
                  Save
                </a>
                <span id="o_website_form_result"></span>
              </div>
            </div>
          </form>
        </section>
      </div> <!-- rows -->
    </div> <!-- container -->
  </t> <!-- website.layout -->
</template>
```

As expected, we can find the Odoo-specific `<t t-call="website.layout">` element, responsible for inserting the template inside the website layout. We also use `<t t-set="additional_title">`, which sets an additional title to the page. This is a standard feature of the website layout.

For the content, most of what we can see in this template can be found on a typical Bootstrap CSS form, but we also have a few attributes and CSS classes that are specific to the website forms. We marked them in bold in the code so that it's easier for you to identify them.

The CSS classes are needed for the JavaScript code to correctly perform the form handling logic. Then, we have a few specific attributes on the `<form>` element:

- `action` is an HTML standard form attribute, but must have the `"/website_form/"` value. The trailing slash is required.
- `data-model_name` identifies the model to write to, and will be passed to the `/website_form` controller.
- `data-success_page` is the URL to redirect to after a successful form submission. In this case, we will be sent back to the `/todos` list.

We won't need to provide our own controller method to handle the form submission. The generic `/website_form` route will do that for us. It takes all the information it needs from the form, including the specific attributes just described, performs essential validations on the input data, and then creates a new record on the target model.

For advanced use cases, we can force a custom controller method to be used. For that, we should add a `data-force_action` attribute to the `<form>` element, with the keyword for the target controller to use. For example, `data-force_action="todo-custom"` would have the form submission call the `/website_form/todo-custom` URL. We should then provide a controller method attached to that route, but here we won't need a custom controller and will stick to the generic handling provided by the `website_form` addon module.

We still need to finish our form, adding the fields to get inputs from the user. Inside the `<form>` element, add:

```html
<!-- Description text, required field: -->
<div class="form-group form-field">
  <div class="col-md-3 col-sm-4 text-right">
    <label class="control-label" for="name">To do*</label>
  </div>
  <div class="col-md-7 col-sm-8">
    <input name="name" type="text" required="True"
      class="o_website_form_input form-control" />
  </div>
</div>

<!-- Attachment file upload field: -->
<div class="form-group form-field">
  <div class="col-md-3 col-sm-4 text-right">
    <label class="control-label" for="file_upload">
      Attach file
    </label>
  </div>
  <div class="col-md-7 col-sm-8">
    <input name="file_upload" type="file"
      class="o_website_form_input form-control" />
  </div>
</div>
```

Here, we are adding two fields, a regular text field for the description and a file field to upload an attachment. All the markup can be found in regular Bootstrap forms, except for the `o_website_form_input` class, which is needed for the website form logic to prepare the data to submit.

The user selection list is not that different, except that we need to explicitly build the list of selection options, using a `t-foreach` QWeb directive. We are able to do this because the controller makes that recordset available to the template under the `users` variable:

```
<!-- User selection field: -->
<div class="form-group form-field">
  <div class="col-md-3 col-sm-4 text-right">
    <label class="control-label" for="user_id">
      For Person
    </label>
  </div>
  <div class="col-md-7 col-sm-8">
    <select name="user_id"
      class="o_website_from_input form-control" >
      <t t-foreach="users" t-as="user">
        <option t-att-value="user.id">
          <t t-esc="user.name" />
        </option>
      </t>
    </select>
  </div>
</div>
```

Our form still won't work until we do some additional security setup.

Accessing the security and menu item

Since this generic form handling is quite open, and processes untrusted data sent by the client, the creation of new records is done in `sudo` mode (with the same powers as the Admin), which means that potentially anyone can insert records into the database.

For security reasons, we need some server-side setup on what the client is allowed to do. Because of this, Models accepting `website_form` data must be whitelisted, as well as the specific list of fields that can be written on.

Still, the `/website_form/<string:model_name>` route is public and will happily insert data into any model that has been whitelisted, unless you implement some extra security checks. This can be done using the `website_form_input_filter()` method, which is shown in the following section.

To add fields to this whitelist, a helper function is provided and we can use it from an XML data file. We should create the `todo_website/data/config_data.xml` file with:

```xml
<?xml version="1.0" encoding="utf-8"?>
<odoo>

    <record id="todo_app.model_todo_task" model="ir.model">
      <field name="website_form_access">True</field>
      <field name="website_form_label">Add a To-Do</field>
    </record>

    <function model="ir.model.fields"
      name="formbuilder_whitelist">
      <value>todo.task</value>
      <value eval="[
        'name',
        'user_id',
        'date_deadline',
      ]"/>
    </function>

</odoo>
```

For a model to be able to be used by forms, we must do two things: enable a flag on the model and whitelist the fields that can be used. These are the two actions being done in the preceding data file.

Don't forget that for our addon module to know about this data file, it needs to be added to the `data` key of the manifest file.

It would also be nice for our Todo page to be available from the website menu. Let's add that:

```xml
<record id="menu_todo" model="website.menu">
  <field name="name">Todo</field>
  <field name="url">/todos</field>
  <field name="parent_id" ref="website.main_menu"/>
  <field name="sequence" type="int">50</field>
</record>
```

As you can see, to add a website menu item, we just need to create a record in the `website.menu` model with a name, URL, and the identifier of the parent menu item. The top level of this menu has as parent the `website.main_menu` item.

Adding custom logic

Website forms allow us to plug in our own validations and computations to form processing. This is done by implementing a `website_form_input_filter()` method with the logic on the target model. This method should expect a `values` argument, containing a dictionary, performing validations, and even modifying it, and then return the final `values` dictionary to be used.

We will make use of it to implement two features:

- Removing any leading and trailing spaces from the task title
- Ensuring that the task title is at least three characters long

Add the `todo_website/models/todo_task.py` file containing the following code:

```
from odoo import api, models
from odoo.exceptions import import ValidationError

class TodoTask(models.Model):
    _inherit = 'todo.task'

    @api.model
    def website_form_input_filter(self, request, values):
        if values.get('name'):
            # Modify values
            values['name'] = values['name'].strip()
            # Validate values
            if len(values['name']) < 3:
                raise ValidationError(
                    'Text must be at least 3 characters long')
        return values
```

The `website_form_input_filter` method actually expects two parameters: the `request` object and the `values` dictionary. Errors preventing form submission should raise a `ValidationError` exception.

Most of the time, this extension point for forms should allow us to avoid custom form submission handlers.

As usual, we must make this new file Python imported by adding `from . import models` in the `todo_website/__init__.py` file, and then adding the `todo_website/models/__init__.py` file containing a `from . import todo_task` line.

Summary

You should now have a good understanding of the essentials of website features. We have seen how to use web controllers and QWeb templates to render dynamic web pages. We then learned how to use the website addon and create our own pages for it. Finally, we introduced the website forms addon that helped us create a web form. These should provide us with the core skills needed to create website features.

Now that we have seen the essentials of developing the main Odoo components, its time to learn more about how to debug our Odoo programs and how to add automated tests to them. This is what we will discuss in the following chapter.

13
Debugging and Automated Tests

A good part of a developer's work consists of testing and debugging code. Automated tests are an inestimable tool to build and maintain robust software. In this chapter, we will learn how to add automated tests to our addon modules to make them more robust. Server-side debugging techniques are also presented to help developers inspect and understand what is happening in their code.

Unit tests

Automated tests are generally accepted as a best practice in software. They not only help us ensure our code is correctly implemented, but more importantly they provide a safety net for future code changes or rewrites.

In the case of dynamic programming languages, such as Python, since there is no compilation step, syntax errors can go unnoticed. This makes it even more important to have unit tests going through as many lines of code as possible.

The two goals described can provide a guiding light when writing tests. The first goal for your tests should be to provide good test coverage, designing test cases that go through all your lines of code.

This alone will usually make good progress on the second goal – to show the functional correctness of the code, since after this we will surely have a great starting point to build additional test cases for non-obvious use cases.

Adding unit tests

Python tests are added to addon modules by using a `tests/` subdirectory. The test runner will automatically discover tests in the subdirectories with that particular name.

To add tests for the wizard logic created in the `todo_stage` addon module, we can start by creating the `tests/test_wizard.py` file. As usual, we will also need to add the `tests/__init__.py` file:

```
from . import test_wizard
```

This would be the basic skeleton for `tests/test_wizard.py`:

```
from odoo.tests.common import TransactionCase

class TestWizard(TransactionCase):

    def setUp(self, *args, **kwargs):
        super(TestWizard, self).setUp(*args, **kwargs)
        # Add test setup code here...

    def test_populate_tasks(self):
        """Populate tasks button should add two tasks"""
        # Add test code
```

Odoo provides a few classes to use for tests. The `TransactionCase` tests uses a different transaction for each test, which is automatically rolled back at the end. We can also use `SingleTransactionCase`, which runs all tests in a single transaction and is rolled back only at the end of the last test. This can be useful when you want the final state of each test to be the initial state for the following test.

The `setUp()` method is where we prepare data and variables to be used. We will usually store them as class attributes, so that they are available to be used in the test methods.

Tests should then be implemented as class methods, like `test_populate_tasks()`. The test cases method names must begin with a `test_` prefix. They are automatically discovered, and this prefix is what identifies the methods implementing test cases. Methods will be run in the order of the test function names.

When using the `TransactionCase` class, a rollback will be done at the end of each. The method's `docstring` is shown when the tests are run, and should provide a short description for it.

These test classes are wrappers around `unittest` test cases, part of the Python standard library. For more details on this, you may refer to the official documentation at `https://docs.python.org/3/library/unittest.html`.

Setting up tests

We should begin by preparing the data to be used in the tests.

It is convenient to perform the test actions under a specific user in order to also test that access control is properly configured. This is achieved using the `sudo()` model method. Recordsets carry that information with them, so after being created while using `sudo()`, later operations in the same recordset will be performed using that same context.

This is the code for the `setUp` method, and a few additional import statements that are also needed:

```
from datetime import date
from odoo.tests.common import TransactionCase
from odoo import fields

class TestWizard(TransactionCase):

    def setUp(self, *args, **kwargs):
        super(TestWizard, self).setUp(*args, **kwargs)
        # Close any open Todo tasks
        self.env['todo.task']\
            .search([('is_done', '=', False)])\
            .write({'is_done': True})
        # Demo user will be used to run tests
        demo_user = self.env.ref('base.user_demo')
        Todo = self.env['todo.task'].sudo(demo_user)
        # Create two Todo tasks to use in tests
        t0 = date.today()
        self.todo1 = Todo.create({
            'name': 'Todo1',
            'user_id': demo_user.id,
            'date_deadline': fields.Date.to_string(t0),
            })
        self.todo2 = Todo.create({
            'name': 'Todo2',
```

```
            'user_id': demo_user.id,
            })
    # Create Wizard instance to use in tests
    Wizard = self.env['todo.wizard'].sudo(demo_user)
    self.wizard = Wizard\
        .with_context(active_ids=None)\
        .create({})
```

To test our wizard, we want to have exactly two open Todos. So, we start by closing any existing Todos so that they don't get in the way of our tests, and using the Demo user create two new Todos for tests. We finally create a new instance of our wizard using the Demo user and assign it to `self.wizard` so that is available to the test methods.

Writing test cases

Now, let's expand the `test_populate_tasks()` method seen in our initial skeleton. The simplest tests run some code from the tested object, get a result, and then use an assert statement to compare it with an expected result.

The `test_populate_tasks()` method will test the `do_populate_tasks()` method of the Todo wizard. Since our setup made sure we have two open Todos, after running it we expect the wizard's `task_ids` to be referencing these two records:

```
# class TestWizard(TransactionCase):
# ...
    def test_populate_tasks(self):
        """Populate Tasks button should add two tasks"""
        self.wizard.do_populate_tasks()
        count = len(self.wizard.task_ids)
        self.assertEqual(
            count, 2,
            'Expected 2 populated tasks')
```

The `docstring`, at the first line of the method definition, is useful to describe the test and is printed out when running it.

The check verifying whether the test succeeded or failed is the `self.assertEqual` statement. It compares the `count` variable with the expected result, 2. The last parameter provides a more informative message when the test fails. It is optional, but recommended.

The `assertEqual` function is just one of the assert methods available. We should use the assert function appropriately for each case, since this will be more helpful in understanding the cause of failing tests. For example, instead of comparing the length of `task_ids`, one could have prepared a recordset with the two expected tasks, and then used:

```
self.assertItemsEqual(
    self.wizard.task_ids, expected_tasks,
    'Incorrect set of populated tasks')
```

This would give the best output in case of failure, with a full comparison of the expected tasks versus the actual tasks.

 The `unittest` documentation provides a good reference for all the methods, and is available at `https://docs.python.org/3/library/unittest.html#test-cases`.

To add a new test case, add another method to the class with its implementation. Next, we will test the `do_mass_update()` wizard method. This is the method doing the work when we click on the wizard's **OK** button:

```
def test_mass_change(self):
    """Mass change deadline date"""
    self.wizard.do_populate_tasks()
    self.wizard.new_deadline = self.todo1.date_deadline
    self.wizard.do_mass_update()
    self.assertEqual(
        self.todo1.date_deadline,
        self.todo2.date_deadline)
```

We start by running `do_populate_tasks()` again. Remember that with `TransactionCase` tests, a rollback is done at the end of each test. So, the operations done in the previous test were reverted, and we need to again populate the wizard's Todo Task list. Next, we simulate the user, filling in the new deadline field and performing the mass update. At the end, we check whether both Todo Tasks ended up with the same date.

Testing exceptions

Sometimes, we need our tests to check whether an exception was generated. A common case is when testing whether some validations are being done properly.

In our example, the `test_count()` method uses a `Warning` exception as a way to give information to the user. To check whether an exception is raised, we place the corresponding code inside a `with self.assertRaises()` block.

We first need to import the `Warning` exception at the top of the file:

```
from odoo.exceptions import Warning
```

Then, add another method with a test case to the test class:

```
def test_count(self):
    """Test count button"""
    with self.assertRaises(Warning) as e:
        self.wizard.do_count_tasks()
    self.assertIn(' 2 ', str(e.exception))
```

If the `do_count_tasks()` method does not raise an exception, the check will fail. If it does raise that exception, the check succeeds and the exception raised is stored in the `e` variable.

We use that to further inspect it. The exception message contains the number of tasks counted, which we expect to be two. In the final statement, we use `assertIn` to check that the exception text contains the ` 2 ` string.

Running tests

The tests are written, so now it's time to run them. For that, we just need to add the `--test-enable` option to the Odoo server start command, while installing or upgrading (`-i` or `-u`) the addon module.

The command will look like this:

```
$ ./odoo-bin -d todo --test-enable -u todo_stage --stop-after-init
```

Only the modules installed or upgraded will be tested. If some dependencies need to be installed, their tests will run too. If you want to avoid this, you can install the module you wish to test the usual way, and then run the tests while performing an upgrade (`-u`) of the module to test.

About YAML tests

Odoo also supports tests described using YAML data files. Originally, all tests used YAML, and only later were `unittest`-based tests introduced. While both are supported, and many core addons still include YAML tests, the official documentation currently does not mention the YAML tests. The last documentation on it is available at `https://doc.odoo.com/v6.0/contribute/15_guidelines/coding_guidelines_testing/`.

Developers with a Python background will probably feel more at home with `unittest`, since it is a standard Python feature, while YAML tests are Odoo-specific. Clearly, the trend is to prefer `unittest` over YAML.

 Consider YAML tests as an undocumented feature that might be removed without warning in a future Odoo version.

For these reasons, we will not have in-depth coverage of YAML tests. It might still be useful to have some basic understanding of how they work.

YAML tests are data files, similar to CSV and XML. In fact, the YAML format was intended to be a more compact data format that can be used in place of XML. Unlike Python tests, where tests must be in a `test/` subdirectory, the YAML test files can be anywhere inside the addon module, but frequently they will be inside a `tests/` or `test/` subdirectory.

While Python tests are automatically discovered, YAML tests must be declared in the `__manifest__.py` manifest file. This is done with the `test` key, similar to the `data` key we already know.

In Odoo 10, YAML tests are not used anymore, but here is an example from the `02_order_to_invoice.yml` file in the Odoo 9.0 `point_of_sale` addon module:

```
  -
    I click on the "Make Payment" wizard to pay the PoS order
  -
    !record {model: pos.make.payment, id: pos_make_payment_2, context:
'{"active_id": ref("pos_order_pos1"), "active_ids":
[ref("pos_order_pos1")]}' }:
      amount: !eval >
          (450*2 + 300*3*1.05)*0.95
  -
    I click on the validate button to register the payment.
  -
    !python {model: pos.make.payment}: |
```

```
        self.check(cr, uid, [ref('pos_make_payment_2')], context={'active_id':
ref('pos_order_pos1')} )
```

The lines that begin with a ! are YAML tags, equivalent to the tag elements we find in XML files. In the preceding code, we can see a !record tag, equivalent to the XML <record>, and a !python tag, which allows us to run Python code on a model, pos.make.payment, in the example.

As you can see, YAML tests use a Odoo-specific syntax that needs to be learned. In comparison, Python tests use the existing unittest framework, only adding Odoo-specific wrapper classes such as TransactionCase.

Development tools

There are a few techniques developers should learn to aid them in their work. Early in this book, we introduced the **Developer Mode** user interface. We also have a server option available, providing some developer-friendly features. We will be describing this in more detail next. After that, we will discuss another relevant topic for developers: how to debug server-side code.

Server development options

The Odoo server provides the --dev option to enable some developer features to speed up our development cycle, such as:

- Entering the debugger when an exception is found in an addon module
- Reloading Python code automatically once a Python file is saved, avoiding a manual server restart
- Reading view definitions directly from XML files, avoiding manual module upgrades

The --dev option accepts a comma-separated list of options, and the all option will be suitable most of the time. We can also specify the debugger we prefer to use. By default, the Python debugger, pdb, is used. Some people might prefer to install and use alternative debuggers. ipdb and pudb are also supported here.

Until Odoo 9, instead of `--dev=all`, the `--debug` option was available, allowing you to open the debugger on an addon module exception.

When working on Python code, the server needs to be restarted every time the code is changed so that it is reloaded. The `--dev` command-line option deals with that reloading. When the server detects that a Python file is changed, it automatically repeats the server loading sequence, making the code change immediately effective.

To use it, just add the `--dev=all` option to the server command:

```
$ ./odoo-bin -d todo --dev=all
```

For this to work, the `watchdog` Python package is required. It can be installed using `pip`:

```
$ pip install watchdog
```

 Note that this is useful only for Python code changes and view architectures in XML files. For other changes, such as model data structure, a module upgrade is needed, and reloading it is not enough.

Debugging

We all know that a good part of a developer's work is to debug code. To do this, we often make use of a code editor that can set breakpoints and run our program step by step.

If you're using Microsoft Windows as your development workstation, setting up an environment capable of running Odoo code from a source is a nontrivial task. Also the fact that Odoo is a server that waits for client calls, and only then acts on them, makes it quite different to debug compared to client-side programs.

The Python debugger

While it may look a little intimidating for newcomers, the most pragmatic approach to debug Odoo is to use the Python integrated debugger, `pdb`. We will also introduce extensions to it that provide a richer user interface, similar to what sophisticated IDEs usually provide.

To use the debugger, the best approach is to insert a breakpoint into the code we want to inspect, typically a model method. This is done by inserting the following line in the desired place:

```
import pdb; pdb.set_trace()
```

Now, restart the server so that the modified code is loaded. As soon as the program execution reaches that line, a (pdb) Python prompt will be shown in the Terminal window where the server is running, waiting for our input.

This prompt works as a Python shell, where you can run any expression or command in the current execution context. This means that the current variables can be inspected and even modified. These are the most important shortcut commands available:

- h (help) displays a summary of the pdb commands available
- p (print) evaluates and prints an expression
- pp (pretty print) is useful to print data structures such as dictionaries or lists
- l (list) lists the code around the instruction to be executed next
- n (next) steps over to the next instruction
- s (step) steps into the current instruction
- c (continue) continues execution normally
- u (up) moves up in the execution stack
- d (down) moves down in the execution stack
- bt (backtrace) shows the current execution stack

If the dev=all option is used to start the servers, when an exception is raised, the server enters a *post mortem* mode at the corresponding line. This is a pdb prompt, such as the one described earlier, allowing us to inspect the program state at the moment where the error was found.

A sample debugging session

Let's see what a simple debugging session looks like. We can start by adding a debugger breakpoint in the first line of the do_populate_tasks wizard method:

```
def do_populate_tasks(self):
    import pdb; pdb.set_trace()
    self.ensure_one()
    # ...
```

Now, restart the server, open a **To-do Tasks Wizard** form, and click on the **Get All** button. This will trigger the `do_populate_tasks` wizard method on the server, and the web client will stay in a **Loading...** state, waiting for the server's response. Looking at the Terminal window where the server is running, you will see something similar to this:

```
> /home/daniel/odoo-dev/custom-
addons/todo_stage/models/todo_wizard_model.py(54)do_populate_tasks()
-> self.ensure_one()
(Pdb)
```

This is the `pdb` debugger prompt, and the two first lines give you information about where you are in the Python code execution. The first line states the file, line number, and function name you are in, and the second line is the next line of code to be run.

During a debug session, server log messages can creep in. These won't harm our debugging, but they can disturb us. We can avoid that by reducing the verbosity of the log messages. Most of the time, these log messages will be from the `werkzeug` module. We can silence them using the `--log-handler=werkzeug:CRITICAL` option. If this is not enough, we can lower the general log level using `--log-level=warn`. Another option is to just enable the `--logfile=/path/to/log` option so that the log messages are redirected from the standard output to a disk file.

If we type h now, we will see a quick reference of the commands available. Typing l shows the current line of code and the surrounding lines of code.

Typing n will run the current line of code and move on to the next. If we just press *Enter*, the previous command will be repeated. Do that three times and we should be at the method's return statement.

We can inspect the content on any variable, such as the `open_tasks` used in this method, and typing p `open_tasks` or `print open_tasks` will show the representation of that variable. Any Python expressions are allowed, even variable assignments. For example, to show a friendlier list with the Task names, we could use:

```
(pdb) p open_tasks.mapped('name')
```

Running the return line, using n once more, we will be shown the returning values of the function. Something like this will appear:

```
--Return--
> /home/daniel/odoo-dev/custom-
addons/todo_stage/models/todo_wizard_model.py(59)do_populate_tasks()->{'res
_id': 14, 'res_model': 'todo.wizard', 'target': 'new', 'type':
'ir.actions.act_window', ...}
-> return self._reopen_form()
```

The debugging session will continue on the caller's lines of code, but we can finish it and continue normal execution by typing c.

Alternative Python debuggers

While pdb has the advantage of being available out of the box, it can be quite terse, and a few more comfortable options exist.

The Iron Python debugger, ipdb, is a popular choice that uses the same commands as pdb, but adds improvements such as tab completion and syntax highlighting for more comfortable use. It can be installed with:

```
$ sudo pip install ipdb
```

And a breakpoint is added with the following line:

```
import ipdb; ipdb.set_trace()
```

Another alternative debugger is pudb. It also supports the same commands as pdb and works in text-only Terminals, but uses a graphical display similar to what you can find in an IDE debugger. Useful information, such as the variables in the current context and their values, is readily available on the screen in their own windows:

```
PuDB 2017.1.4 - ?:help  n:next  s:step into  b:breakpoint  !:python command line
 38 @api.multi                                          Variables:
 39 def _reopen_form(self):                             pudb: <module 'pudb' from
 40     self.ensure_one()                                '/usr/local/lib/python3.
 41     action = {                                         5/dist-packages/pudb/__i
 42         'type': 'ir.actions.act_window',             nit__.py'>
 43         'res_model': self._name,                     self: todo.wizard(16,)
 44         'res_id': self.id,
 45         'view_type': 'form',                         Stack:
 46         'view_mode': 'form',                         >> do_populate_tasks [todo
 47         'target': 'new',                                call_kw_multi  api.py:68
 48     }                                                   call_kw  api.py:689
 49     return action                                      call_kw  [DataSet] main
 50                                                         call_button [DataSet] m
 51 @api.multi                                             response_wrap  http.py:5
 52 def do_populate_tasks(self):                           call    [EndPoint] htt
 53     import pudb; pudb.set_trace()                    Breakpoints:
>  54     self.ensure_one()
 55     Task = self.env['todo.task']
Command line: [Ctrl-X]

>>>                                            < Clear >
```

It can be installed either through the system package manager or through `pip`, as shown here:

```
$ sudo apt-get install python-pudb  # using Debian OS packages
$ sudo pip install pudb  # or using pip, possibly in a virtualenv
```

Adding a `pudb` breakpoint is done just the way you would expect it to be:

```
import pudb; pudb.set_trace()
```

But a shorter and easier-to-remember alternative is available:

```
import pudb; pu.db
```

Printing messages and logging

Sometimes, we just need to inspect the values of some variables or check whether some code blocks are being executed. A Python `print` statement can do the job perfectly without stopping the execution flow. As we are running the server in a Terminal window, the printed text will be shown in the standard output, but it won't be stored to the server log if it's being written to a file.

The `print` statement is only being used as a development aid, and should not make its way to final code, ready to be deployed. If you suspect that you need more details about the code execution, use debug level log messages instead.

Adding debug level log messages at sensitive points of our code allow us to investigate issues in a deployed instance. We would just need to elevate that server logging level to debug and then inspect the log files.

Killing running processes

There are also a few tricks that allow us to inspect a running Odoo process.

For that, we first need to find the corresponding process ID (PID). To find the PID, run another Terminal window and type:

```
$ ps ax | grep odoo-bin
```

The first column in the output is the PID for that process. Take a note of the PID for the process to inspect, since we will need it next.

Now, we want to send a signal to the process. The command used to do that is `kill`. By default, it sends a signal to terminate a process, but it can also send other friendlier signals.

Knowing the PID for our running Odoo server process, we can print the traces of the code currently being executed using:

```
$ kill -3 <PID>
```

If we look at the Terminal window or log file where the server output is being written, we will see the information on several threads being run, as well as detailed stack traces on what line of code they are running.

Summary

Automated tests are a valuable practice, both for business applications in general, and for ensuring code robustness in a dynamic programming language such as Python.

We learned the basic principles of how to add and run tests for an addon module. We also discussed some techniques to help us debug our code.

Next, in our final chapter, we will learn about how to deploy our Odoo server for production use.

14
Deploying and Maintaining Production Instances

In this chapter, you will learn how to prepare your Odoo server for use in a production environment.

There are many possible strategies and tools that can be used to deploy and manage an Odoo production server. We will guide you through one way of doing it.

This is the server setup checklist that we will follow:

- Installing dependencies and a dedicated user to run the server
- Installing Odoo from the source
- Setting up the Odoo configuration file
- Setting up multiprocessing workers
- Setting up the Odoo system service
- Setting up a reverse proxy with SSL support

Let's get started.

Available prebuilt packages

Odoo has a Debian/Ubuntu package available for installation. Using it, you get a working server process that automatically starts on system boot. This installation process is straightforward, and you can find all you need at `https://nightly.odoo.com`. You can also find the `rpm` builds for CentOS and the `.exe` installers there.

While this is an easy and convenient way to install Odoo, most integrators prefer to deploy and run version-controlled source code. This provides better control over what is deployed and makes it easier to manage changes and fixes once in production.

Installing dependencies

When using a Debian distribution, by default your login is root with administrator powers, and your Command Prompt shows #. On Ubuntu systems, the root account is disabled, and the initial user configured during the installation process is a *sudoer*, meaning that it is allowed to use the sudo command to run commands with root privileges.

First, we should update the package index and then perform an upgrade to ensure that all installed programs are up to date:

```
$ sudo apt-get update
$ sudo apt-get upgrade -y
```

Next, we will install the PostgreSQL database and make our user a database superuser:

```
$ sudo apt-get install postgresql -y
$ sudo su -c "createuser -s $(whoami)" postgres
```

We will be running Odoo from source, but before that, we need to install the required dependencies. These are the Debian packages required:

```
$ sudo apt-get install git python3-pip python3-dev -y
$ sudo apt-get install libxml2-dev libxslt1-dev libevent-dev \
libpq-dev libjpeg-dev poppler-utils -y # for Python dependencies
$ sudo apt-get install libldap2-dev libsasl2-dev -y  # for LDAP
$ sudo apt-get install node-less node-clean-css -y
```

We should not forget to install wkhtmltox, which is needed to print reports:

```
$ wget "https://github.com/wkhtmltopdf/wkhtmltopdf/releases/download"\
"/0.12.1/wkhtmltox-0.12.1_linux-trusty-amd64.deb" -O /tmp/wkhtml.deb
$ sudo dpkg -i /tmp/wkhtml.deb
$ sudo apt-get -fy install  # In case of dependency errors
```

It is possible for the package installation to report a missing dependencies error. In this case, the last command will force the installation of those dependencies and correctly finish the installation.

Now, we are only missing the Python packages required by Odoo. Many of them also have Debian/Ubuntu system packages. The official Debian installation package uses them, and you can find the package names in the Odoo source code, in the `debian/control` file.

However, these Python dependencies can be also installed directly from the **Python Package Index (PyPI)**. This is friendlier for those who prefer to install Odoo in `virtualenv`. The required package list is in Odoo's `requirements.txt` file, as is usual for Python-based projects. We can install them with these commands:

```
$ sudo -H pip3 install --upgrade pip   # Ensure pip latest version
$ wget https://raw.githubusercontent.com/odoo/odoo/11.0/requirements.txt
$ sudo -H pip3 install -r requirements.txt
```

On Ubuntu 16.04, the last command may print a red warning about uninstalling PyYAML and pyserial in case older versions were already installed through system packages. It can be safely ignored.

Now that we have all dependencies, database server, system packages, and Python packages installed, we can install Odoo.

Preparing a dedicated system user

A good security practice is to run Odoo using a dedicated user, with no special privileges on the system.

We need to create the system and database users for that:

```
$ sudo adduser --disabled-password --gecos "Odoo" odoo
$ sudo su -c "createuser odoo" postgres
$ createdb --owner=odoo odoo-prod
```

Here, `odoo` is the username and `odoo-prod` is the name of the database supporting our Odoo instance.

The `odoo` user was made the owner of the `odoo-prod` database. This means that it has create and drop privileges over that database, including the ability to drop the full database. If you are running a multitenant server, you should create an `odoo`-like specific system user for each tenant.

Odoo is designed to work correctly even if the system user is not the owner of the database. While it complicates the setup, a security hardening good practice is to have a master system user as the owner of the databases, and create a specific system user for each of the instances to run on the server, without superuser privileges.

Note that these are regular users without any administration privileges. A home directory is automatically created for the new system user. In this example, it is /home/odoo, and the user can refer to their own home directory with the ~ shortcut symbol. We will use it for that user's Odoo specific configurations and files.

We can open a session as this user using the following command:

```
$ sudo su odoo
```

The exit command terminates that session and returns to our original user.

Installing from the source code

Sooner or later, your server will need upgrades and patches. A version control repository can be of great help when the time comes. We use git to get our code from a repository, just like we did to install the development environment.

Next, we will impersonate the odoo user and download the code into its home directory:

```
$ sudo su odoo
$ git clone https://github.com/odoo/odoo.git /home/odoo/odoo-11.0 \
-b 11.0 --depth=1
```

The -b option ensures that we get the right branch, and the --depth=1 option ignores the change history and retrieves only the latest code revision, making the download much smaller and faster.

Git will surely be an invaluable tool to manage the versions of your Odoo deployments. We just scratched the surface of what can be done to manage code versions. If you're not already familiar with Git, it's worth learning more about it. A good starting point is http://git-scm.com/doc.

By now, we should have everything needed to run Odoo from source. We can check whether it starts correctly and then exit from the dedicated user's session:

```
$ /home/odoo/odoo-11.0/odoo-bin --help
$ exit
```

Next, we will set up some system-level files and directories to be used by the system service.

Setting up the configuration file

Adding the `--save` option when starting an Odoo server saves the configuration used in the `~/.odoorc` file. We can use this file as a starting point for our server configuration, which will be stored at `/etc/odoo`, as shown in the following code:

```
$ sudo su -c "~/odoo-11.0/odoo-bin -d odoo-prod" \
" --db-filter='^odoo-prod$' --without-demo=all" \
" --save --stop-after-init" odoo
```

This will have the configuration parameters to be used by our server instance.

> The former `.openerp_serverrc` config file is still supported, and it is used if found. This can cause some confusion when setting up Odoo 10 or 11 in a machine that was also used to run the previous Odoo versions. In this case, the `--save` option might be updating the `.openerp_serverrc` file instead of `.odoorc`.

Next, we need to place the config file in the expected location for system configuration files, the `/etc` directory:

```
$ sudo mkdir /etc/odoo
$ sudo cp /home/odoo/.odoorc /etc/odoo/odoo.conf
$ sudo chown -R odoo /etc/odoo
$ sudo chmod u=r,g=rw,o=r /etc/odoo/odoo.conf  # for extra hardening
```

The last command from the preceding block is optional, but it improves your security; it ensures that the user running the Odoo process can read but can't change the configuration file. With this, you won't be able to change the master database password, but for a production service this should not be a problem, since the web database manager should be disabled with the `list_db=False` server configuration.

We should also create the directory where the Odoo service will store its log files. This is expected to be somewhere inside `/var/log`:

```
$ sudo mkdir /var/log/odoo
$ sudo chown odoo /var/log/odoo
```

Now, we should edit the configuration file and ensure that a few important parameters are configured:

```
$ sudo nano /etc/odoo/odoo.conf
```

Here are suggested values for the most important ones:

```
[options]
addons_path = /home/odoo/odoo-11.0/odoo/addons, /home/odoo/odoo-11.0/addons
admin_passwd = False
db_name = odoo-prod
dbfilter = ^odoo-prod$
list_db = False
logfile = /var/log/odoo/odoo-prod.log
proxy_mode = True
without_demo = all
workers = 6
http_port = 8069
```

Let's explain them:

- `addons_path` is a comma-separated list of the paths where add-on modules will be looked up. It is read from left to right, with the leftmost directories having a higher priority.
- `admin_passwd` is the master password to access the web client database management functions. It's critical to set this with a strong password or, even better, to set it to `False` to deactivate the function.
- `db_name` is the database instance to initialize during the server startup sequence.
- `dbfilter` is a filter for the databases to be made accessible. It is a Python-interpreted regex expression. For the user to not be prompted to select a database, and for unauthenticated URLs to work properly, it should be set with `^dbname$`, for example, `dbfilter=^odoo-prod$`. It supports the `%h` and `%d` placeholders, which are replaced by the HTTP request hostname and subdomain name.
- `list_db = False` blocks database listing, both at the RPC level and in the UI, and it also blocks the database management screens and the underlying RPC functions.
- `logfile` is where the server log should be written. For system services, the expected location is somewhere inside `/var/log`. If left empty, the log prints to standard output instead.
- `proxy_mode` should be set to `True` when Odoo is accessed behind a reverse proxy, as we will do.

- `without_demo` should be set to `all` in production environments so that new databases do not have demo data on them.
- `workers` with a value of two or more enables multiprocessing mode. We will discuss this in more detail in a bit.
- `http_port` is the port number at which the server will listen. By default, port `8069` is used.

> The `http_port` parameter was introduced in Odoo 11 to replace the `xmlrpc_port` parameter, which was used in the previous versions but deprecated.

The following parameters can also be helpful:

- `data_dir` is the path where session data and attachment files are stored; remember to have backups on it.
- `http_interface` sets the addresses that will be listened to. By default, it listens to all `0.0.0.0`, but when using a reverse proxy, it can be set to `127.0.0.1` in order to respond only to local requests. It was introduced in Odoo 11 to replace the deprecated `xmlrpc_interface` parameter.

We can check the effect of the settings made by running the server with the `-c` or `--config` option, as follows:

```
$ sudo su -c "~/odoo-11.0/odoo-bin -c /etc/odoo/odoo.conf" odoo
```

Running Odoo with the preceding settings won't display any output to the console, since it is being written to the log file defined in the configuration file. To follow what is going on with the server, we need to open another terminal window and run the following there:

```
$ sudo tail -f /var/log/odoo/odoo-prod.log
```

> To run multiple terminal sessions on the same terminal window, you can use multiplexing applications such as `tmux` or GNU screen. You also might like to try Byobu (`https://help.ubuntu.com/community/Byobu`), which provides a nice user interface on top of GNU Screen or Tmux.

It is also possible to use the configuration file and still force the log output to be printed to the console by adding the `--logfile=` option, like this:

```
$ sudo su -c "~/odoo-11.0/odoo-bin -c /etc/odoo/odoo.conf" \
" --logfile=" odoo
```

Multiprocessing workers

A production instance is expected to handle a significant workload. By default, the server runs one process and can use only one CPU core for processing, because of the Python language GIL. However, a multiprocess mode is available so that concurrent requests can be handled, taking advantage of multiple cores.

The `workers=N` option sets the number of worker processes to use. As a guideline, you can try setting it to `1+2*P`, where `P` is the number of processor cores. The best setting to use needs to be tuned for each case, since it depends on the server load and what other load intensive services are running on the server, such as PostgreSQL.

It is better to set workers too high for the load than too low. The minimum should be six due to the parallel connections used by most browsers, and the maximum is generally limited by the amount of RAM on the machine.

There are a few `limit-` configuration parameters to tune the workers. Workers are recycled when they reach these limits—the corresponding process is stopped and a new one is started. This protects the server from memory leaks and from particular processes overloading the server resources.

The official documentation already provides good advice on the tuning of the worker parameters, and you may refer to it for more details, at `https://www.odoo.com/documentation/11.0/setup/deploy.html`.

Setting up Odoo as a system service

Next, we will want to set up Odoo as a system service and have it started automatically when the system boots.

In Ubuntu/Debian, the `init` system is responsible for starting services. Historically, Debian (and derived operating systems) has used `sysvinit`, and Ubuntu has used a compatible system called `Upstart`. Recently, this has changed, and the `init` system used in the latest version is now `systemd`.

This means that there are two different ways to install a system service, and you need to pick the correct one depending on the version of your operating system.

On the last Ubuntu LTS (long term support) version, 16.04, we should be using systemd. However, older versions such as 14.04 are still used in many cloud providers, so there is a good chance that you might need to use it.

To check whether systemd is used in your system, try this command:

```
$ man init
```

This opens the documentation for the currently used init system, and you will be able to check what is being used.

Creating a systemd service

If the operating system you are using is recent, such as Debian 8 or Ubuntu 16.04, you should be using systemd for the init system.

To add a new service to the system, we just need to create a file describing it. Create a /lib/systemd/system/odoo.service file with the following content:

```
[Unit]
Description=Odoo
After=postgresql.service

[Service]
Type=simple
User=odoo
Group=odoo
ExecStart=/home/odoo/odoo-11.0/odoo-bin -c /etc/odoo/odoo.conf

[Install]
WantedBy=multi-user.target
```

 The Odoo source code includes a sample odoo.service file inside the debian/ directory. Instead of creating a new file, you can copy it and then make the required changes. At least the ExecStart option should need to be changed, according to your setup.

Next, we need to register the new service:

```
$ sudo systemctl enable odoo.service
```

To start this new service, use the following command:

```
$ sudo systemctl start odoo
```

Also, to check its status, run this:

```
$ sudo systemctl status odoo
```

Finally, if you want to stop it, use this command:

```
$ sudo systemctl stop odoo
```

Creating an Upstart/sysvinit service

If you are using an older operating system, such as Debian 7, Ubuntu 15.04, or even 14.04, chances are that your system is sysvinit or Upstart. For the purpose of creating a system service, both should behave the same way. Many cloud VPS services are still based on Ubuntu 14.04 images, so this might be a scenario you may encounter when deploying your Odoo server.

The Odoo source code includes an init script used for the Debian packaged distribution. We can use it as our service init script with minor modifications, as follows:

```
$ sudo cp /home/odoo/odoo-11.0/debian/init /etc/init.d/odoo
$ sudo chmod +x /etc/init.d/odoo
```

At this point, you might want to check the content of the init script. The key parameters are assigned to variables at the top of the file. A sample is as follows:

```
PATH=/sbin:/bin:/usr/sbin:/usr/bin:/usr/local/bin
DAEMON=/usr/bin/odoo
NAME=odoo
DESC=odoo
CONFIG=/etc/odoo/odoo.conf
LOGFILE=/var/log/odoo/odoo.log
PIDFILE=/var/run/${NAME}.pid
USER=odoo
```

These variables should be adequate, and we will prepare the rest of the setup with their default values in mind. However, of course you can change them to better suit your needs.

The USER variable is the system user under which the server will run. We have already created the expected odoo user.

The DAEMON variable is the path to the server executable. Our executable used to start Odoo is in a different location, but we can create a symbolic link to it:

```
$ sudo ln -s /home/odoo/odoo-11.0/odoo-bin /usr/bin/odoo
$ sudo chown -h odoo /usr/bin/odoo
```

The CONFIG variable is the configuration file to use. In a previous section, we created a configuration file in the default expected location /etc/odoo/odoo.conf.

Finally, the LOGFILE variable is the directory where log files should be stored. The expected directory is /var/log/odoo, which we created when we were defining the configuration file.

Now we should be able to start and stop our Odoo service, as follows:

```
$ sudo /etc/init.d/odoo start
Starting odoo: ok
```

Stopping the service is done in a similar way, as shown:

```
$ sudo /etc/init.d/odoo stop
Stopping odoo: ok
```

In Ubuntu, the service command can also be used:

```
$ sudo service odoo start
$ sudo service odoo status
$ sudo service odoo config
```

Now, we only need to make this service start automatically on system boot:

```
$ sudo update-rc.d odoo defaults
```

After this, when we reboot our server, the Odoo service should be started automatically and with no errors. It's a good time to verify that all is working as expected.

Checking the Odoo service from the command line

At this point, we can confirm whether our Odoo instance is up and responding to requests.

If Odoo is running properly, we should now be able to get a response from it and see no errors in the log file. We can check inside the server if Odoo is responding to HTTP requests using the following command:

```
$ curl http://localhost:8069
<html><head><script>window.location = '/web' +
location.hash;</script></head></html>
```

Also, to see what is in the log file, we can use the following:

```
$ sudo less /var/log/odoo/odoo.log
```

In case you are just starting with Linux, you will like to know that you can follow what is going on in the log file using `tail -f`:

```
$ sudo tail -f /var/log/odoo/odoo.log
```

Using a reverse proxy

While Odoo itself can serve web pages, it is strongly recommended to have a reverse proxy in front of it. A reverse proxy acts as an intermediary managing the traffic between the clients sending requests and the Odoo servers responding to them. Using a reverse proxy has several benefits.

On the security side, it can do the following:

- Handle (and enforce) HTTPS protocols to encrypt traffic
- Hide the internal network characteristics
- Act as an *application firewall*, limiting the URLs accepted for processing

Also, on the performance side, it can provide significant improvements:

- Cache static content, thus reducing the load on the Odoo servers
- Compress content to speed up loading time
- Act as a load balancer, distributing load between several servers

Apache is a popular option to use as a reverse proxy. Nginx is a recent alternative with good technical arguments. Here, we will choose to use Nginx as a reverse proxy and show how it can be used to perform the security and performance-side functions mentioned here.

Setting up Nginx as a reverse proxy

First, we should install Nginx. We want it to listen on the default HTTP ports, so we should ensure that they are not already taken by some other service. Performing this command should result in an error, as follows:

```
$ curl http://localhost
curl: (7) Failed to connect to localhost port 80: Connection refused
```

If not, you should disable or remove that service to allow Nginx to use those ports. For example, to stop an existing Apache server, you should use this command:

```
$ sudo service apache2 stop
```

Better yet, you should consider removing it from your system, or reconfigure it to listen on another port, so that the HTTP and HTTPS ports (80 and 443) are free to be used by Nginx.

Now we can install Nginx, which is done in the expected way:

```
$ sudo apt-get install nginx -y
```

To confirm that it is working correctly, we should see a **Welcome to nginx** page when visiting the server address with a browser or using curl http://localhost inside our server.

Nginx configuration files follow the same approach as Apache: they are stored in /etc/nginx/available-sites/ and activated by adding a symbolic link in /etc/nginx/enabled-sites/. We should also disable the default configuration provided by the Nginx installation, as follows:

```
$ sudo rm /etc/nginx/sites-enabled/default
$ sudo touch /etc/nginx/sites-available/odoo
$ sudo ln -s  /etc/nginx/sites-available/odoo /etc/nginx/sites-enabled/odoo
```

Using an editor, such as nano or vi, we should edit our Nginx configuration file, as shown:

```
$ sudo nano /etc/nginx/sites-available/odoo
```

First, we add the upstreams and the backend servers; Nginx will redirect traffic to the Odoo server in our case, which is listening on port 8069, as follows:

```
upstream backend-odoo {
  server 127.0.0.1:8069;
}
server {
  location / {
    proxy_pass http://backend-odoo;
  }
}
```

To test whether the edited configuration is correct, use the following command:

```
$ sudo nginx -t
```

If you find errors, verify that the configuration file is correctly typed. Also, a common problem is for the default HTTP to be taken by another service, such as Apache or the default Nginx website. Double-check the instructions given before to ensure that this is not the case, then restart Nginx. After this, we can have Nginx reload the new configuration, as demonstrated:

```
$ sudo /etc/init.d/nginx reload
```

If your operating system is using `systemd`, the appropriate version for the mentioned command is this:

```
$ sudo systemctl reload nginx
```

We can now confirm that Nginx is redirecting traffic to the backend Odoo server:

```
$ curl http://localhost
<html><head><script>window.location = '/web' +
location.hash;</script></head></html>
```

Enforcing HTTPS

Next, we should install a certificate to be able to use SSL. To create a self-signed certificate, use these commands:

```
$ sudo mkdir /etc/nginx/ssl && cd /etc/nginx/ssl
$ sudo openssl req -x509 -newkey rsa:2048 -keyout key.pem -out cert.pem \
-days 365 -nodes
$ sudo chmod a-wx *           # make files read only
$ sudo chown www-data:root *  # access only to www-data group
```

This creates an `ssl/` directory inside the `/etc/nginx/` directory and creates a passwordless self-signed SSL certificate. When running the `openssl` command, some additional information will be asked and a certificate and key files are generated. Finally, the ownership of these files is given to the `www-data` user used to run the web server.

Using a self-signed certificate can pose some security risks, such as man-in-the-middle attacks, and may not even be allowed by some browsers. For a robust solution, you should use a certificate signed by a recognized certificate authority. This is particularly important if you are running a commercial or e-commerce website.

The **Let's Encrypt** service at `https://letsencrypt.org` provides free certificates. An Odoo add-on module exists to handle the automatic requesting of SSL certificates for the Odoo server, but at the time of writing, it wasn't yet ported to 11.0. You can learn more details at `https://github.com/OCA/server-tools/tree/10.0/letsencrypt`.

Now that we have an SSL certificate, we are ready to configure Nginx to use it.

To enforce HTTPS, we will redirect all HTTP traffic to it. Replace the `server` directive we defined previously with the following:

```
server {
  listen 80;
  add_header Strict-Transport-Security max-age=2592000;
  rewrite ^/.*$ https://$host$request_uri? permanent;
}
```

If we reload the Nginx configuration now and access the server with a web browser, we will see that the `http://` address will be converted into an `https://` address.

However, it won't return any content before we configure the HTTPS service properly, by adding the following server configuration:

```
server {
  listen 443 default;
  # ssl settings
  ssl on;
  ssl_certificate     /etc/nginx/ssl/cert.pem;
  ssl_certificate_key /etc/nginx/ssl/key.pem;
  keepalive_timeout 60;
  # proxy header and settings
  proxy_set_header Host $host;
  proxy_set_header X-Real-IP $remote_addr;
  proxy_set_header X-Forwarded-For $proxy_add_x_forwarded_for;
```

```
    proxy_set_header X-Forwarded-Proto $scheme;
    proxy_redirect off;
    location / {
      proxy_pass http://backend-odoo;
    }
  }
```

This will listen to the HTTPS port and use the /etc/nginx/ssl/ certificate files to encrypt the traffic. We also add some information to the request header to let the Odoo backend service know that it's being proxied.

For security reasons, it's important for Odoo to ensure that the proxy_mode parameter is set to True. The reason for this is that when Nginx acts as a proxy, all requests will appear to come from the server itself instead of the remote IP address; setting the X-Forwarded-For header in the proxy and enabling --proxy-mode solves that. However, enabling --proxy-mode without forcing this header at the proxy level will allow anyone to spoof their remote address.

At the end, the location directive defines that all requests are passed to backend-odoo upstream.

Reload the configuration, and we should have our Odoo service working through HTTPS, as shown in the following commands:

```
$ sudo nginx -t
nginx: the configuration file /etc/nginx/nginx.conf syntax is ok
nginx: configuration file /etc/nginx/nginx.conf test is successful
$ sudo service nginx reload  # or: sudo systemctl reload nginx
* Reloading nginx configuration nginx
...done.
$ curl -k https://localhost
<html><head><script>window.location = '/web' +
location.hash;</script></head></html>
```

The last output confirms that the Odoo web client is being served over HTTPS.

> For a particular case where an Odoo POSBox is being used, we need to add an exception for the /pos/ URL to be able to access it in HTTP mode. The POSBox is located in the local network but does not have SSL enabled. If the POS interface is loaded in HTTPS, it won't be able to contact the POSBox at all.

Nginx optimizations

Now, it is time for some fine-tuning of the Nginx settings. They are recommended to enable response buffering and data compression that should improve the speed of the website. We also set a specific location for the logs.

The following configurations should be added inside the server listening on port `443`; for example, just after the proxy definitions:

```
# odoo log files
access_log /var/log/nginx/odoo-access.log;
error_log  /var/log/nginx/odoo-error.log;
# increase proxy buffer size
proxy_buffers 16 64k;
proxy_buffer_size 128k;
# force timeouts if the backend dies
proxy_next_upstream error timeout invalid_header http_500  http_502
http_503;
```

An optimization is to enable the `gzip` data compression, but this comes enabled by default, at least in the Ubuntu package default configurations, at `/etc/nginx/nginx.conf`. In case you need to manually enable them, here's a sample configuration:

```
# enable data compression
gzip on;
gzip_min_length 1100;
gzip_buffers 4 32k;
gzip_types text/plain text/xml text/css text/less application/x-javascript
application/xml application/json application/javascript;
gzip_vary on;
```

We can also activate static content caching for faster responses to the types of requests mentioned in the preceding code example, and to avoid their load on the Odoo server. After the `location /` section, add the following second location section:

```
location ~* /web/static/ {
  # cache static data
  proxy_cache_valid 200 60m;
  proxy_buffering on;
  expires 864000;
  proxy_pass http://backend-odoo;
}
```

With this, the static data is cached for 60 minutes. Further requests on top of those requests in that interval will be responded to directly by Nginx from the cache.

Long polling

Long polling is used to support the instant messaging app, and when using multiprocessing workers, it is handled on a separate port, which is `8072` by default.

For our reverse proxy, this means that the long polling requests should be passed to this port. To support this, we need to add a new upstream to our Nginx configuration, as shown in the following code:

```
upstream backend-odoo-im { server 127.0.0.1:8072; }
```

Next, we should add another location to the server handling the HTTPS requests, as follows:

```
location /longpolling { proxy_pass http://backend-odoo-im;}
```

With these settings, Nginx should pass these requests to the proper Odoo server port.

Server and module updates

Once the Odoo server is ready and running, there will come a time when you need to install updates on Odoo. This involves two steps: first to get the new versions of the source code (server or modules), and second to install them.

If you have followed the approach described in the *Installing from the source code* section, we can fetch and test the new versions in the staging repository. It is strongly advised that you make a copy of the production database and test the upgrade on it. If `odoo-prod` is your production database, this can be done with the following commands:

```
$ dropdb odoo-stage
$ createdb odoo-stage
$ pg_dump odoo-prod | psql -d odoo-stage
$ sudo su odoo
$ cd ~/.local/share/Odoo/filestore/
$ cp -al odoo-prod odoo-stage
$ ~/odoo-11.0/odoo-bin -d odoo-stage --xmlrpc-port=8080 \
-c  /etc/odoo/odoo.conf
```

Before we can use this copy of the database, some cleanup should be done, such as deactivating scheduled actions, email servers (both for sending and fetching messages), and more. The specific steps needed here depend on your setup, but they can probably be automated by a script. For this, remember that the `psql` command can be used to run SQL directly from the command line, using something like `psql -d odoo-stage -c "<SQL command>"`.

If everything goes okay, it should be safe to perform the upgrade on the production service. Remember to make a note of the current version Git reference in order to be able to roll back by checking out this version again. Keeping a backup of the database before performing the upgrade is also highly advised.

> The database copy can be made in a much faster way, using the following `createdb` command: `$ createdb --template odoo-prod odoo-stage`. The caveat here is that for it to run, there can't be any open connections to the `odoo-prod` database, so the Odoo server needs to be stopped to perform the copy.

After this, we can pull the new versions to the production repository using Git and complete the upgrade, as shown here:

```
$ sudo su odoo
$ cd ~/odoo-11.0
$ git pull
$ exit
$ sudo service odoo restart   # or: sudo systemctl restart odoo
```

Regarding the Odoo release policy, no minor versions are released anymore. GitHub branches are expected to represent the latest stable version. The nightly builds are considered the latest official stable release.

On the update frequency, there is no point in updating too frequently, but also not to wait for one year between updates. Performing an update every few months should be fine. Also, usually a server restart will be enough to enable code updates, and module upgrades shouldn't be necessary.

Of course, if you need a specific bug fix, an earlier update should probably be made. Also, remember to watch out for security bugs disclosures on public channels such as GitHub Issues for Odoo (in particular, the ones displaying the **Security** tag), at the Odoo official mailing lists, which can be subscribed to at `https://www.odoo.com/groups`. As part of the service, enterprise contract customers can expect early email notifications of this type of issue.

Summary

In this chapter, you learned about the additional steps to set up and run Odoo in a Debian-based production server. The most important settings in the configuration file were visited, and you learned how to take advantage of the multiprocessing mode.

For improved security and scalability, you also learned how to use Nginx as a reverse proxy in front of our Odoo server processes.

This should cover the essentials of what is needed to run an Odoo server and provide a stable and secure service to your users.

To learn more about Odoo, you should also look at the official documentation at `https://www.odoo.com/documentation`. Some topics are covered in more detail there, and you will also find topics not covered in this book.

There are also other published books on Odoo that you might also find useful. Packt Publishing has a few in its catalog, and in particular, *Odoo Development Cookbook* provides more advanced material, covering more topics not discussed here.

Finally, Odoo is an open source product with a vibrant community. Getting involved, asking questions, and contributing is a great way not only to learn but also to build a business network. On this, we can't help mentioning the **Odoo Community Association** (**OCA**), promoting collaboration and quality open source code. You can learn more about it at `odoo-comunity.org`.

Other Books You May Enjoy

If you enjoyed this book, you may be interested in these other books by Packt:

Odoo 11 Development Cookbook - Second Edition
Alexandre Fayolle, Holger Brunn

ISBN: 978-1-78847-181-7

- Install and manage Odoo environments and instances
- Use Models to define your application's data structures
- Add business logic to your applications
- Add automated tests and learn how to debug Odoo apps
- Learn about the access security model and internationalization features
- Customize websites built with Odoo, by writing your own templates and providing new snippets for use in the website builder
- Extend the web client with new widgets and make RPC calls to the server

Odoo 10 Implementation Cookbook
Mantavya Gajjar

ISBN: 978-1-78712-342-7

- Learn the modern way of doing sales and managing sales contracts.
- Create and configure your products and manage your sales quotations
- Set up an online shop and start selling online with Odoo eCommerce
- Manage multi-currency transactions and create a deferred revenue plan and link it with products
- Administer vendors and products and request quotations, confirm orders, and get them delivered
- Manage quality control in the warehouse and manual and real-time inventory stock valuations.
- Manage projects and project forecasting via grid and Gantt views
- Implement Human Resource apps and manage the employee appraisal process
- Manage Workcenters and the product lifecycle
- Track worker activity with tablets and launch new changes in production

Leave a review - let other readers know what you think

Please share your thoughts on this book with others by leaving a review on the site that you bought it from. If you purchased the book from Amazon, please leave us an honest review on this book's Amazon page. This is vital so that other potential readers can see and use your unbiased opinion to make purchasing decisions, we can understand what our customers think about our products, and our authors can see your feedback on the title that they have worked with Packt to create. It will only take a few minutes of your time, but is valuable to other potential customers, our authors, and Packt. Thank you!

Index